P9-DXE-124

LOVE FOR LIBERATION

LOVE FOR LIBERATION

AFRICAN INDEPENDENCE, BLACK POWER, AND A DIASPORA UNDERGROUND

ROBIN J. HAYES

UNIVERSITY OF WASHINGTON PRESS
Seattle

Love for Liberation was made possible in part by a grant from the
V Ethel Willis White Endowment, which supports the publication
of books on African American history and culture.

25 24 23 22 21   5 4 3 2 1

Printed and bound in the United States of America

UNIVERSITY OF WASHINGTON PRESS
uwapress.uw.edu

LIBRARY OF CONGRESS CATALOGING-IN-PUBLICATION DATA
Names: Hayes, Robin J., author.
Title: Love for liberation : African independence, Black Power, and a diaspora
    underground / Robin J. Hayes.
Other titles: African independence, Black Power, and a diaspora underground
Description: Seattle : University of Washington Press, [2021] | Includes
    bibliographical references and index.
Identifiers: LCCN 2020054664 (print) | LCCN 2020054665 (ebook) |
    ISBN 9780295749051 (hardcover) | ISBN 9780295749075 (paperback) |
    ISBN 9780295749068 (ebook)
Subjects: LCSH: National liberation movements—Africa—History—20th century. |
    Black power—History—20th century. | Political activists—Africa—History—
    20th century. | Political activists—United States—History—20th century. |
    African American political activists—United States—History—20th century. |
    African diaspora—History—20th century. | Pan-Africanism. | Africa—Politics
    and government—20th century. | United States—Race relations—History—20th
    century.
Classification: LCC DT31 .H38 2021 (print) | LCC DT31 (ebook) |
    DDC 322.4089/96—dc23
LC record available at https://lccn.loc.gov/2020054664
LC ebook record available at https://lccn.loc.gov/2020054665

For activists living underground,
their families,
and the communities that continue to resist in non-self-governing territories

CONTENTS

ILLUSTRATIONS

ORGANIZATIONS AND ABBREVIATIONS

AAPC	All-African People's Conference
AAPRP	All-African People's Revolutionary Party
ABAKO	Alliance des Bakongo
BLA	Black Liberation Army
BLM	Black Lives Matter
BPP	Black Panther Party
CAWAH	Cultural Association for Women of African Heritage
CCM	Chama Cha Mapinduzi
CIA	Central Intelligence Agency
CONAKAT	Confédération des Associations Tribales du Katanga
CORE	Congress on Racial Equality
CPP	Convention People's Party
FBI	Federal Bureau of Investigation
FLN	Front de Libération Nationale
IMF	International Monetary Fund
LCFO	Lowndes County Freedom Organization
MFDP	Mississippi Freedom Democratic Party
MMI	Muslim Mosque, Inc.
MNC	Mouvement National Congolais
NAACP	National Association for the Advancement of Colored People
NAG	Nonviolent Action Group
NOI	Nation of Islam
OAAU	Organization of Afro-American Unity

OAU	Organization of African Unity
PDG	Parti Démocratique de Guinée
RDA	Rassemblement Démocratique Africain
SCLC	Southern Christian Leadership Conference
6PAC	sixth Pan-African Congress
SNCC	Student Nonviolent Coordinating Committee (pronounced "Snick")
TANU	Tanganyika African National Union
UAACC	United African Alliance Community Center
UGCC	United Gold Coast Convention
UNIA	Universal Negro Improvement Association

LOVE FOR LIBERATION

INTRODUCTION

I FIRST LEARNED HOW much Black lives matter from my glamorous grandmother, Mrs. Willie Belle David Hayes. She was proud to say she is the granddaughter of Mrs. Georgiana Broady, who was born enslaved in South Carolina. Each year Mrs. Hayes eagerly anticipated her Brooklyn church's "Africa Day" by purchasing a new caftan and coordinating headwrap from Senegalese vendors on Fulton Street. However, after leaning forward with her bifocals to read the first few pages of my dissertation—while sitting in her front room beneath portraits of Nelson Mandela and Martin Luther King Jr.—my grandmother asked me pointedly, "Die-asss-pore-uh . . . what is that?!"

In straightforward terms, a diaspora is a community that continues to be bound by a shared identity in spite of being dispersed from their original geographic homeland to a variety of locations throughout the world for a significant period of time. There are many diasporas, including Irish, Chinese, Jewish, Puerto Rican, and Greek. The *African* diaspora, which is the focus of this book, is an international community of millions of people who have African ancestors and "contend with the everyday realities of anti-Black racism."[1]

Diaspora studies focuses on how and why community members remain connected and mutually invested in each other given this longtime physical separation from their place of origin.[2] For example, how did my eighty-six-year-old grandmother, a lifelong resident of the US, feel empowered and affirmed by wearing a traditional headwrap to a celebration of Africa at her church? Based on commonsense understanding of human connection, the intuitive answer to this question is simple: love. The kind of love that people experience only when they feel truly at home.

The concept of home helps us reconcile our vision of the future with our ancestral past, as well as our present-day relationship to power dynamics in society. Home can be an idyllic homeland or "imagined community" from which our ethnic group—and therefore our families and ourselves—originates.[3] A (healthy, functioning) home is also a private space for contemporary family connections, which provide affirmation and a validated sense of who we are. Being at home in a family, community, ethnic group, or nation involves knowing and being comfortable with how we as individuals fit into a larger narrative of human history. As scholars including Sidney Lemelle, Robin D. G. Kelley, and Saidiya Hartman have suggested, this idea is particularly complicated for members of the African diaspora, who feel far from home in many ways.

Diasporans (members of diasporas) have a persistent discomfort because their community's dispersal from their homeland is usually due to traumatic circumstances, such as famine, civil war, or the transatlantic slave trade. In addition, diasporan experiences of hostility and oppression in the countries that receive them are not uncommon. History has demonstrated that the same othering logics—which justify the violence of colonialism (in the case of the Irish), the marginalization necessitated by imperialism (in the case of Puerto Ricans), and the exploitation enshrined by White supremacy (in the case of Africans)—ride along with diasporans into their new countries. These logics adapt expertly over time to these communities' efforts to organize and fully enjoy their human rights.[4]

Inevitably, these communities are forced to cope with loss and the grief that it causes. To this end, profoundly intimate traditions, moral lessons, and strategies of survival are shared within families and memorialized within ethnic groups across generations. Through this sharing and memorializing, struggles emerge to imagine ourselves before the loss in the past, to reshape the present, and to envision a different future. And so home for diasporans becomes the gap (or *décalage*) between now and then, homeland and hostland, how a community sees itself and how dominant elites see that same community.[5] In addition, home for diasporans involves the work of healing that gap.[6]

Scholars including Kim Butler and Tiffany Patterson explain that a diaspora's efforts to reconcile the old and the new is as significant to its identity as the original cause of its separation.[7] Diasporans continuously develop new empowering meanings of their roots, travel different routes to cultivate relationships in spite of geographic and generational distances, and revise dominant cultural and political ideas about their community's relationship to power. This healing work, as well as the ideas, creative expression, and physical spaces that result from this effort, provide diaspora members with a source of love and affirmation for self, family, and community.[8] This affirmation may be more significant to diasporans because they are severed from home as an idyllic place of origin, as safety in the present, and as a valorized place in society. So, for example, my grandmother Mrs. Willie Belle David Hayes, remembering her own grandmother's resistance to slavery and Jim Crow as well as her personal struggles with intersectionality, redlining, and the War on Drugs, unites her honor of the past, her resistance to an unjust present, and her hope for her granddaughter's future by donning a custom-made headwrap and matching caftan to celebrate Africa Day with her friends at a church in Bed-Stuy, Brooklyn. This book explores how this healing diasporic engagement—when conducted by Black social movements—reflects and generates a love for liberation.

METHODS AGAINST EMPIRE

Love for Liberation: African Independence, Black Power, and a Diaspora Underground explores how and why passionate idealists came together and fought for self-determination between 1957 and 1974. This unique era in the broader story of engagement between Africans and African Americans is told from the perspective of the activists who lived through it. I use a crucial case study of the relationship between several African independence and Black Power organizations during this period to build the original theory of a diaspora underground, which articulates the motivations, methods, and impact of transnational engagement between Black social movements.

African independence movements organized to end European colonialism and then struggled to govern as national parties. The often misrepresented Black Power movement sought to build autonomous institutions in Black communities. Both are significant examples of social movements that involve collective action, which seek to create meaningful political change using a variety of tactics (e.g., marches, civil disobedience, and popular education).

I chose the African organizations included in this study—Ghana's Convention People's Party, Guinea's Parti Démocratique de Guinée, Algeria's Front de Libération Nationale, Congo's Mouvement National Congolais, and Tanzania's Tanganyika African National Union—because they represent the breadth of tactics and ideas in African anticolonialism. Each of these organizations profoundly influenced other independence efforts on the continent and combated the various techniques of domination that were used by European colonizers. These techniques included deportation, exile, forced labor, corporal and capital punishment, imprisonment, and the introduction of highly authoritarian social institutions such as missions, schools, hospitals, mines, and plantations.[9]

African independence also intended to dismantle the racial hierarchies perpetuated by segregation and violence.[10] The ideology and tactics of African independence varied significantly and were shaped by the specific cultural, political, and economic contexts of the colonizing governments and indigenous ethnic dynamics in each country. However, frequently recurring repertoires of action included the use of violence to overthrow colonial regimes, petitioning the international community for intervention, nonviolent civil disobedience, and intracontinental pan-Africanism.

The Black Power movement, unique to the latter half of the twentieth century, was composed of organizations that sought increased political, economic, and cultural autonomy for communities of African descent in the United States. This generation of activists was part of a complex tradition of African American resistance, reform, and rebellion that originated with efforts to abolish slavery. They considered themselves distinct from the civil rights movement because of their radicalism. Black Power rigorously challenged claims about the physical, cultural, and intellectual superiority of people defined as White by the social construct of race. It also imagined African Americans as bound together by ties of history, culture, and kinship in a finite, sovereign community, regardless of the inequality and exploitation that existed within.[11] I chose to examine the Student Nonviolent Coordinating Committee (SNCC), founded in 1960; the Organization of Afro-American Unity (OAAU), founded in 1964; and the Black Panther Party (BPP), founded in 1966, because they are important examples of the political philosophies, tactics, and aesthetics that continue to be associated with Black Power. Each of these organizations had a different trajectory of engagement with African independence, as well as close interactions and mutual influences on each other.

Using the process-tracing method of theory development, I constructed a detailed narrative of how and why encounters between African independence and Black Power evolved into political relationships. I also analyze the broader motivations, content, and effects of diasporic engagement among Black social movements.[12] I compiled evidence by walking in the footsteps of these organizations through routes of resistance and commemoration in the US and Africa. I interviewed surviving activists and institutional participants; analyzed correspondence, fliers, speeches, and periodicals found in archival collections; and reviewed activist memoirs and historical accounts. By examining and coding my observations, I mined the data for patterns (and anomalies). I also observed the meanings ascribed to these encounters by activists, organizations, and institutions. My research methods reflect my commitment to giving voice to underrepresented communities and cultivating the existing archive for new insights into the political praxis of the African diaspora.

In order to carefully trace the processes through which encounters between African independence and Black Power took place, my research addresses the following questions:

- What factors drove these activists and organizations to look for opportunities outside of their nation-state's borders?
- Which institutions, organizations, and individuals based in the African diaspora aided connections between these movements?
- When and how did these activists and organizations exchange ideas and tactics?
- What was the impact of these exchanges on their political philosophies, strategies, leadership, and constituencies?

I conducted interviews with over twenty subjects, including surviving activists and participants in Black institutions between 1957 and 1974. Through my review of archival and secondary sources and the recommendations of interviewees, I determined which individuals would be best able to provide information about how indigenous institutions organized encounters between these movements and how their relationships influenced their ideas and tactics. The breadth of the sample was limited by the availability of subjects. Unfortunately, many activists and institutional participants who could have been key informants for this study are no longer with us. However, the subjects whom I was able to interview represent the diversity of participants in Black activism and indigenous institutions. Among the interviewees are rank-and-file members, those who held key organizational leadership positions, and individuals with a variety of educational, class, geographic, and ethnic backgrounds. Wherever I found these subjects—from Oakland, California, to Lusaka, Zambia—I discovered that they all shared a vivid recollection of their involvement in African independence, Black Power, or indigenous institutions. They also remained dedicated to antiracist activism, which, in the light of the murders of George Floyd and Breonna Taylor, clearly remains as urgently needed as ever. Some interviewees, like Kathleen Neal Cleaver, have evolved into enduring inspirations for the Black Lives Matter activists who valiantly contest racial injustice today. These interviews, which took place in the location of the subject's choosing (most often their homes and offices), were recorded using digital video or audio.

The archival collections I reviewed typically included correspondence between activists, organizational records, speeches, and audiovisual materials. I used these sources to garner information about the evolution of these movements' ideas and tactics, meetings between activists, and relationships between organizations and Black institutions. The vivid details about events, decision-making processes, and activist perspectives found in these materials offered rich data that directly addressed the questions central to my research.

The evidence I gathered shows that Black Power and African independence activists were drawn together by the frustrations they experienced while fighting for citizenship equality in the US and formerly colonized Africa. Their relationships were made possible by the efforts of secular

Black institutions such as New York's *Amsterdam News* and Howard University, as well as havens for progressive activists created in African cities such as Accra, Algiers, Conakry, and Dar es Salaam. Through their profound connection, Black Power and African independence activists discovered that racial discrimination is an international human rights issue that requires education, sustained collective action, and solidarity among communities throughout the African diaspora. The relationships, physical spaces, and institutional bonds that bloomed from their connection built a diaspora underground, which continued to support racial justice activism after the African independence and Black Power movements subsided.

THE JOURNEY TO COME

Chapter 1 of *Love for Liberation* details the original theory of a diaspora underground. A diaspora underground is a transnational space-time that connects Black social movement organizations, activists, and constituencies across national borders through a configuration of spaces, routes that connect these spaces, and a shared understanding of the past, present, and future. Motivated by movement frustrations with domestic elites, these connections are also facilitated by the work of institutions indigenous to Black communities. A diaspora underground is distinct from the broader diaspora, because it is explicitly created by and for contentious social movement politics.

Chapters 2–9 are a narrative history of the African independence and Black Power organizations included in this case study, their encounters with each other, and the impact of those encounters on the activists and constituencies involved. In chapter 2—"New African in the World"—the story begins on March 6, 1957, when Ghana became one of the first African countries to gain its independence during a wave of decolonization in the latter half of the twentieth century. Bedecked in traditional kente cloth, new Ghanaian president and social movement activist Dr. Kwame Nkrumah articulated his dream for this infant nation to fifty thousand of his countrymen, while flanked by dignitaries, including the Duchess of Kent, Vice President Nixon, and Martin Luther King. Black media outlets in the US, such as *Amsterdam News* and the *Baltimore Afro-American*, broadcast compelling images of the highs of the African independence movement. These inspirational representations contrasted sharply with the experiences of young African Americans, who were routinely attacked by police for challenging Jim Crow segregation.

Chapter 3—"A Free Black Mind"—begins in Algeria, where conflict raged between the French military and the Front de Libération Nationale (National Liberation Front, FLN). The FLN was an uncompromising armed independence organization led by Muslim youths, including Ali LaPointe and Ahmed Ben Bella. Their guerrilla tactics, along with the French military's counterinsurgency, escalated into the three-year-long Battle of Algiers. Each side contended with the questionable ethical choices of involving civilians in this violent confrontation and abandoning the Geneva Conventions by torturing prisoners for intelligence. The grisly and apparently boundaryless nature of the battle seared the Algerian Revolution into international consciousness and stimulated a broad conversation about the cost of continuing colonialism.

Meanwhile, an increasing number of politicized young Africans arrived at historically Black colleges and universities (HBCUs), including Howard University. They made an impression on one suit-wearing Harlem-raised student in particular, Stokely Carmichael. Carmichael became a member of the Nonviolent Action Group (NAG), the Howard chapter of the Student Nonviolent Coordinating Committee (SNCC, pronounced "Snick"). SNCC was a collective of organizers who used civil disobedience tactics to challenge the racial segregation of public facilities. He and the other group members embraced NAG's motto, "A free Black mind is a concealed weapon," and delved into learning about African and African American history. Eventually Stokely joined the SNCC Freedom Rides in the South. After being imprisoned in the notorious Parchman Farm, he traded his suit for the trademark denim overalls of a full-time SNCC voting rights organizer in Mississippi. Working with SNCC, Stokely befriended activists Charles Cobb Jr., James Forman, John Lewis, Bob Moses, Dona Richards, and Fannie Lou Hamer.

Chapter 4—"Independence with Danger"—introduces affable yet politically uncompromising beer salesman, husband, and father Patrice Lumumba. He quickly expanded the ranks of the Mouvement National Congolais (National Congolese Movement, MNC) as he inspired people to fight for the country's independence from Belgium with his fiery speeches and displays of defiance after being incarcerated by colonial authorities. He traveled to Accra for the first All-African People's Conference—a summit for emerging African independence movement leaders. He witnessed Ghanaian attendees proudly bearing a sign that stated, "We prefer independence with danger to servitude in tranquility." There he met Ghana president Kwame Nkrumah, who deepened Patrice's commitment to Pan-Africanist ideas.

Less than a year after he became prime minister of the Congo, Patrice was arrested and assassinated illegally with the sanction of Belgian authorities. Human rights activists argue Patrice was murdered partly because of his commitment to keeping his country "nonaligned"—outside of the Cold War between the US and the Soviet Union—which was making some African countries politically and economically dependent on either superpower. African American activists, including Maya Angelou and Abbey Lincoln, protested the UN's failure to protect Patrice and his democratically elected government. Black newspapers question why the US State Department failed to intervene. Although his earnest rebellion continues to inspire a younger generation in Africa and the US, Lumumba's death foreshadowed the challenges that would soon diminish the continent's independence euphoria.

The start of chapter 5—"Our Problem Is Your Problem"—reveals how Patrice Lumumba's daring and sacrifice made a strong impression on Malcolm X, leader of the Harlem mosque of the Nation of Islam. After being expelled from the Nation of Islam due to conflicts with the organization's leadership, Malcolm traveled to Ghana in May 1964. At that time, its capital, Accra, had become a haven for progressive activists, writers, and artists of African descent under Kwame Nkrumah's leadership. The previous year, Kwame had founded the Organization of African Unity (OAU), a collective of independent African nations committed to work together for the continent's economic and political autonomy. Malcolm was welcomed in Accra by a small group of African American expats—including Maya Angelou and Julian Mayfield—who called themselves the "Malcolm X Committee" and escorted him around town.

Kwame Nkrumah invited Malcolm to his home. Malcolm was aware that, like his deceased father, Earl Little, Kwame had been strongly influenced by Marcus Garvey. Nkrumah and Malcolm dialogued about the struggles that Africans and African Americans have in common. Inspired by Nkrumah's example and his time in Ghana, Malcolm founded the Organization of Afro-American Unity (OAAU) and made an appeal to African political leaders in Cairo during the second meeting of the Organization of African Unity—which the OAAU was named after. After he returned from Cairo, every Sunday at the Audubon Ballroom, the OAAU brought together everyday Harlemites, African American activists, and African diplomats from the UN. They had lively discussions about the promise of African and African American collaboration as well as how racism and colonialism are international human rights issues.

Chapter 6—"Mississippi Eyes"—details how in the heat of 1964, while Malcolm X visited with Kwame Nkrumah in Ghana and appealed to African heads of state in Cairo to support African Americans, Freedom Summer inspired hundreds of predominately White and Northern college student volunteers to travel to the Jim Crow South and fight for voter equality. Freedom Summer built on years of work by Stokely Carmichael; Fannie Lou Hamer; James Forman; Bob Moses; his wife, Dona Richards Moses; and other SNCC activists. The campaign involved committed young people collaborating with locally based African American organizers to challenge poll taxes, arbitrary exams, and other practices that inhibited Black Mississippians from exercising their right to vote. There was an immediate backlash by Southern White supremacists against SNCC activists and Freedom Summer volunteers. Over one thousand organizers were arrested, eighty brutally beaten, and seven murdered. In spite of these setbacks, SNCC activists worked with their colleagues in the Council of Federated Organizations (COFO) to forge ahead. The organizers helped create a network of voluntary summer Freedom Schools that offered an alternative curriculum to what was taught in segregated Mississippi public schools.

After being harassed, beaten, bombed, and losing some of their friends to homicidal racism, alumni of Freedom Summer described themselves as having "Mississippi Eyes"—meaning that they saw the world with skepticism of authorities and compassion toward marginalized communities. Having heard about some of the events in Mississippi during Freedom Summer, Guinea president Sékou Touré invited leaders of SNCC to visit his country. Touré, a Pan-Africanist and collaborator of Kwame Nkrumah's, was a leader among the emerging movement for nonalignment among African nations. Longtime friend of the civil rights movement Harry Belafonte encouraged the group to accept the invitation and funded the trip. Harry supported the activists going to Guinea because they needed to be renewed after the tribulations and disappointments of Freedom Summer. The SNCC delegation to Guinea included James Forman, John Lewis, Bob and Dona Richards Moses, Prathia Hall, Julian Bond, Ruby Doris Robinson, Bill Hansen, Donald Harris, Matthew Jones, and Fannie Lou Hamer.

During their time in Guinea, the SNCC delegation met with African leaders and political activists. They were outraged to learn that the US State Department was fundamentally distorting the information that Africa received regarding race in America, in order to boost their bid for support among African nations in the Cold War. After returning from their transformative experience, Mrs. Hamer traveled to Harlem to participate in an event organized by the OAAU, Malcolm X's Pan-African human rights organization. SNCC activists relayed their new outlook to the organization's strategy and shared what they learned with their colleagues, including SNCC chairman Stokely Carmichael.

Chapter 7—"Love Our Community"—reveals that just as African independence and Black Power leaders began discovering how much they have in common, external pressures and their own questionable decision-making drove many of them underground and into exile. During a gathering of the Organization of Afro-American Unity, Malcolm X was assassinated by members of the Nation of Islam, on February 21, 1965 His funeral in Harlem was attended by tens of thousands of mourners. After alienating his colleagues in the National Liberation Front (FLN) and being perceived as too enamored of his international celebrity, Algerian president Ahmed Ben Bella and his wife, Zohra Sellami, were forced under house arrest and deposed by a military coup led by his close friend Houari Boumédiène. Kwame Nkrumah—perceived as insensitive to local needs in Ghana—was overthrown and forced into exile in Guinea. His wife, Fathia, and children fled to Egypt.

Chapter 8—"We Have Come Back"—follows SNCC as it began working with an antiracist group called the Black Panther Party for Self-Defense, which was founded in Oakland, California, by community college students Huey P. Newton and Bobby Seale in October 1966. The party's *Ten-Point Program*, which included demands for full employment and affordable housing, along with its signature style and rebellious rhetoric catapulted the organization to national prominence. In Oakland, Chicago, and other chapters, the Black Panther Party drew the attention of local police departments and the FBI. Stokely fled to Guinea, where he became a student of Kwame Nkrumah and Sékou Touré's with political asylum. Stokely changed his name to Kwame Ture and remained based in Conakry, where he founded the All-African People's Revolutionary Party.

After Reverend Dr. Martin Luther King Jr. was assassinated in April 1968, the Black Panther Party's minister of information, Eldridge Cleaver, led an ambush against Oakland police in which two officers and teenaged Panther Bobby Hutton were killed. He fled the US and ended up in Algiers, which had become a sanctuary for African revolutionaries and progressive activists under the leadership of Houari Boumédiène. Boumédiène was empowered in his nonalignment strategy by Algeria's considerable oil wealth.

Eldridge was soon joined by his wife, Kathleen Neal Cleaver, and other Panther couples, including Don and Barbara Easley Cox and Connie Matthews and Mike Tabor, as well as Pete and Charlotte O'Neal. They set up the International Section of the Black Panther Party, where they hosted celebrity visitors during the Pan-African Cultural Festival and discussed political strategies with representatives from the dozen or so anticolonial movements that were also enjoying refuge in Algiers.

Tensions between the International Section and the Algerian government heightened as a number of African Americans hijacked planes to join Eldridge and Kathleen in what they perceived to be a revolutionary utopia. Relationships within the section also deteriorated due to allegations of marital infidelity, domestic violence, and murder, as well as the extraordinary stress of exile. The BPP's Central Committee, led by increasingly dictatorial Huey P. Newton, became increasingly frustrated with Eldridge and expelled him and all International Section members from the Black Panther Party. As the International Section collapsed, some Panthers headed to Tanzania.

Chapter 9—"Ready for the Revolution"—shows how a number of veterans of the Black Power movement, including Charles Cobb, were also drawn to Tanzania due to the pull of President Julius Nyerere's encouragement of African American migration there as well as the push of the movement's decline, which was brought on by internal conflicts, activist fatigue, and the impact of the FBI's Counterintelligence Program (COINTELPRO). Nyerere's Ujamaa—"familyhood" in Swahili—was a socialist economic policy and a vision for a united, autonomous Africa and African diaspora. Ujamaa was especially appealing to certain embattled Black Power activists who embraced Nyerere's extolling of "traditional African values"—a return that was also popular in certain segments of the African American community in the US.

In 1974, Tanzania hosted the sixth Pan-African Congress. By this time, this incarnation of a diaspora underground had facilitated the establishment of Black studies programs and brought the wearing of the daishiki, the embrace of natural hairstyles, and the adoption of African names into mainstream Black culture. The sixth Pan-African Congress was attended by many activists who were involved in the African Liberation Support Committee (ALSC) in the US. The committee raised awareness about the second wave of African independence struggle in colonized regions that would become Angola, Mozambique, Namibia, Rhodesia, and postapartheid South Africa.

This book's epilogue, "Black Lives Matter," explores the legacy of the relationship between African independence and Black Power, especially its influence on the current cycle of transnational contention known as the Black Lives Matter movement. It also explores this legacy's implications for the theory of a diaspora underground. Although African independence and Black Power leaders were not able to fully realize their vision for complete self-determination, today's Black Lives Matter activists appear to be taking cues from the best of their examples. Participants have appealed to the United Nations for intervention on behalf of the African American community to investigate racial profiling and police misconduct. Interviews with the founders of the movement show how they have been inspired by their activist ancestors in their efforts to advance racial justice and defund the police. According to SNCC activist turned congressperson

John Lewis, Black Lives Matter "is so much more massive and all inclusive" than the activism of his time. "There will be no turning back."[13]

DEPARTURES

My research about the political philosophies, tactics, and achievements of African independence and Black Power uncovers the significance of diversifying interest and commemoration of Black social movements beyond slavery, abolition, and civil rights. The work of African independence illustrates how what has become known as the Black freedom struggle was waged in part by activists who were neither descendants of enslaved Africans in the US nor particularly invested in American citizenship as a strategy for emancipation. In fact, the freedoms these activists sought were

- a freedom from dependence on dominant elites who perpetuated racial subjection; and
- a freedom to build and support indigenous institutions and networks that transcended national boundaries.

Encounters between African independence and Black Power reflect how transnational interactions between social movements can be shaped by shared experiences of historical marginalization. Although each of these movements forged alliances with non-Black social movements and nation-states, they were in some ways drawn together and in other ways linked together by diasporic currents. *Love for Liberation* is important today because it highlights how contemporary connections between Africans and African Americans can be rooted in collaboration and reciprocal empowerment.

This study integrates academic and activist concerns about transnational collective action by Black communities. I interrogate the notion that divisions between the academy and the multitude are intransigent. This notion is perpetuated by the calcified thinking reflected in terms such as "public intellectual," "ivory tower," and "town and gown." My approach to research design and theory building is inspired and informed by the work of African independence and Black Power activists, who considered the production of knowledge and creation of educational experiences for their constituencies vital to their organizing efforts. This was exemplified by the Organization of Afro-American Unity's Liberation School, the Black Panther Party's required political education classes, and the Freedom Schools organized by SNCC.[14] Scholars and teachers were not presumed to be intrinsically incapable of dedicated participation in these movements or in possession of a rarefied expertise about racial injustice that could not be challenged or enhanced by community members. These activists also recognized the academy as a politically and intellectually diverse institution that could provide significant resources for the growth and sustenance of social movement organizations. A crucial element of African independence and Black Power's effectiveness was their ability to see through the artifice of the university entrance (often guarded by minimum wage workers) and recognize that the gates to ivory towers should not separate communities of people opposed to White supremacy.

African independence and Black Power mobilized their constituencies and allies throughout the world to engage in a variety of political activities, including electoral participation, mass demonstrations, autonomous institution-building, and creative work. This illustrates how Black politics occurs on a broad spectrum that spans the divides of what is often considered formal or informal, governmental and nongovernmental.[15] The reciprocal effects of exchanges between African independence and Black Power reveal the necessity of expanding our perceptions about the arenas in which Black politics take place, as well as how these politics are not always concerned primarily with attaining citizenship rights or negotiating with nation-state institutions. There are significant distinctions between objectives and philosophies born out of Black politics that are driven to create national belonging and those that are motivated to achieve racial justice. A group's assimilation into dominant institutions does not necessarily lead to the democratic distribution of resources and power to all members of that group.

The theory of a diaspora underground maps specific pathways for activists who are developing strategies to address marginalization, which lowers the life chances of people of African descent. Black social movement activists can forge connections between themselves by participating in, and helping to create, autonomous emancipated spaces in which interpersonal encounters and discursive exchanges may occur. Institutions that are grounded in the African diaspora, or indigenous institutions, can use their resources, credibility, and audiences to facilitate transnational exchanges by providing information that validates antiracist activism in other countries as relevant to domestic struggles. Black social movements are well served by transnational exchanges with each other because these relationships help expand the resources available to organizations, add complexity to the political philosophies that drive an organization's efforts, and introduce leadership to new tactics and constituencies. This research shows that transnational engagement between social movements can also help rejuvenate activists from the spiritual and intellectual fatigue created by the political frustrations, personal conflicts, and profound loss that accompany the work of grassroots organizing.

1

Diaspora Underground
Diaspora Souterraine
الشتات تحت الأرض
Ugenini chini ya Ardhi

AFRICAN INDEPENDENCE'S ENGAGEMENT with Black Power
between 1957 and 1974 demonstrates how the efforts of institutions
based in the African diaspora, combined with activists' frustrations with
political elites, facilitate transnational exchanges between Black social
movements. As collectives, Black social movements strive to transform
policies and practices that perpetuate racism as a system of inequality.
They also seek to challenge dominant society's persistent dehumanizing
of Black identities, cultures, and bodies. Connections between such movements occur in a geography of antiracist praxis that I describe as a diaspora underground. A diaspora underground consists of

- a configuration of spaces and routes of travel between these
  spaces;
- a shared historical experience, which includes discourses and
  action created by international exchanges between activists; and

- long term international relationships between social movements and their constituencies.

Drawing from scholarly literatures about Black politics, social movements, diaspora, and comparative politics, I argue a diaspora underground is the transnational space-time created during heightened periods of Black insurgency. Its transnationalism arises from how the underground functions as a coalescer of diasporic communities across nation-state boundaries. Within this space-time, activists develop political philosophies that deepen racial solidarities and operationalize a global antiracist praxis, which can dismantle intersections of inequalities based on race, class, citizenship, sexuality, and gender.[1] Institutions indigenous to Black communities help facilitate a diaspora underground by providing information about—and offering opportunities for relating to—activists and organizations in other countries in the diaspora.

How is it a space-time? Activists and their constituencies experience and construct a diaspora underground as a single continuum that simultaneously involves three dimensions of space as well as one dimension of time.[2] Traveling through and engaging with this space-time creates distinct and long-lasting perspectives about the most impactful events in diasporic communities. By generating new ideas and tactics—as well as strengthened and prolonged identification with international Black communities—a diaspora underground empowers activists to articulate their roots, envision alternatives to present-day racial regimes, and strategize for futures in which systemic change enables universal human rights enjoyment.[3]

Why is a diaspora underground constructed? Because transnational engagement offers Black social movements distinct methods to gain leverage with existing targets and pursue new avenues of contention when all others seem exhausted. Therefore, a diaspora underground is strongly influenced by activist perceptions of diminished domestic political opportunities. Information about social movements in other areas of the African diaspora resonates deeply with antiracist activists and their constituencies when efforts to achieve first-class citizenship appear nearly futile (see figure 1.1). For example, encounters between African independence and Black Power developed into longer-term engagement as each of these movements grappled with the challenges of facing state-sponsored

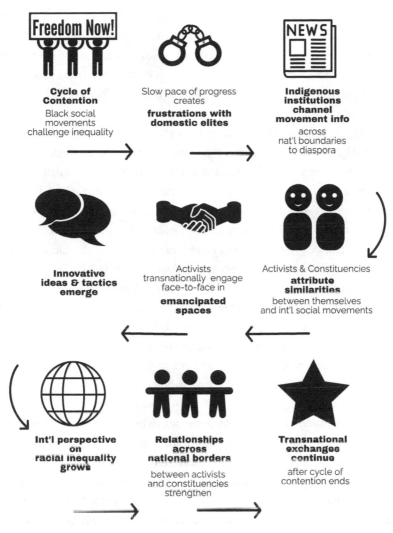

Cycle of Contention
Black social movements challenge inequality

Slow pace of progress creates **frustrations with domestic elites**

Indigenous institutions channel movement info
across nat'l boundaries to diaspora

Innovative ideas & tactics emerge

Activists transnationally engage face-to-face in **emancipated spaces**

Activists & Constituencies **attribute similarities** between themselves and int'l social movements

Int'l perspective on racial inequality grows

Relationships across national borders between activists and constituencies strengthen

Transnational exchanges continue after cycle of contention ends

1.1. Model of a diaspora underground. Infographic by author.

counterinsurgency, remaining "nonaligned" in a world increasingly divided by the Cold War, and resolving bitter divisions in organizational leadership.[4] As Black social movements are repeatedly excluded from elite corridors of power (e.g., "the room where it happens")—as well as subjected to psychological and physical brutality because of their insurgency—activists and their constituencies become increasingly skeptical that continued participation in dominant domestic political institutions is a legitimate route to emancipation.[5] Transnational relationships between social movements in the African diaspora are thus fashioned from activists' perceptions about how racism works as a system of oppression and how this system prevents conventional forms of citizenship from offering justice and freedom to Black community members.

Love for Liberation also considers the processes through which institutions indigenous to the African diaspora facilitate transnational engagement between Black social movements. The term "indigenous institutions" refers to stalwart civic, media, and educational organizations based in communities of African descent. These include, for example, the National Association for the Advancement of Colored People (NAACP), Black press publications like New York's *Amsterdam News* and the *Chicago Defender,* and historically Black colleges and universities (HBCUs), such as Howard University. Indigenous institutions are informed by the resistance traditions, affinities, and networks produced by experiences of racial marginalization. They challenge dominant and dehumanizing representations of Black constituencies, mark the boundaries of group membership, and help community members understand the meaning of their shared historical and cultural experiences.[6] Because indigenous institutions are owned and/or managed by Black people and primarily serve that community, they are understood by their constituencies to be "for us, by us." They also act as channels that direct information and arrange encounters between Black social movements through nation-state boundaries.[7]

Similarly, emancipated spaces are areas within the African diaspora that are organized by antiracist activists for the purpose of facilitating transnational dialogue and exchange. Examples of these spaces include the Pan-African Congresses (1900–1994) and the All-African People's Conferences (1958–61). These spaces are emancipated because they offer activists opportunities to devise, learn about, and exemplify alternatives to White supremacist practices in zones perceived to be independent from the control of dominant elites. They are crucial to the construction of a diaspora underground, because they provide safe outlets for the expression of frustration that precedes transnational engagement. Emancipated spaces also encourage collaboration that can forge solutions.

Exchanges between African independence and Black Power indicate that a diaspora underground can have a long-term impact on Black social movement constituencies. One of my colleagues—an American who specializes in African history—once asked me, "Why do so many African Americans speak Swahili? Tanzania was not part of the transatlantic slave trade. It's like, all the way on the Eastern side." I laughed because it was a completely fair question that I would not have asked before researching this book. Having grown up in an African American household with an uncle who wore daishikis and played conga drums, I knew there are certain specific forms of *kongo*, Twi, Yoruba, and Bembe culture (among others) that are embedded in African American life. Some of these practices are the result of cultural retention, as acclaimed art historian Robert Farris Thompson and others have pointed out.[8] However, the relationship between African independence and Black Power continues to shape African American engagement with Africa. Tanzania, Ghana, Congo, Algeria, and Guinea loom large in the African American community because of their connections with SNCC, the OAAU, and the Black Panther Party. A diaspora underground creates a model for future transnational social movement engagement and empowers Black communities to frame racial justice as a human rights issue long after a cycle of contention has ended.

FRUSTRATIONS WITH DOMESTIC ELITES

The theory of a diaspora underground argues that transnational exchanges between Black social movements are motivated by frustrations with domestic elites during cycles of contention. According to sociologist Sidney Tarrow, cycles of contention are characterized by

- the rapid spread of collective action;
- innovation in forms of protest (for example, sit-ins, glitter bombing, or hashtag flooding);
- the creation of new political opportunities; and
- changes in how social problems, groups, and dynamics of power are explained and understood.[9]

The academic field of political theory explains that domestic elites are individuals (or groups of individuals) who have a disproportionate amount of access to capital and/or decision-making power within a nation's most powerful and well-resourced institutions.[10] Domestic elites can be beloved or reviled by a community. For example, media mogul Oprah Winfrey, Congresswoman Nancy Pelosi, and Republican Party supporters David and Charles Koch are all people who could be considered domestic elites. Within the field of social movement studies, the terms "cycle of contention" and "protest cycle" describe a sustained period of conflict. These conflicts can be between institutional leadership (or "the establishment," in 1960s slang) and opposing organizations, coalitions of organizations (e.g., the Fight for 15 campaign to increase the minimum wage), or self-directed groups of local activists, such as Ferguson Action.[11]

Love for Liberation examines a specific cycle of contention within the African diaspora. The social movements for Black Power and African independence were able to make considerable gains. Yet, ultimately, they were frustrated by the resistance of domestic elites. For example, the creativity and tenacity of youth activists within the Student Nonviolent Coordinating Committee (SNCC) contributed significantly to the passing of the Civil Rights Act in 1964—which prohibited segregation of public facilities and employment discrimination—and the Voting Rights Act of 1965—which bars state and local governments from creating barriers to African American enfranchisement. This scaffolding for democracy and equality, which benefited all Americans, required SNCC organizers to endure numerous beatings, arrests, and in some cases murder. While these youths continued to be willing to put their lives and bodies on the line to end anti-Black racism, the slow nature of the social change produced by their considerable sacrifice eviscerated their confidence in the American political system as the best path to reach their social justice goals. Ten years after desegregation sit-ins by Morgan State University students successfully integrated lunch counters at a Baltimore drugstore chain, in 1966 SNCC leader Stokely Carmichael suffered his twenty-seventh arrest for his opposition to Jim Crow. Shortly after he was detained, during the March against Fear in Greenwood, Mississippi, Carmichael declared, "I ain't goin' to jail no more!"[12]

The assertion that frustrations with domestic elites motivate Black social movements' transnational engagement draws from the social movement studies literature. In their frequently cited text, *Activists beyond Borders*, scholars Margaret Keck and Kathryn Sikkink establish that transnational advocacy networks (TANs) consist of coalitions of social movements and nongovernmental organizations working across national boundaries. TANs are most likely to emerge when communication between activists and domestic governments breaks down or when activists believe engaging with such networks will advance the movement toward its goals.[13] Sociologists agree that the international spread, or "cross-national diffusion," of social movements is spurred by activist perception that better political opportunities lie outside of domestic contexts.[14] For example, after Carmichael's fiery speech in Greenwood, SNCC increased its efforts to connect with African independence. In addition, the organization began to frame racial discrimination as an international human rights issue rather than simply a national civil rights issue in the US.

Concerns about racism impact how social movement activists and their constituencies understand, articulate, and respond to frustrations with domestic elites. Race is an "unstable complex of social meanings constantly being transformed by political struggle," which also signifies dynamics of power in society by describing different kinds of human bodies, according to sociologists Howard Winant and Michael Omi.[15] Racism is a system of inequality that involves "the state-sanctioned or extralegal production and exploitation of group-differentiated vulnerability to *premature death*."[16] By continuously challenging the dehumanization of Black bodies, social movements in the African diaspora—beginning with the slavery abolitionists and continuing with prison abolitionists today—have engaged in what Marxist scholar Cedric Robinson named "the Black Radical Tradition."[17]

While frustrations with domestic elites push Black social movement activists outward to seek and recognize political opportunities, their place in the Black Radical Tradition pulls them toward transnational engagement with other activists and constituencies in the African diaspora. Scholars including Doug McAdam, Hanspeter Kriesi, David A. Snow, and Robert Benford agree that transnational exchanges between social movements are usually based on some form of mutual identification between the organizations or activists involved.[18] The notion that activists and their constituencies would have to believe they had something in common with their counterparts in another country before they attempted to mentor or emulate them appeals to our commonsense understanding of human behavior. Social movement theorists build on this commonsense approach by explaining that the "attribution of similarity" between constituencies and activists can be the result of "cultural proximity" or "shared problem definition" between groups.[19]

THE BLACK CHANNELS: INSTITUTIONS BROKERING IDENTITY

Scholars have consistently established that exchanges between social movements across borders are facilitated by channels, through which information and representations flow. These channels help social movements identify with their counterparts in other countries and form perceptions about potentially advantageous political opportunities outside of domestic contexts.[20] Due to their unique community role as articulators of group identity and trusted sources of information, institutions indigenous to the African diaspora serve as channels of cross-national diffusion between Black social movements. For example, this study reveals how the *Amsterdam News* (a Black press publication) and Howard University (a historically Black university) consistently provided information to their African American constituencies about African independence and shaped understanding about that movement's relevance to domestic antiracist efforts. These institutions also influence opinions about international and domestic political opportunity for their constituencies.[21] Black institutions use and develop the complex repertoires of images and narratives that constitute the "oppositional cultures" of their communities to reinforce group identity as well as an understanding of racial marginalization as unjust.[22]

According to some of the most well-known social movement scholars, political identities are shaped by "identity-transforming mechanisms" that can change political perceptions of social movement activists/constituents, as well as their opinions about relationships with other groups.[23] One identity-transforming mechanism is *category formation*, which creates and recognizes boundaries that observably exclude or include certain groups and provides instructions for intergroup relationships. Another mechanism is *brokerage*, which facilitates "communication and coordination" between groups.[24] The theory of a diaspora underground suggests that Black institutions engage in category formation by drawing upon their communities' cultures and behavioral guidelines to delineate, and sometimes expand, the boundaries of group membership along international lines. In addition, these institutions engage in brokerage by serving as communication networks that connect Black social movements across borders.

Acclaimed cultural studies theorist Paul Gilroy explains that identity is "increasingly shaped in the marketplace, modified by the cultural industries, and managed and orchestrated in localized institutions."[25] Along with individual consciousness and social structure, indigenous institutions are part of the social processes that help constituencies "understand the significance and meaning of their kinship."[26] To gain recognition from dominant elites for their marginalized communities, these institutions act as sites for the expression of constituencies' desires and experiences.[27] Their role in shaping community identity also enables indigenous institutions to foster political protest because "institutional life . . . draws people into the settings within which collective action can erupt."[28] As Gunnar Myrdal observed in *An American Dilemma*, Black institutions help create a community that is "a special and psychological reality for the individual" and "for this reason [they are] far more than a mere expression . . . of protest"; they also magnify it, "acting like a huge sounding board."[29] By challenging dominant representations of their constituencies and marking the boundaries of group membership, indigenous institutions help create political consciousness and relational networks that are significant to building and sustaining a diaspora underground.[30]

However, in their efforts to consolidate a collective sense of self that can serve as the basis for political action and recognition, indigenous institutions can ignore the needs of the most vulnerable members of Black communities. These institutions help their constituencies understand that their kinship is based in shared experiences of struggle, but these experiences can be centered on male, straight, cis-gendered, and lighter-skinned group members' perspectives. Black institutions also help their communities calculate how acting as a political collective can make their demands more viable or attractive to dominant elites.[31] Using the "politics of respectability," which involves the regulation of individual behavior in order to discredit justifications for Black communities' subjugation, indigenous institutions create specific parameters for "appropriate" individual and collective action.[32] In her frequently cited classic, *Boundaries of Blackness*, political scientist Cathy Cohen explains that these "moralistic character evaluations" further marginalize "the most resource-poor and alienated" people in Black communities.[33] In her study of transnational Yoruba networks, anthropologist Kamari Clarke agrees that institutions in the Black Atlantic have "substantive rules and regulations that legitimate norms" and "protocol and procedures by which norms can be derived."[34] Therefore, the identity-shaping work of indigenous institutions in a diaspora underground is not uniformly beneficial to constituencies. It is often oppressive to community members with intersectional identities, for example those who are Black while being women, lesbian, gay, bisexual, transgendered, queer, gender nonbinary, lower income, dark skinned, disabled, or otherwise defined as Other.[35]

Drawing from their resources and "cultural tool kits," indigenous institutions make up communication networks that facilitate mutual identification between movements across borders.[36] In a diaspora underground, these communication networks are sites of transnational political, social, and cultural exchanges where current events, interpersonal relationships, communal history, and strategies for struggling against oppression are discursively engaged and negotiated. These discussions in institutional spaces are prompted by the formal presentation of information (e.g., news outlets or conferences) or the types of informal sharing (e.g., barbershop debates and homecoming parties) that occur during "everyday talk."[37]

By using their resources to facilitate discursive exchanges between community members, indigenous institutions are sites where the thought worlds of Black communities materialize and change. They play an essential role in helping activists and their constituencies understand themselves as belonging to, and benefiting from, participating in a diaspora underground. While they enlighten their audiences, these institutions function as what political prisoner/theorist Antonio Gramsci described as "organic intellectuals"—those who give their community "homogeneity and awareness of its own function" through the pedagogical work of informing, organizing, and leading.[38] Black institutions also offer "alternative, oppositional perspectives that can help form group consciousness" and determine the standards by which their audiences evaluate issues and events.[39] These functions enable activists and their constituencies to consider international alternatives once they experience frustrations with domestic elites. Through the manner in which they disseminate information, indigenous institutions shape community perceptions of domestic and international political opportunities as well as the relevance of international Black social movements to domestic struggles.

SPACE-TIME AND AUTHENTICITY

Frustrations with domestic elites during cycles of contention turn the focus of Black social movements outward. At the same time, indigenous institutions channel these movements' discursive and physical engagement across borders through routes within a diaspora underground. A diaspora underground facilitates travel through space-time to reclaim power as well as the envisioning of alternatives to racist institutions, practices, and policies. It is created and bounded more by a shared investment in the struggle against racism than by genetics or cartography. As an underground, this space-time reflects and shapes how antiracist social movements and their constituencies view past, present, and future dynamics of power between themselves and dominant elites. Their efforts to build relationships across nation-state borders are not often secret, but simply invisible or less visible to dominant elites because they occur in the social margins.

Diaspora plays an important role in the "social construction of similarity" between Black constituencies that's necessary for international exchanges between social movements to take place.[40] Like all social constructions—including race, class, and gender—the significance of diaspora to Black communities emerges from tensions between knowledge produced by the marginalizing practices of dominant institutions (which are international in scope) and resistance traditions by subaltern groups that seek to challenge and transform this oppressive reality.[41] According to political scientist Bernard Magubane, "Pan-African consciousness has always been a determined effort on the part of Black peoples to rediscover their shrines from the wreckage of history. It was a revolt against the [W]hite man's ideological suzerainty in culture, politics, and historiography."[42] For example, long-standing tropes in mainstream institutions define Africa (and the African) as savage, strange, and chaotic.[43] These messages are countered by representations of the continent from Black institutions that posit Africa as a homeland—both geographically "real" and culturally, politically, and historically "imagined." These counter-representations affirm Africa as the source of roots and kin from which Black people outside the continent were traumatically and forcibly dispersed.[44] This transnational imagining, and the meanings that are invested in these visions by Black institutions and social movements, are the consequences of social practices that involve negotiations between individuals and "globally defined fields of possibility."[45] For Black social movement actors and their constituencies, the reality of diaspora—as it is reproduced by systems of knowledge in their communities—lights physical and discursive routes for exchanges across national boundaries that are distinct from other forms of international engagement.

Activists and their constituencies look most to their diaspora as a bounded—but not sealed—space of the world because it reflects and valorizes the historical experiences of Black communities. Historian Penny Von Eschen acknowledges that the Black Radical Tradition includes African diasporic engagement as a "global analysis [of race] and vision of Black solidarity" that can be traced back to the Pan-African aspirations of some slave revolts, as well as to abolitionist Martin Delany's "presentation of slavery as an international system of economic exploitation" during the eighteenth century.[46] In their foundational texts *The Black Atlantic* and *In Search of Power*, Paul Gilroy and Brenda Gayle Plummer illuminate how Black activists, artists, intellectuals, and politicians have articulated their diasporic consciousness by seeking opportunities to connect in a manner that allows them to travel through space—across borders—and through time to erase previous disruptions caused by factors outside of the control of Black communities.[47]

In addition to gaining an affirming understanding of their "home" as past and present, participants in a diaspora underground are empowered to envision radical antiracist futures for their communities based on present-day exchanges of ideas and tactics with their diasporic counterparts. For example, when Mrs. Fannie Lou Hamer—a Mississippian activist and sharecropper—observed for the first time in her life Black airline pilots, judges, and presidents during a SNCC delegation to Guinea—she gained, by her own account, a broader view of the possibilities of successful racial justice organizing for her own lifetime and the future.[48] Her journey to a recently decolonized African country to meet with activists was not a journey to an idealized past. It was a path forward.

The term "underground" has gained romantic allure due to its association with insurgency such as the Underground Railroad and the French Resistance to Nazi occupation. "Going underground" in the Black Radical Tradition describes removing oneself from the gaze and persecution of dominant authorities as well as placing oneself in a safe haven—often with the assistance of allies. In youth cultures such as hip hop, the "underground" signifies a physical space and community mindset that are truly authentic in that they are indigenous to its participants and committed to remaining free from corrupting dominant influences. The phrase "diaspora underground" describes an oppositional yet constructive transnational space-time in which Black social movements can freely articulate community-based desires for social justice and freedom, as well as the true value of Black lives (which are degraded by racist policies and practices). In this sense, a diaspora underground functions as a "structure of feeling"—which cultural theorist Raymond Williams describes as a set of "meanings and values as they are actively lived and felt" with a "specific set of internal relations."[49]

The issue of authenticity is crucial to how activists and their constituencies experience a diaspora underground as discursive, interpersonal, and physical spaces that are emancipated from White supremacist policies and practices. According to philosopher Charles Taylor, personal authenticity involves the construction and discovery of "original" ideas, beliefs, and identities that frequently oppose the rules of society. It also involves a person's definition of self that results from developing an understanding of what is significant through a dialogue with external ideas and values.[50] Although the modern ideal of authenticity had several interpretations during its early development in the eighteenth century, the commonsense version that persists today derives from political theorist Jean-Jacques

Rousseau's assertion that a "natural" inner moral compass exists within all of us and that intimate isolated contact with this compass is a source of joy and contentment.[51] Present-day discourses on authenticity emphasize the importance of achieving the goal of self-fulfillment and having the freedom to "do [y]our own thing."[52]

This concept of individual authenticity is more problematic for Black people, who have a sense of "linked fate" with others in their group and are often forced to witness the misrepresentation of their cultures, beliefs, and behaviors because of cultural imperialism.[53] For these communities, the issue of authenticity is concerned mostly with the ability to make meaningful choices about aspects of life that affect their individual and collective selves. This kind of authenticity enables Black social movement activists and their constituents to create alternative narratives of heritage and relations of power. It should not be conflated with homophobic, misogynist, classist, or ethnocentric rhetoric disguised as self-empowerment. For example, affirming that "Black Is Beautiful!" or "Black Lives Matter!" is radical in its challenge to racial regimes that consistently represent Blackness as ugly and inhuman, and therefore killable.[54] On the other hand, dubiously claiming that the financial independence of Black women is interfering with the well-being of Black men, or that homosexuality is the result of negative White influences, is conservative minstrelsy.

FACE-TO-FACE IN EMANCIPATED SPACES

Counterinsurgency tactics suffered by Black social movements—including unlawful arrests, agents provocateurs, censorship, false imprisonment, and assassination—require the existence of physically and intellectually safe social spaces that are at least somewhat insulated from the control of dominant elites.[55] As Kathleen Neal Cleaver, head of the Black Panther Party's International Section in Algiers, explains, this safety is particularly important to activists who have been exiled or censored by their governments. Without intervention, "the essential anonymity of the life of the fugitive . . . eventually leads to the death of [their] political identity."[56] In a diaspora underground, face-to-face interpersonal interactions occur in emancipated spaces—including conferences, associations, and neighborhoods—which are organized by antiracist activists for the purpose of facilitating frank dialogues and earnest exchanges between activists of African descent.

These emancipated spaces offer opportunities for intellectual and tactical expressions of "positive freedom," through which activists may help their communities autonomously develop value systems and ideologies that interrogate racialized international relations of power.[57] They embody the process of deterritorialization, in which "new self-conceptions and self-fashionings are made, and remade, outside of the structures of territorially-based place," where domestic elites are often more powerful.[58] Emancipated spaces are also sites of struggle and contestation between different national groups in the African diaspora, whose economic, cultural, and political statuses vary in the international arena. Similar to indigenous institutions, such as the Black press and HBCUs, emancipated spaces are based on a sense of group consciousness that they also help perpetuate.

Within the Black Radical Tradition, emancipated spaces produce a discursive articulation (or joining together) of the diaspora through the relationships and correspondence that they engender.[59] In addition, they empower activists to build group consciousness while contesting imperialist values.[60] For example, literary critic Brent Hayes Edwards reveals that "innovative dialogic spaces that were assembled by Black women," such as writers' salons and les cercles des amis in Paris between World Wars I and II, "played an often under-appreciated role in transnational cultural circuits."[61] Similarly, Von Eschen points to the emancipated spaces of the Pan-African Congresses of the early twentieth century (1900, 1919, 1921, 1927) and the Bandung Conference in 1955 as examples of diasporic gatherings in which transnational strategies for combating White supremacy were discussed and relationships between activists were developed and strengthened.[62]

In a diaspora underground, emancipated spaces provide occasions for activists and constituents to elevate their transnational engagement from the indirect discourse that occurs via indigenous institutions to direct dialogues, strategizing, and interpersonal relationship building. Emancipated spaces are characteristic of what Gramsci described as subaltern counterpublics, because they serve as "parallel discursive arenas where members of subordinated social groups invent and circulate counter-discourses to formulate oppositional interpretations of their identities, interests, and needs."[63] The candid debates and long-lasting friendships produced by emancipated spaces in a diaspora underground help transnational social justice praxis fulfill its potential to tangibly address the everyday struggles and often grim realities of historically marginalized communities.

A LONG-TERM UNDERSTANDING
OF "A WORLD PROBLEM"

Antiracist social movements often employ a repertoire of political ideas and strategies that connect their concerns with White supremacy to dominant discourses about fairness, self-determination, and authority. In a diaspora underground, encounters between activists and their constituencies develop into the longer-term engagement between constituencies after specific cycles of contention end. As evidenced by the relationship between African independence and Black Power, diminished domestic political opportunities as well as violence, sabotage, imprisonment, and other state-sponsored counterinsurgency tactics breed doubt among Black communities about the legitimacy of dominant institutions and liberal political discourse. Engagement within a diaspora underground appears to produce consensus among activists that an international human rights framework is the best strategy for combating racial discrimination.[64] As Malcolm X—founder of the Organization of Afro-American Unity (OAAU)—explained to an audience in the emancipated space of the second meeting of the Organization of African Unity in Cairo, thinking about racial discrimination in a transnational context allows it to become "a world problem; a problem for humanity."[65] Although the following chapters focus on the relationship between African independence and Black Power and how it evolved into a diaspora underground, the period between 1957 and 1974 is one of many cycles of transnational social movement engagement that have addressed racial inequality. Each iteration creates additional ideas, discourses, and spaces that enhance the possibility for all of our human rights enjoyment.

2

"New African in the World"
Nouvel Africain dans le Monde
الأفريقي الجديد في العالم
Mwafrika mpya Ulimwenguni

A FEW MINUTES AFTER midnight on March 6, 1957, in the West African city of Accra, hundreds of thousands of tribal chiefs, market women, dignitaries, and drummers fell silent. They were gathered at the Polo Grounds—one of several spaces built by the British winners of a colonizing war against the peoples of the Gold Coast in order to make settlers feel more at home and to tutor the indigenous elite in "civilized" British culture. Roughly 150 kilometers south lay a "door of no return" at the Cape Coast fort, from which thousands of members of the Ashanti, Ewe, and other tribes were shipped to the Americas after being kidnapped, enslaved, and tortured between the sixteenth and nineteenth centuries as part of the transatlantic slave trade.[1] At the fort, those who challenged British authorities or attempted to escape were confined to a cell marked with a skull and bones until they died from dehydration or starvation.[2]

Generations later, West African rebels were able to achieve a different outcome from their resistance. Like dozens of other attendees, movement leader and recently elected prime minister Kwame Nkrumah rode into these festivities on a motorbike clad in a green and white striped prisoner's uniform cap.[3] When he and his political organization—the Convention People's Party—were elected to a majority in the General Assembly in 1956, he was serving a jail sentence for "unlawful agitation" related to his anticolonial activism. At 12:05 a.m., the red, gold, and green flag representing a freshly independent nation ascended above the hushed crowd. At 12:20 a.m., Nkrumah stepped to the microphone on the main stage's podium and led the crowd in singing their new national anthem: "May we unite together, proclaim the dawn of our new day!"[4] Following the anthem, Nkrumah acknowledged the diverse national community—"the chiefs, the youth, the farmers, the women"—that had come together to make that moment possible.[5] They were no longer of the Gold Coast, a title for their land conferred by "slave traders and gold hunters" after their ancestors were forced to succumb to British forces in 1901. Fifty-six years later, they were now the people of Ghana.[6] Like the juxtaposition in the crowd between the chiefs' headdresses and kente cloth and the Ghanaian Supreme Court justices' powdered white wigs and black robes, the naming of this country highlighted the tensions between old and new, indigenous and colonial, with which Ghana and other newly independent African nations would soon struggle.[7]

A DUCHESS AND THE RADICAL KING

Foreign dignitaries in attendance revealed the breadth of international stakes in the success of Ghanaian independence. Wearing opera-length white gloves and a feathered hat, Her Royal Highness the Duchess of Kent—daughter-in-law of the British Empire's King George V and Queen Mary—shared a message from Queen Elizabeth II: "It is my earnest and confident belief that my people in Ghana will go forward in freedom and justice."[8] Queen Elizabeth II—as leader of the British Empire—was also the queen of the Gold Coast. A few days earlier, the White duchess electrified the international press by dancing at a preindependence ball with Black prime minister Nkrumah. She wore a diamond tiara and white ball gown. He wore an indigenous kente cloth shawl. Mainstream press outlets represented the gesture as one of goodwill. However, African American newspapers were more skeptical that the duchess's actions were rooted in British imperial paternalism. For example, *Chicago Defender* columnist Ethel Payne reported British dignitaries were eager "to be pictured as the fond parent assisting a toddler to walk, instead of an iron-handed colonial tyrant."[9]

Vice President Nixon attended the celebration as a representative of US president Dwight Eisenhower. During the Eisenhower Administration (1953–61), tensions between the US and the then Soviet Union escalated, which resulted in the heated competition between the two nations that became characteristic of the Cold War. Eisenhower's drive to ally with the civil rights movement was due in part to how the Soviet Union used anti-Black racism to delegitimize America's reputation as a harbinger of democracy and freedom abroad—especially in rapidly decolonizing Africa.

Nixon arrived in Ghana with an entourage that included accomplished campaigner Mrs. Pat Nixon and two prominent African American politicians: Representative Charles Diggs of Detroit and Representative Adam Clayton Powell Jr. of Harlem.[10] The presence of Diggs and Powell is unlikely to have been an ambiguous gesture to either African American constituents or Ghanaian allies. Representative Diggs was the only congressman to attend the 1955 trial of the lynchers of fourteen-year-old Emmett Till. He requested President Eisenhower call a special congressional session on civil rights following the trial's "not guilty" verdict turned in by an all-White Mississippi jury.[11] Rep. Adam Clayton Powell—a former pastor of the influential Abyssinian Baptist Church and stalwart of the African American political community—attended the Bandung Conference in 1955, which was an emancipated space filled with representatives from African and Asian nations who opposed colonialism and neocolonialism.[12] Powell gained favor with President Eisenhower by making a speech at Bandung that addressed his concerns about racism in the US with a fervent anticommunist stance.

Diggs and Powell were among a larger group of African American dignitaries in attendance, which included Nobel Peace Prize winner and coarchitect of the United Nations' Declaration of Human Rights Ralph Bunche, leader of the Brotherhood of Sleeping Car Porters A. Phillip Randolph, Executive Secretary of the National Urban League Lester Granger and his wife, as well as Rev. Martin Luther King and Mrs. Coretta Scott King.[13] The young Kings were "official guests" of Nkrumah because of their leadership of the thirteen-month-long Montgomery, Alabama, bus boycott—which played a key role in the desegregation of US public transportation in 1956. The *Amsterdam News* (a Black press publication) reported that the Kings' invitation to Ghana's independence celebration, where they would mingle with heads of state, was "an expression of world interest in the struggle of Negro Americans to achieve full civil and democratic rights."[14] The invitation was coordinated by activists Bayard Rustin and Bill Sutherland—who worked for Ghanaian finance minister K. A. Gbedemah.

At the same preindependence gala where the duchess danced with Nkrumah, a tuxedoed Reverend King confronted Nixon and reportedly said, "I want you to come visit us down in Alabama where we are seeking the same kind of freedom."[15] During a radio interview in Accra, King reflected that Ghana's independence showed him that "somehow the universe itself is on the side of freedom and justice. So this gives new hope to me in the struggle for freedom."[16] A few weeks later, back in his preacher's collar at the pulpit of Montgomery's Dexter Avenue Baptist Church, King hinted that his experience at the Polo Grounds radicalized his worldview and strengthened his resolve. "[These] half a million people . . . waited for this moment for years," he recalled. "I was crying for joy. . . . I knew about all of the struggles, and all of the agony that these people had gone through for this moment. . . . It reminded me of the fact that freedom never comes easy."[17]

BLACK STAR

As the radical King and dutiful duchess looked on, the new red, gold, and green Ghanaian flag ascended above hundreds of thousands of onlookers.[18] The top stripe of red commemorated the blood sacrifice many Ghanaians made to make independence possible. The center stripe of gold symbolized the wealth of the region and its prior colonial name, the Gold Coast. The bottom color of green saluted the nation's forests and farms. In front of the stripes lay a black star that signified Ghana's commitment to Pan-Africanism and a broader hope for the human rights enjoyment of all people of African descent.

"Pan-Africanism" is an umbrella term for a number of political views, which agree that transnational collaboration and mutual affirmation are the most effective means for Black communities to achieve equality and self-determination.[19] Black press journalists and Ghanaian officials framed this victory over British colonialism as a triumph for the entire African diaspora. The *Afro-American* reported, "The new state of Ghana is concerned with the treatment meted out to all people of African descent." Ghanaian minister of justice Ako Adjei asserted, "We consider our independence to be meaningless unless it is closely linked up with the . . . ultimate liberation of our brothers and sisters in other parts of the African continent."[20] For this infant government, the raising of the flag was the conclusion of one nationalist struggle for human rights and the beginning of a diasporic one.

The black star adorning the Ghanaian flag is likely to have been inspired by the Universal Negro Improvement Association's Black Star Line.[21] Led by Jamaican activists Marcus Garvey and Amy Jacques Garvey, the Universal Negro Improvement Association (UNIA) evolved into an international movement with hundreds of thousands of members advocating for racial self-determination during the early twentieth century.[22] The short-term objective of the organization was to mobilize an emigration to Liberia (without the Liberian government's permission), where UNIA members would establish a self-governing colony. Members of the UNIA were to travel to Africa via a shipping entity called the Black Star Line. This and many other UNIA plans did not come to fruition. However, the Garveys' pioneering "Black Is Beautiful" message, as well as their vision of an autonomous utopian Black nation, profoundly inspired millions of Black people throughout the world. This fact is simple to understand in historical context. With its promise of equality, abundance, empowerment, and racial success, the UNIA offered an alternative to the grim realities of discrimination, relative economic scarcity, cultural imperialism, and White supremacist violence with which all Black people struggle.[23]

Kwame Nkrumah asserted that Garvey's philosophy influenced him more than anything else during his stay in the US between 1935 and 1945 as a student and lecturer at Lincoln University—a historically Black college and university (HBCU) in Pennsylvania.[24] During his studies of economics, sociology, theology, and education in the US, Nkrumah's Pan-African and anticolonial ambitions emerged.[25] As the *Chicago Defender* reported, it was common for a small cadre of Gold Coast citizens to be selected for an educational track that led to universities in the United Kingdom and the US.[26]

Nkrumah developed important political connections as the president of the African Student Association of the US and Canada and as an organizer of the Pan-African Conference in New York in 1944.[27] During this period, he also began longtime friendships with diaspora scholar-activist C. L. R. James, as well as community organizer Grace Lee Boggs. He also traveled to Harlem and learned from progressive street corner speakers (self-appointed grassroots leaders who stood on stepladders and espoused antiracist philosophies).[28] The capitalist civil rights orientation of African American dignitaries who attended these independence celebrations—such as King and Powell—differed significantly from the human rights–oriented socialist radicalism in which Nkrumah immersed himself while in the US.

After the newly ascended Ghanaian flag blew in the breeze for a few moments, former political prisoner Nkrumah stepped before the microphone again to begin his address. "Once upon a time [Marcus Garvey] said he looked through the whole world to see if he could find a government of a Black people," Nkrumah noted. "He did not find one and he said he was going to create one. Marcus Garvey did not succeed. But here today the work of Rousseau, the work of Marcus Garvey . . . the work of our illustrious men who have gone before us has come to reality."[29] On March 6, 1957, that reality was that an anticolonial social movement organization named the Convention People's Party had evolved under the leadership of Nkrumah and his collaborators into the dominant political party of Ghana's first national government. Just ten years earlier, in 1947, Nkrumah returned to Accra from the US with his radical diasporic education as an anticolonial coalition of tribal chiefs and professionals called the United Gold Coast Convention (UGCC) was gaining momentum. A former Lincoln University classmate invited Nkrumah to become general secretary of the organization.

THE PEOPLE'S PARTY

At that time, resentment brewed among Gold Coast citizens about the two faces of the British Empire. West African soldiers had been recruited into service during World War II by a pledge of commonwealth unity and implied equity.[30] "Together," declared a popular poster crafted by the British military, which portrayed valiant officers from Asia, Africa, Australia, and New Zealand standing tall during the war to end all wars. However, in the post–Third Reich world, Britain doubled down on its exploitation of Africa by restabilizing its economy with help from the new International Monetary Fund (IMF) and continuing its imperial practices. By 1948, World War II veterans in the Gold Coast were discontent with the British Empire's failure to provide pensions and other promised rewards.

They channeled their disappointment into collective action.[31] Black veterans, who had helped protect the world from the expansion of genocidal fascism, marched peacefully to the colony governor's residence. When they came face-to-face with British police, officers shot and killed three decorated former soldiers and wounded dozens of others in the unarmed crowd. Following this human rights violation, resentment erupted into rebellion. For five days, violence and looting took hold of Accra and other Gold Coast cities.

Colonial authorities held the leadership of the United Gold Coast Convention responsible for the Accra Rebellion (or Accra Riots) and briefly imprisoned them.[32] Policy advising panels assembled by the British government, called the Watson Commission and the Coussey Committee, suggested the UK address this unrest by implementing a series of constitutional reforms that would enhance, yet continue to manage, local input into colonial governance.[33] Frustrated by the slow pace of change, Kwame Nkrumah led a faction that split from the United Gold Coast Convention and formed the more populist Convention People's Party (CPP) in 1949.[34] The renegade party's slogan? "Full Self-Government NOW."[35] (This divergence foreshadowed a similar conflict that would occur within the African American freedom struggle over a decade later, when the progressive youth activists of the Student Nonviolent Coordinating Committee (SNCC) traded their mainstream media–friendly slogan of "Freedom Now" for the more provocative "Black Power."[36])

According to Gold Coast governor Sir Charles Arden-Clarke, to achieve its aims the CPP began a campaign of nonviolent civil disobedience that party members labeled "positive action" and the colonial government described as "the subversion of lawful authority and the creation of chaos."[37] Nkrumah recollected that during this period, labor unions, students, women, and farmers played significant roles in the independence movement by making strikes and boycotts effective.[38] This broad base of support among the Gold Coast's less affluent enabled the CPP to survive counterinsurgency efforts long enough to be elected as the majority party in the new constitutional government in 1951.[39] Between 1951 and 1956, under Nkrumah's leadership, the Convention People's Party mobilized international support for the Gold Coast's development and independence, while it chipped away at local and international stereotypes about Africans' ability to lead and self-govern.[40] Once the Convention People's Party won a sweeping victory in the 1956 parliamentary elections, making the people's will to be autonomous indisputable, Britain finally agreed to grant the Gold Coast its independence.

THE END AND THE BEGINNING

For Gold Coast citizens and communities in the African diaspora, Ghana's independence victory signified the end of an old world order in which their self-image, heritage, and aspirations had no autonomous flag to wave. In the US, Black newspapers noted how Ghanaian independence disproved dehumanizing images of African life that were common in travelogues and textbooks such as "half-naked women with their breasts bared."[41] An editorial from the *Afro-American* proclaimed, "We can take justifiable pride in the continent from which our forebears came . . . we should refer to ourselves as Africans, rather than colored people."[42] New foreign minister K. A. Gbedemah explained that at institutions such as the International Monetary Fund, he and other officials had transformed in status from mere observers of decisions about their country to participants who were invited to a seat at the table.[43] The nation's new constitution guaranteed full suffrage to all and explicitly barred racial discrimination.[44]

Ghana's independence also represented the beginning of a cycle of contention about what the alternative national order would be. In front of the independence celebration crowd Nkrumah declared: "From now on there is a new African in the world [who] is ready to fight his own battle and show that, after all, the Black man is capable of managing his own affairs."[45] However, the country remained a voluntary member of the British Commonwealth, which is an association of colonies and former colonies. After independence, Queen Elizabeth II continued on as head of state in Ghana's constitutional monarchy until 1960. The disjunctive landscape of Accra that lay outside the Polo Grounds—simple farmlands and roadside market stands next to gleaming high-rise hotels, banks, and television studios—indicated the tensions created by the hybridization of Western and indigenous in this new nation.

The question of how to fashion a singular, cohesive national identity out of many identifications with tribes, genders, classes, and sexual orientations—or one diasporic identity out of many nationalities and ethnicities—shadowed Nkrumah's optimism about the transformative possibilities of self-determination and Pan-Africanism. At the dawn of this nation's existence, it was unclear just how Africans would be new in this world. There were no guarantees about how long they would have a seat at the table or if that seat would ever be equal to those long held by European colonizers and their American and Soviet allies.

Ghana's struggle to emerge as an independent nation and the event's influence on African American antiracist activists illuminate the pathways of a diaspora underground. Frustrations with domestic elites over the slow process of attaining racial equality led activists such as Rev. Dr. Martin Luther King to seek inspiration from the example of African independence. Indigenous institutions—such as the historically Black Lincoln University and the Black press publication the *Chicago Defender*—provided resources for activists to exchange ideas and strategies for action across borders. In addition, these institutions framed the success of Ghana's independence struggle as directly relevant to the ability of African American constituents to value their African heritage, capacity for self-governance, and increasing distaste for racist stereotypes (which were sometimes camouflaged as benevolent paternalism). Nkrumah had come to his work as an anticolonial leader after traveling through the routes of a prior, World War II–era diaspora underground. Ten years later, as a black star–adorned flag flew over the ecstatic African crowd at the Polo Grounds, he and his colleagues in the Convention People's Party began to help build a new one.

3

"A Free Black Mind"
Un Esprit Noir Libre
عقل أسود حر
Akili ya Bure Nyeusi

WHILE THE PEOPLE of Ghana celebrated in 1957, the people of Algeria remained embroiled in a grisly independence war that was reaching its nadir with the Battle of Algiers. France's colonizing violence toward the indigenous people of Algeria began with an invasion of the North African country in 1830. The aggression continued with the racist and Islamophobic Indigenous Code (Code de l'Indigénat) and other oppressive policies. By the time the National Liberation Front (FLN) declared war in November 1954 to secure both Algerian independence and Muslim sovereignty, metropolitan French and local governments had failed to respond to decades of Algerians' nonviolent advocacy for their human rights.[1]

Techniques of domination used by the French against Algerians were similar to those employed by British institutions against Ghanaians and Tanzanians, as well as by Belgian institutions against the Congolese. Euphemistically described as "indirect rule" in many American and

European history textbooks, this system created a power structure in which a small minority of White settlers controlled and disciplined the greater colonized majority of people of color through a cadre of administrative institutions including schools, churches, and colonial legislatures.[2] All of this surveillance and control serves the purpose of extracting human, cultural, and natural resources from colonies for the disproportionate benefit of externally based enterprises and governments.

Much like Jim Crow laws in the US South, the Indigénat implemented a segregated society in French colonies with different sets of rules for citizens based on their race and ethnicity.[3] In Algeria, *les indigènes* (majority indigenous Muslim population) were largely excluded from voting, educational opportunities, sustainable employment, and adequate housing. On the other hand, the minority community of European descent—predominantly Spanish and Portuguese with some French (nicknamed *les pieds-noirs*, or "the black footed")—enjoyed privileged socioeconomic status and disproportionate influence in the electorate.[4] For example, a 1954 study revealed *pied-noir* farmers owned over ten times more land than their Muslim counterparts did.[5] The salaries of *les indigènes* were, on average, thirty times less than those of European Algerians.[6]

Within the French Empire—which included Guinea and Martinique—the Code and other colonial institutions legitimized this day-to-day practice of subjection by criminalizing and objectifying "native" identity.[7] Just as it was commonplace in the US during the mid-twentieth century for Whites to address adult African Americans as "boy" or "girl" instead of "Sir" or "Miss," the *pieds-noirs* in Algeria would routinely *tutoyer* any Muslim (*tutoyer* is a French form of speech usually directed at children and animals).[8] Similar to how African Americans have been stereotyped in US popular culture as lazy, intellectually feeble, criminal, and rapacious, the Muslim Algerian was consistently articulated by the *pieds-noirs* as incompetent and violent.[9] Renowned French author, World War II veteran, and anticolonial activist Jules Roy recalled of his childhood in the Algerian village of Sidi Moussa, "I was always being told . . . 'They don't have the same needs we do.' . . . I was glad to believe it. . . . Who suffers seeing oxen sleep on straw or eating grass?"[10] In other words, French discourse naturalized the observable suffering of *les indigènes*, as well as validated the French Empire as a benevolent civilizing mission.

After World War II—as activists in the Gold Coast and other colonies in the British Commonwealth questioned the consequences of being "Together" with the United Kingdom—a counterdiscourse also emerged among intellectuals, artists, and activists from throughout the Francophone colonies. For example, in Paris in 1947, the Pan-African journal *Présence Africaine* (founded by Senegalese professor Alioune Diop and edited by Martinican poet Aimé Césaire, among others) published essays and literature that challenged the alleged universality of French humanism.[11] Though children in French colonial public schools from Caribbean Guadeloupe to African Guinea were learning the French Revolution's ideals of "Liberté, Egalité, Fraternité" (Liberty, Equality, Fraternity) and were encouraged to think of themselves as French citizens, Césaire argued that in reality the French concept of the "rights of man" was "narrow and fragmentary, incomplete, and biased, and all things considered, sordidly racist."[12]

By 1957, the amplifying voice of *la France d'outre-mer* ("overseas France," a euphemism for the nation's empire) was vigorously critiquing the colonial power. The anticolonial movement was at times supported by in-country progressives, including Jean-Paul Sartre. This burgeoning coalition consistently highlighted France's hypocrisy as a colonizer given the self-destructiveness that is bred from being defined as a savage, the impoverishment caused by enduring marginalization, the alienation that arises by being able to succeed only by dominating others in your community, and the premature death caused by extraction and forced participation in an international capitalist system.[13]

LA TORTURE

During the same period in Algeria, two strands of independence activism emerged.[14] One was led by Ferhat Habbas, who advocated for the full inclusion of Muslim Algerians into French citizenship. Another was led by the militant nationalist Messali Hadj. This militant strand—along with hardening French opposition to reform—eventually inspired the Front de Libération Nationale (National Liberation Front, FLN). The first nine founders of the FLN, known as *les neuf historiques*, or the historic nine, included World War II veteran Ahmed Ben Bella. Ben Bella and several others had followed Hadj and, after being imprisoned, became so radicalized (and perhaps frustrated) that they believed armed confrontation was the only solution to French dominance. From the beginning, the founders adopted a collective leadership principle to diminish divisions between members of two indigenous Algerian ethnic groups: Arab and Kabyle.

Emboldened by the victory of the communist anticolonial Vietminh forces in Vietnam, the FLN leaders and a larger group of revolutionary operatives voted to begin an "unlimited revolution" that would not end until full independence.[15] A message spread through the Algerian underground: "Arm, Train, Prepare!" On November 1, 1954, the FLN began the Algerian Revolution in a guerrilla style that would become its signature, with fewer than four hundred firearms and homemade bombs. Although orders called for "no attacks on European civilians," Muslims, *pieds noirs*, and Frenchmen were killed. Millions of dollars' worth of property was destroyed. The FLN followed the attack with its proclamation of objectives via Cairo radio and pamphlets scattered throughout the country.

Between 1954 and 1956, the French government's response to the FLN transformed from dismissiveness to sometimes extralegal counterinsurgency. The escalating violence reflected the intransigence of the three sides of the conflict. FLN founders had pledged to struggle "by any means until the realization of [their] goal."[16] French officials and military leaders believed a defeat in Algeria—following the humiliation of Nazi occupation during World War II and their loss in the First Indochina War (known as the French War in Vietnam)—would have been an intolerable blow to France's status as a global power.[17] "We want to halt the decadence of the West," a French colonel explained, unironically. "That is our duty. That is why we must win the war in Algeria."[18] The *pieds-noirs* felt as if they were too alienated from Europe to return and too economically and socially invested in the racial privileges they enjoyed to embrace an inclusive society.[19] This commitment to victory at all costs seduced FLN leadership, French officers, and KKK-like *pied-noir* paramilitary groups into rationalizing the terrorism against civilians and the systemic human rights violations that came to characterize the Battle of Algiers.

According to historians, one's beliefs about which of the following events provoked the Battle of Algiers may depend on one's sympathies in the conflict.[20] First, to appease *pied-noir* outrage, in June 1956 French authorities executed FLN operatives Ahmed Zabane, who was found guilty of killing a gamekeeper, and Abdelkader Ferradj, who was found guilty of participating in an ambush that killed eight civilians, including a child. The sentence was carried out by guillotine, the streamlined beheading device made famous during the French Revolution. Members of the Muslim community found these executions particularly atrocious given Ferradj was unable to walk and had only one eye. Shortly afterward, the FLN attempted to make good on their vow that one hundred French would be killed for every guillotined comrade by gunning down civilians in front of the chic cafés in the European quarter of Algiers. Toward the end of the summer, a *pied-noir* terrorist group took responsibility for bombing a house in the overcrowded Casbah—the segregated Muslim ghetto of Algiers—where FLN operatives involved in the shootings earlier that summer had stayed. The bomb also razed three neighboring houses, killing seventy Muslims, including women and children.

In more rural areas, FLN squads had mercilessly targeted Muslim men they believed were sympathetic to the French or simply too moderate politically. However, the intensification of French and *pied-noir* violence against the disabled, women, and children along with increasingly oppressive curfews helped leaders Saadi Yacef, Ali LaPointe, and Djamila Bouhired recruit educated middle-class youths in Algiers to the independence effort. For example, on September 30, 1956, law students Zohra Drif and Samia Lakhdari traded their *hijabs* for sundresses and beach bags in order to smuggle bombs past checkpoints at the Casbah perimeter to the *pied-noir* hangouts Milk-Bar and Caféteria.[21] The bombs were made by a chemistry student at the local university.[22] In the months that followed, under the direction of *neuf historiques* member Ben M'Hidi, Saadi Yacef—a slick-talking baker's son—mobilized over a thousand clandestine operatives as well as an extensive network of bomb factories and weapons caches in the Casbah.[23]

FLN leadership's prior order to not kill women, children, or elders was abandoned. The use of violence against civilians created a moral dilemma for a number of devoted FLN members. While sitting at the Milk-Bar among young civilians, bomber Zohra Drif reportedly endured revulsion symptoms before carrying through with her task. She was able to steel herself only by remembering the *pied-noir* attack of a home in the Casbah earlier that summer.[24] As the battle continued through 1957, Yacef began visiting the sites of bombings he ordered disguised as a woman.[25] While holding a machine gun, he confessed to French anthropologist and concentration camp survivor Germaine Tillion that on one visit, he wept after discovering that one of these explosions had killed a *pied noir* "football friend" and dismembered the friend's fiancée. Devoid of his charming smile and slick talk, Yacef told Tillion, "We are assassins. It's the only way in which we can express ourselves." Following through on their commitment to pursue self-determination "by any means," some FLN operatives empowered themselves against their colonizers but began a war with their own consciences.

In order to suppress the FLN's attacks in Algiers, French forces routinely employed counterinsurgency tactics that violated the 1949 Geneva Conventions' standards for governments' wartime treatment of people who are nonparticipants in a conflict. Nonparticipants include combatants who have surrendered and parties who are *hors de combat* (outside the fight) because they are incapacitated due to being ill or detained.[26] These standards require providing medical assistance for the wounded and prohibit torture, humiliating treatment, and extrajudicial executions.[27] In addition, the conventions forbade discriminatory treatment based on race, color, religion, or wealth.[28] The boundaries of wartime engagement set by the Geneva Conventions can be understood as similar to boxing match rules for a fair fight—bystanders can observe unscathed, one can survive by throwing in the towel, or one can opt out if too hurt to continue.

In spite of the Geneva Conventions, French World War II and First Indochina War veteran General Jacques Massu ordered that known or suspected FLN operatives be subjected to *la torture*.[29] Casbah inhabitants were cordoned off and, by the thousands, routinely stopped, frisked, and detained indefinitely without cause or due process.[30] Soldiers employed battery, waterboarding, and electrocution against suspected and known FLN operatives and independence supporters to acquire "human intelligence."[31] One interrogation method involved suspending a male detainee naked by his feet—with his hands bound behind his back—and plunging his head repeatedly into a bucket of water until he was half drowned. A popular method of interrogation used the *gègène*, a device that fastened electrodes to sensitive areas, including fingers, mouths, ears, and genitals.[32]

Other techniques included pouring cold water in the mouths of detainees until their bellies and lungs filled with fluid, thrusting foreign objects into women's vaginas, and inserting high pressure hoses into rectums.[33] Some suspects were disappeared via mass graves in the countryside, watery graves in the sea, and in the case of FLN leader Ben M'Hidi, barely credible "suicides."[34] After the war, Massu admitted that he was "not frightened of the word" torture and that French forces used extralegal counterinsurgency tactics against the FLN, as well as the larger Muslim community.[35]

In the short term, Massu's technique of *guerre revolutionnaire*—"fighting terrorist fire with fire"—succeeded.[36] French forces were able to dismantle the FLN's organization in Algiers from the bottom to the top. On September 24, 1957, a little over a year after the Battle of Algiers began, Saadi Yacef and Zohra Drif surrendered after a standoff with French forces at No. 4 Rue Canton in the Casbah. On October 8, French soldiers discovered FLN leader Hassiba Ben Bouali (age nineteen), along with twelve-year-old Petit Omar, crouched in a compartment behind a wall at 5 Rue Aberdames.[37] They had spent weeks making paper cutouts in silence to pass the time with their comrade, twenty-seven-year-old Ali LaPointe.

Dangerously handsome, LaPointe was recruited by FLN militants a year or so earlier while serving a prison sentence for resisting arrest in Barberousse prison, where disabled Abdelkader Ferradj was guillotined to FLN outrage in 1956.[38] In prison, LaPointe began to awaken his political consciousness and understand himself as a "victim of colonialism" (in FLN language) due to education by fellow inmates. Before prison, he had carved out a living as a pimp after surviving a childhood characterized by poverty, homelessness, violence, and sexual abuse. After escaping Barberousse, LaPointe contacted Saadi Yacef and mobilized his Casbah street network to serve the FLN. In a short time, he transformed from small-time hustler to FLN lieutenant and revolutionary political assassin.

Outside of the house with the compartment where LaPointe, Omar, and Ben Bouali were cornered and unarmed, French soldiers called for the FLN soldiers to surrender three times. When the calls went unanswered, they detonated bombs. The explosion obliterated 5 Rue Aberdames along with several neighboring houses in the Casbah. The corpses of these two young men and one child were found underneath the rubble, along with the bodies of seventeen other Muslim civilians. Four French soldiers were also injured. LaPointe had survived life as a hustler and a prisoner, but he could not outlive his radical opposition to the colonial system that had put him on the street and in captivity. His body was able to be identified only by the tattoo on his chest, "Go Forward or Die."[39]

DEFEAT LEADS TO TRANSNATIONAL STRENGTH

After Yacef's arrest and LaPointe's death, the surface of Algerian life returned to normal.[40] However, the new peace obscured two fundamental shifts that would ultimately work in the FLN's favor. First, the "luminous glare" that mainstream media focused on Algiers during the battle increased international support for Algerian independence by the international left.[41] For example, writers and intellectuals—including feminist pioneer Simone de Beauvoir and existentialist philosopher Jean-Paul Sartre—signed the *Manifeste des 121*, which "advocated for military disobedience" by French soldiers against further torture orders and asserted that the FLN was waging a legitimate independence struggle.[42] Popular Black newspaper the *Chicago Defender* reported the war to its African American readers, who were also engaged in a bloody struggle for human rights. "Algerians want independence and apparently no sacrifice either in blood or money is too costly for them. . . . France cannot shut her eyes to the grim reality of a people's unswerving right to freedom."[43] Ironically, France's willingness to fight "fire with fire" in order to avoid being further diminished following its occupation by Nazi forces and defeat in Vietnam led to an erosion of the nation's credibility at home and abroad.

The defeated FLN leaders also recognized that terrorist acts in cities and direct confrontation with French forces were futile strategies.[44] They created a new base in neighboring Tunisia to further internationalize their efforts. Prior to the Battle of Algiers, FLN leader Ahmed Ben Bella had greater difficulties gaining significant material aid from their North African neighbors.[45] After the battle, the publicized human rights violations endured by Muslim Algerians rallied newly independent nations in the region to offer greater support.

The groundwork for internationalizing FLN work in Tunis (the capital of Tunisia) had been laid by a number of previously exiled supporters, including Afro-Caribbean psychiatrist Frantz Fanon. Fanon began his unlikely journey to becoming part of the FLN by traveling to France in 1943 to fight for the Allies in World War II, during which he earned the Croix de Guerre. During a brief return to his home island of Martinique, he worked with his mentor—poet, anticolonial activist, and *Présence Africaine* editor Aimé Césaire. Afterward, Fanon attended the University of Lyon in France to pursue his medical degree with a specialization in psychiatry. During his studies, Fanon wrote the classic 1952 text *Black Skin, White Masks*. In this work, he described realizing that although he was taught to think of himself as a first-class French citizen while growing up middle-class and lighter skinned in Martinique, in the eyes of metropolitan France he was simply a Black man. "As I begin to recognize that the Negro is the symbol of sin," Fanon wrote, "I catch myself hating the Negro. But then I recognize that I am a Negro . . . I have only one solution . . . to reach out for the universal."[46]

Shortly before the eruption of the Algerian Revolution, Fanon accepted a position in Algiers as psychiatric chief of staff at Blida-Joinville hospital.[47] While offering psychological trauma treatment to both Muslim torture victims and French soldiers ordered to carry out abuse, he became more radicalized.[48] Through Dr. Pierre Chaulet, Fanon joined the FLN. For years, he used his anthropological studies of rural Algerian communities as a cover for his clandestine revolutionary activities. By the beginning of the Battle of Algiers, Fanon resigned from Blida through a letter that was later published posthumously in the book *Toward the African Revolution*. He wrote, "One did not have to be a psychologist to divine . . . beneath [the Algerian's] stripped humility, a fundamental aspiration to dignity." "A society that drives its members to desperate solutions," he continued, "is a non-viable society, a society to be replaced."[49] His increasing militancy attracted the attention of the French military as the Algerian revolution escalated.

Fanon fled to Tunis, where he served in the FLN Press Services by writing a number of anonymously published essays for the organization's news organ, *El Moudjahid* (The Holy Warrior). Fanon's writing emphasized his theories that all anticolonial struggle was linked, that the FLN was the vanguard of the African revolution, and that colonialism was a manifestation of racism.[50] As a representative of the Algerian independence movement, Fanon addressed the First Congress of Negro Writers and

Artists in Paris, which was an emancipated space whose attendees included Aimé Césaire, Sengalese anticolonialist Léopold Senghor, and African American author Richard Wright. "A country that . . . draws its substance from the exploitation of other peoples, makes those peoples inferior." Fanon continued, "[However], racism is . . . not a constant of the human spirit."[51] The FLN's expansion of their efforts across nation-state borders was due to their inability to win concessions with French authorities. This led them to a diaspora underground.

JIM CROW'S DIPLOMATIC EXPERIENCE

As Fanon and other FLN leaders kept fighting the Algerian independence war, Guinea's anticolonial struggle was embodied by Ahmed Sékou Touré—a gifted political organizer and ardent labor advocate. In 1953, Touré rose to prominence by leading the Postal Workers Union (Postes, Télégraphes, et Téléphones) in an unprecedented strike, which won a number of concessions from the French colonial administration.[52] He became leader of the Parti Démocratique de Guinée (Democratic Party of Guinea, PDG). The PDG was the Guinean chapter of the Rassemblement Démocratique Africain, or African Democratic Rally (RDA)—a regional independence organization with participants from throughout French West Africa (including Senegal and Ivory Coast).[53]

As the RDA's mobilization for independence gained momentum in the mid-1950s, Touré's popularity within Guinea grew due to his, and the PDG's, embrace of participation by less educated members of the community. The educated elite of the Francophone colonies, which Fanon would later describe in his classic text *The Wretched of the Earth* as the "national bourgeoisie," were known at the time in Guinea as *les évolués*, or the evolved.[54] Self-taught and self-made, Touré stated in the trade union newsletter *L'Ouvrier*, "You must never believe that ability lies in the so-called évolué element . . . some of our best leaders are illiterates. . . . They are most apt . . . [to] make better understood the aspirations of the masses."[55] By encouraging everyday Guineans to see themselves as leaders, Touré addressed colonialism's psychology of subjection and self-doubt.

In 1958, a year after Ghanaian independence and the end of the Battle of Algiers, the entire French Union (formerly the French Empire) participated in a referendum about whether or not to accept a new French constitution. A "yes" vote by a territory indicated a desire to remain part of France. A "no" vote indicated a choice of independence. In response to France's threats to withdraw all aid from territories who chose autonomy, Touré stated plainly—at an event where French prime minister Charles de Gaulle was also in attendance—"We prefer poverty in freedom to wealth in slavery."[56] Due to the mass mobilization of the PDG, which rallied with the slogan "Say 'NO' to Inequality, 'NO' to Irresponsibility," over 95 percent of Guinean voters voted against remaining a colony.[57] The *Afro-American* (a Black press publication distributed widely in Washington, DC, and surrounding areas) reported that Touré and his people were "jubilant over the fact that freedom at last was theirs and prepared for their new nation."[58] The *Defender* optimistically opined to its predominantly Black American readership that Guinea's "economy can be made self-supporting . . . with a little diligence."[59]

By the time the people of Guinea boldly chose self-determination, the US civil rights movement had arrived at a critical junction. On one hand, activists (including the Reverend Dr. Martin Luther King Jr.) realized two achievements scholars acknowledge are significant to social movement success.[60] First, activist leadership networks were developing within and between indigenous institutions such as local kinship affiliations, progressive Black churches, the Black press, and historically Black colleges and universities (HBCUs).[61] Second, more and more African Americans were developing what sociologist Doug McAdam describes as cognitive liberation, which is a group's awareness that its situation is unjust and—equally important—that collective action can transform its circumstances.[62] African American institutions were challenging White supremacist invalidation of the value of Black life and providing resources that helped their participants to get involved politically. For example, the response to *Jet* magazine's publication of the heartbreakingly gruesome photo of teen lynching victim Emmett Till in 1955, as well as the internationally recognized successes of efforts such as the Montgomery Bus Boycott, illustrated that organizing worked to expand racial equality.[63]

On the other hand, the slow pace of change and hardening segregationist resistance planted seeds of doubt among activists about the ability of pacifism or less confrontational direct action to gain leverage with decision makers. The frustrations with US elites that would lead African American organizers to engage a diaspora underground were already beginning to fester. Some participants in the movement began to advocate for armed self-defense.

In 1959, World War II veteran Robert F. Williams was building his Monroe, North Carolina, chapter of the National Association for the Advancement of Colored People (NAACP) by going door-to-door at "beauty parlors, pool halls, and street corners."[64] Williams boasted that unlike most NAACP chapters, Monroe was predominately working-class with a strong contingent of domestic workers.[65] Organizing in the shadow of the Ku Klux Klan—which held local rallies with as many as fifteen thousand in attendance—the military veterans in this NAACP chapter began to teach members of all genders how to use weapons in self-defense.[66] Williams acquired a charter from the National Rifle Association (NRA) after becoming embittered by his neighbors' inability to receive any reasonable consideration in the criminal justice system.

Empowered after fending off illegal attacks by the Klan and local police, Williams stated to the press, "The Negro in the South cannot expect justice in the courts. . . . He must meet violence with violence, lynching with lynching."[67] During a time when Black people in the South were still expected to step into the gutter if a White person were to approach them on the sidewalk, Williams's proclamations about the value of Black life and the community's entitlement to protect it were sensational enough to make national news. Although his statements were condemned by national civil rights leadership, his advocacy for self-defense reflected the grim, dangerous reality of antiracist organizing under Jim Crow, as well as the growing militancy of African American communities.[68] Williams would inspire a younger generation of leaders who articulated this unflinching commitment to self-defense as the slogan "Black Power."

At the same time, a young cadre of diplomats from newly independent Ghana and Guinea arrived in Washington, DC and New York City. Black press coverage of Africans in the diplomatic core reflected how the early successes of the African independence movement further subverted the faulty, White supremacist logic of American segregation. In the article "Ghana Envoy Jim Crowed in Maryland," the *Amsterdam* reported that

Finance Minister K. A. Gbedemah had never been "so insulted in [his] whole life" after stopping for a cold drink and being told that he had to consume his beverage outside of the premises.[69] The headline "Dear Head Nigger" appeared above an article that described a "vicious race-hate letter" received by the leader of Ghana's UN delegation "at his $150,000 home" (approximately $1.2M, adjusted for inflation in 2021).[70] The *Afro-American* newspaper proudly shared with its readership that at HBCU North Carolina A&T College, Ghana's ambassador to the US corrected a White reporter who claimed Great Britain had handed his country independence: "Freedom is never given—it must be fought for."[71]

During an event hosted by the governor of North Carolina, newly elected prime minister Sékou Touré "attacked racial prejudice," according to the *Chicago Defender*.[72] Touré stated, "it was not the color of a man's skin . . . but the spirit of brotherhood in him which counted." The prime minister's visit throughout the US with his wife, Hadja Andrée Touré, took them from North Carolina to New York and Washington, DC. The goodwill tour was also documented by the popular African American magazine *Ebony* and the *Afro-American*. Touré aimed to secure economic aid from the US in exchange for Guinea's allyship in the Cold War.[73] Given France's refusal to support Guinea in its choice of independence—after forcing the country into economic dependence for decades—Touré's government needed new sources of support to avoid the "poverty in freedom" that he'd told French president de Gaulle his people preferred. Cultivating connections with African Americans through a diaspora underground was part of his new government's strategy for survival.

The African American press and members of the Black middle class appeared to be particularly interested in the image and poise of Mrs. Touré as an example of respectable women's leadership. A reporter accompanied Mrs. Touré on a shopping trip to a luxury department store in Washington, DC, where she purchased a "white beaded French purse—price $46.75!" (nearly $400 in 2021 prices).[74] Her ability to shop freely is likely to have made an impression on African American readers, who were in 1959—and continue to be at present—routinely racially profiled in such luxury retail environments. Another Black press publication effusively described a reception for the Guinean first lady that was hosted by the National Council of Negro Women, the civil rights organization that advanced what historian Evelyn Higginbotham describes as a "politics of respectability."[75] Through indigenous institutions, the ability of both masculine and feminine African independence leaders to negotiate the US racial hierarchy from a position of strength was consistently broadcast to the African American community.

HAMBURGERS AND COFFEE

At around the same time, the success of African independence organizations raised the stakes for African American insurgency among the classes of '62, '63, and '64—which were streaming onto the campuses of historically Black colleges and universities. John Lewis, an Alabama sharecropper's son, recalled that when he returned to Nashville's Fisk University, "there was a sense of urgency . . . among Black students. . . . Amazing changes were happening in Africa . . . we couldn't help being thrilled . . . but also a little ashamed. Here were Black people thousands of miles away achieving liberation . . . and we couldn't even get a hamburger and a Coke at a soda fountain."[76] Graduate student James Forman was specifically inspired by the Convention People's Party's effective use of nonviolent direct action in Ghana, which he learned about from groundbreaking sociologist St. Clair Drake and his contact with activists in African independence organizations (including Tanzanian leader Julius Nyerere).[77] Stokely Carmichael—a buttoned-up, Harlem raised, Trinidadian Bronx High School of Science alum—arrived at Howard University in Washington, DC.[78] His classmates were inspired by stories of African diplomats standing up to the humiliation of segregation on a highway from New York City to Washington.[79] Author and activist James Baldwin summed up the youth perspective to a New York Times reporter: "At the rate we are going, all of Africa will be free before we can get a lousy cup of coffee."[80]

The new heightened visibility of African presidents and first ladies may have contributed to this "positive identity crisis," which historian, Spelman professor, and movement ally Howard Zinn observed among this emerging generation of antiracist activists. In his work *SNCC: The New Abolitionists*, Zinn asserted, "[Youths] must detect some meaningful resemblance between what [they] have come to see in [themselves] and what [their] sharpened awareness tells [them] others . . . expect [them] to be." "It would be hard to imagine a more startling contrast," he wrote, "than that between the young Negro as the old South saw him . . . and the vision of himself he suddenly perceived in the glare of the 1960s."[81] Ironically, the African heads of state who helped inspire the boldness of African American student activism would soon confront the tension between their self-image as proud Africans, their visions for their new nations, and how their former colonizers, the US, and the Soviet Union saw Africa's place in the world.

John Lewis's classmate Diane Nash invited him to attend a weekly workshop on nonviolent philosophy led by Rev. James Lawson, an activist with the Fellowship for Reconciliation. Struck by her intelligence, intensity, and movie star looks, Lewis supported Nash as she encouraged her fellow students to evolve from learning about nonviolent resistance to engaging in it.[82] As the Nashville youths were preparing for their campaign, on February 1, 1960, four freshmen named Joe McNeil, Ezell Blair, Frank McCain, and David Richmond gained national media attention when they staged a sit-in at a segregated lunch counter after weeks of contemplating direct action. They were students at North Carolina A&T College in Greensboro, where the Tourés had visited the previous year.

This group, which became known as the Greensboro Four, quickly mushroomed into over fifty thousand youths who staged sit-ins, wade-ins, stand-ins and other actions to challenge Jim Crow across the Southern United States.[83] In the mid-twentieth century, a lunch counter, or luncheonette, could be found in the downtown areas of cities where a Chipotle or Starbucks might be found in 2021. Simple, inexpensive American fare would be quickly served to customers seated on stools. Luncheonettes were popular features in the small department stores or drugstores (similar to Walgreens or CVS) that populated once thriving downtown areas in smaller Southern American cities. Below the Mason-Dixon line, along with advertisements for Coca-Cola and Pepsi, these establishments were adorned with signs such as "We Cater to White Trade Only."[84] In its time, the lunch counter was an institution that embodied the mundane nature of everyday American life, which made it a brilliant choice for a statement about the absurdity of White supremacy. By focusing on the little things— for example, luncheonettes, swimming pools, libraries—youth activists illuminated the pervasively grotesque nature of racial segregation and the viciousness of those who were determined to defend it.

Mainstream press outlets, including the relatively new national television news, portrayed these actions as spontaneous outbursts of rebellion. In reality, young participants placed careful thought and training into the aesthetics and physicality of their political performance.[85] For example, openly gay Bayard Rustin—who advised leaders of the Montgomery Bus Boycott—taught Howard University's student activist collective, the Nonviolent Action Group (NAG), the basic techniques of nonviolent confrontation, which requires near superhuman restraint in the face of vicious taunts and violent behavior. Some students at Claflin College and South Carolina State chose to directly face physical assault from segregationists during sit-ins by placing their hands at their sides unclenched, while others planned to protect themselves with specific positions, such as folding their hands over their heads or lying on their sides with knees to chin.[86] A Nashville activist remembered that her friends at sit-ins "were determined to be courteous and well-behaved. . . . Most of them read or studied . . . for three or four hours."[87] The protesters wore carefully straightened and curled bobs, meticulously lined and faded haircuts, and crisp starched shirts and ties, as well as below-the-knee and over-the-collarbone dresses to convey an image of middle-class respectability and order. This styling and choice of action was intended to depict these young African Americans as undeserving of racist treatment. Of course, nobody deserves racist treatment. But the America they were fighting for did not seem to know that.

By April 1960, just weeks after Greensboro, it was apparent to veteran activist Ella Baker that the courage and radicalism of Black youths could be sustained into an even more impactful force. Baker had served for years as an NAACP field secretary in the South. She effectively built long-term relationships with community-based leaders and promoted the decentralization of authority within the organization.[88] As this wave of protest swept the South, Baker was chief of staff at the Southern Christian Leadership Conference (SCLC)—an uneasy fit given Baker's feminism and support for grassroots leadership that was indigenous to Black communities.[89] Baker persuaded the SCLC, which was headed by Dr. Martin Luther King, to sponsor a South-wide Youth Leadership Conference for sit-in movement activists at her alma mater, the HBCU Shaw University. Over two hundred people attended from nineteen northern colleges and fifty-eight different Southern communities, including Nashville's Diane Nash, John Lewis, and Rev. James Lawson.[90]

Lawson encouraged students to continue embodying the philosophy of nonviolent direct action. He warned that without their continued commitment, "[all] of Africa would be free before the American Negro attains first class citizenship."[91] In Ella Baker's conference address, "Bigger Than a Hamburger," she summarized key takeaways from the students' discussions about the purpose and direction of their movement. "Current sit-ins and other demonstrations are concerned with something much bigger than a hamburger," she said. The movement was concerned with the moral implications of racial discrimination for the "whole world" and the "Human Race." Baker explained that the students' international perspective was connected to its philosophy that "it is important to keep the movement democratic and to avoid struggles for personal leadership."[92] Baker's and Lawson's statements reveal that seeing American racism as an international issue further emboldened student activists to become agents of social change.

Although governing a nation is grander than getting a hamburger, the goal of African independence and what would grow into Black Power was the same: to enjoy self-determination—the human right to define oneself for oneself as an individual and as a community. As a result of Baker's mentorship, the youth activists ultimately agreed to establish an independent organization that would engage in direct action to challenge segregation and mobilize voter registration to end African American disenfranchisement in the South.[93] They decided to call themselves the Student Nonviolent Coordinating Committee (SNCC).

THE COMMON SENSE OF HBCUS

HBCUs like Fisk, Howard, and Shaw were founded because until the late 1960s (or later), predominately White institutions of higher education systemically excluded people of color, women, and people who were openly LGBTQ. Often administered by White philanthropists, HBCUs aimed to train a management class that upheld mainstream bourgeois values and served as a buffer between Black community aspirations and the segregated status quo.[94] Acclaimed sociologist and Howard University professor E. Franklin Frazier observed in his classic text *The Black Bourgeoisie*, "The chief aim [of HBCUs] was Christianization and moral training . . . [students] seemed to suffer from . . . fear that if they did not exhibit a 'spirit of cheerful gratitude' towards the [W]hite northerners, they would be expelled from the school."[95]

Ironically, the sit-in dress code of jackets and ties for men and stockings and heels for women—which helped create the iconic imagery of young Black serenity in the face of hysterical defensive racism that changed American hearts and minds about Jim Crow—was inspired by HBCU dress codes, which demonstrated that there was no difference between these students and those attending Harvard, Amherst, or Wellesley.[96] The esteem placed by the African American community onto the faculty and students of HBCUs influenced the self-image of campus participants. A Howard alumnus reflected, "I was aware of historically black colleges growing up in Tuskegee. . . . I loved the attitude that they had and that they still have . . . a tremendous amount of positive arrogance."[97] This generation's defiance was fostered in part by the upward mobility culture of HBCUs.

Black students from throughout the diaspora were drawn to the HBCU promise of academic training and access to the elite social networks necessary for professional success. However, the manner in which the administrations of HBCUs linked Black leadership with class privilege did not always promote diasporic, class, gender, or even racial unity. Sitting among his classmates from throughout Africa, the Caribbean, and Latin America at Howard's foreign student orientation, Caribbean American scholarship student Stokely Carmichael recalled that an African administrator "planted the fear of 'American Negroes' in our consciousness. We . . . were warned not to venture freely [in DC] because of crime. . . . Had it come out of a White mouth, I'd have unhesitatingly dismissed it as racist."[98]

Although young people are ideal candidates for social movement participation because they are often free from external pressures (such as children) or crystallized notions of what is supposedly impossible or unrealistic, many HBCU administrators did not support the activism of their students.[99] At Voorhees College in North Carolina, the Board of Trustees instructed the school's president to put a stop to demonstrations.[100] Spelman College fired tenured professor Howard Zinn because he and his wife, Roslyn Zinn, advised student activists (including future Pulitzer Prize winner Alice Walker and future Presidential Medal of Freedom winner Marian Wright Edelman), provided a brave space in their home for debating strategies, and applied classroom texts to their daily experiences of racial and economic equality. The Zinns also supplied their car for the diagramming and choreographing of demonstrations.[101] Atlanta would become the headquarters of SNCC operations in part because it was home to the Atlanta University Center (which includes Spelman, Morehouse College, and Clark Atlanta University). Administrative resistance to students' civic engagement reflected the inherent and unsustainable tension within HBCUs between aiming to foster community advancement and defining that advancement as exclusion and privilege.

The SNCC activists on HBCU campuses redefined the terms of racial uplift in a manner that challenged HBCUs and other community leaders to walk the walk of their institutions' stated principles. In an article for the *Nation* entitled "Finishing School for Pickets," Howard Zinn observed the change in his students caused by their antiracist activism in Atlanta. "They will use every method short of violence to end segregation," he wrote. "It would be an exaggeration to say: 'You can always tell a Spelman girl—she's under arrest.' But the statement has a measure of truth."[102] One of these Spelman girls was the plucky and committed Ruby Doris Smith. Inspired by the Montgomery Bus Boycott, Smith asserted to her sister at a young age that her life's goal was to see Black people be free. "I will never rest until it happens," she said. "I will die for that cause."[103]

Working together and enduring the physical and verbal abuse of sit-ins began to democratize gender roles on campuses. Among the Howard activists, a student noted, "the women were articulate and many were as vocal and assertive as the men."[104] Student activism also made an impact on campus workers in a manner that broke down class divides. One Spelman alumnus remembered the impact of sit-ins on the school's cafeteria employees. "I can't explain [their] expressions. . . . They didn't ask us what we wanted; they just started putting everything they could find on our trays," she said. "They were so proud of us. We knew immediately we were doing something that they felt they had not been able to do."[105] Fisk University's Stephen Wright, the first HBCU president to publicly support the sit-in movement, recognized that these "students have been exposed all their lives to the teachings of the great American scriptures of democracy, freedom, and equality, and no literate person should be surprised that they reflect these teachings in their conduct."[106] Similarly, Morehouse president Benjamin Mays informed his students that he "would have been dismayed had they not participated in this South-wide revolution."[107]

Despite his disturbing experience at foreign student orientation, Stokely Carmichael dived into the vibrant intellectual and political life at Howard University's campus in the early 1960s. He joined the campus affiliate of SNCC, the Nonviolent Action Group (NAG), whose motto became "A free Black mind is a concealed weapon."[108] Carmichael and his colleagues, such as South Carolina native Cleveland Sellers and fellow New Yorker Courtland Cox, were influenced by Howard faculty members who were engaged in diasporic culture and politics. They enjoyed informal interactions with celebrated poet and scholar Sterling Brown, during which they would "'drink some likker, an' tell some lies.'"[109] Carmichael remembered, "Those sessions were all oral history—tall tales, folk poems, literary, and music criticism rolled in one. All of it, from or about our people . . . grounding us, so to say, in our African cultural heritage."[110] He also studied with sociologist G. Franklin Edwards, a UN consultant on African development, and first encountered African art at a campus exhibition organized by Dr. Chancellor Williams, author of *The Destruction of Black Civilization*.[111] In addition to targeting segregation along the highway between New York and Washington, where African diplomats had come face-to-face with Jim Crow, NAG staged sit-ins and demonstrations to integrate public places throughout the Washington, DC, metropolitan area.

Fisk had also emerged as a hotbed of student activism under the leadership of Diane Nash and John Lewis. Utilizing their civil disobedience training, in the spring of 1960 hundreds of young people staged dozens of lunch counter sit-ins, during which they endured racist insults and threats of violence, hot coffee thrown in their faces, and being forcibly removed from stools with beatings and dragging. The campaign also instituted a "Jail, No Bail" policy as an additional protest of segregation. After negotiating with the city's mayor, the Nashville campaign successfully integrated luncheonettes in the city. Because of their demonstrated commitment and effectiveness, participants in that campaign were highly regarded. When Diane Nash asked NAG to join them in a direct action campaign to integrate public transportation, Stokely Carmichael, Ruby Doris Smith, and others answered the call.

FREEDOM RIDES

Like sit-ins, the Freedom Rides aimed to directly—but nonviolently—confront the absurdity of segregation, this time highlighting its impact on interstate transportation. Though the Supreme Court ruled in *Morgan v. Virginia* and *Boynton v. Virginia* that the segregation of interstate public buses was illegal, discrimination was still commonplace due to local resistance and lack of federal enforcement. Organized by SNCC ally the Congress on Racial Equality (CORE), the first Freedom Ride, in May 1961, was simple in its strategy: on buses from DC through Alabama, occupy seats from the front (the "For Whites" section) to the back (the "For Coloreds" section), regardless of race. Once the first Freedom Riders arrived in Alabama, they were met with a coalition of local Ku Klux Klan chapters and police officers organized by Birmingham police commissioner Bull Conner.[112] Mobs bombed buses and viciously assaulted protesters. SNCC leaders feared that if the violence against the Freedom Riders went unanswered, it would undo the movement's progress.

Carmichael joined a Freedom Ride from DC to Jackson, where backlash against these legal protests drew hostile crowds, who hurled cans, racial epithets, and lit cigarettes at the riders. Protesters were spat upon and beaten by angry White supremacists. SNCC field secretary Bob Moses, a soft-spoken Harlem native who was drawn to SNCC by televised images of the Greensboro Four, observed that Howard University students had received a political education that fortified their activism by the time they arrived to the front lines of the Deep South.[113] Once Carmichael, then a nineteen-year-old Howard freshman, and his fellow riders arrived in the "For Whites Only" waiting room in the Jackson bus station, they were arrested (see figure 3.1).

The Freedom Rides provoked further suppressive action by local authorities. Due to the movement's "Jail, No Bail" policy—which protested the unlawful incarceration of the activists—nearly 445 students, clergy, and other everyday citizens filled Mississippi jails through the spring and summer of 1961.[114] Some, including Carmichael, Lewis, Cox, Forman, and Smith (see figure 3.2), were transferred to the notoriously brutal Mississippi State Penitentiary, also known as Parchman Farm.[115] The governor of Mississippi offered the warden straightforward instructions for how the protesters should be treated: "Break their spirit . . . but not their bones."[116] Freedom Riders of all genders were subjected to electric cattle prods, bug-ridden food, and beatings.[117] Parchman was a correctional facility only in the sense that it attempted to eradicate every prisoner's sense of themselves as a person entitled to human rights.

Ironically, SNCC activists' time at Parchman proved to be an asset to the organization and the movement as a whole. First, the geographically, philosophically, and culturally diverse group gained the opportunity to deliberate their differences and create a foundation of mutual respect and trust—which is essential for sustained social movement participation.[118] Carmichael remembered that after their time in Parchman, the activists "remained a close [sibling]hood of shared experience." "[Prison] would be life altering, a rite of passage, a turning point," he wrote.[119] Second, incarcerated students received a vigorous political education from the more experienced activists, clergy, and professors who shared their prison cells. According to Carmichael, "the jail term was like a university of social struggle."[120] Third, and perhaps most importantly, while in Parchman SNCC activists developed effective techniques to cope with incarceration and police misconduct. These included singing freedom songs—such as "I'm Gonna Tell God How You Treat Me" and "We Shall Not Be Moved"—staging miniprotests—such as refusing to relinquish mattresses that were seized as punishment for singing—and subjecting racist police officers to the dozens, an African American oral tradition of comedic insults. Such strategies empowered activists to remain nonviolent in the face of segregationist hostility without sacrificing their self-esteem or their commitment to the movement. After Carmichael emerged from Parchman, he traded his sharp collared shirts and pressed slacks for denim overalls and work boots, which were the uniform for SNCC activists promoting voter registration in Greenwood, Mississippi.[121] In Greenwood, he joined Bob Moses and Diane Nash on the next front line of America's struggle for racial equality.[122]

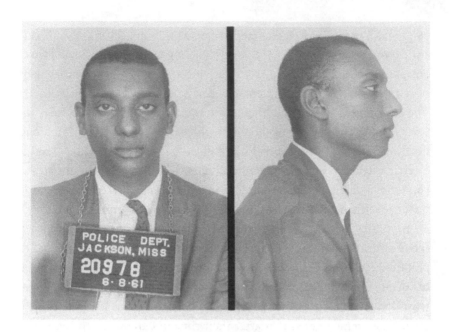

3.1. Mugshot of HBCU student and Freedom Rider Stokely Carmichael, 1961. Courtesy of the Archives and Records Services Division, Mississippi Department of Archives and History. Made available to the public pursuant to *American Civil Liberties Union v. Fordice, 969 F. Supp. 403 (S.D. Miss. 1994).*

As acts of nonviolent civil disobedience, the Freedom Rides were tremendous successes because they focused national attention on Southern states' failure to enforce federal law. This protest tactic revived youths' commitment to antiracist activism by channeling their impatience with the slow pace of social change at the local level into a broader conflict that demanded supportive federal intervention.[123] There is no doubt that the riders anticipated the violence of the mobs and intentionally induced segregationists to disrupt the public order, which dramatized the viciousness of Southern opposition to equality as well as the nobility of Black people's devotion to equality.[124] Diane Nash recalled, "People faced the probability of their own deaths before they ever left. . . . Several made out wills . . . some told me frankly that they were afraid, but they knew . . . freedom was worth it."[125] Like the sit-ins, this push for federal accountability called into question the post-Reconstruction compromise between Northern

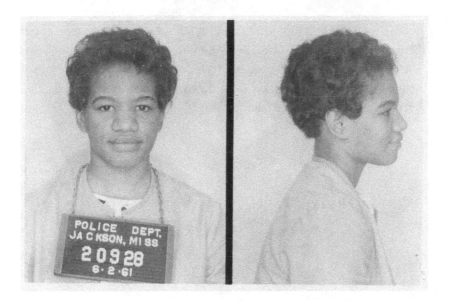

3.2. Mugshot of HBCU student and Freedom Rider Ruby Doris Smith, 1961. Courtesy of the Archives and Records Services Division, Mississippi Department of Archives and History. Made available to the public pursuant to *American Civil Liberties Union v. Fordice, 969 F. Supp. 403 (S.D. Miss. 1994).*

and Southern elites that had enabled Jim Crow and the violation of African Americans' constitutional rights.[126]

By 1961, a new era of the African diaspora underground began to take shape, as Africans and African Americans engaged in social movements to achieve self-determination. African independence organizations in Algeria, Ghana, and Guinea had succeeded in coalescing their constituencies into powerful forces that challenged the cultural and political authority of colonizers. The FLN in Algeria and PDG in Guinea sought international allies as their search for full autonomy was frustrated by colonizers. At the same time, African American institutions—including the Black press and historically Black colleges and universities—lifted up the success of African independence movements as evidence that Black people were capable of self-governance and that the fight for equality could be won, albeit with great sacrifice. These messages inspired young African American activists—such as Stokely Carmichael, Diane Nash, and John Lewis—to identify with African independence and take direct action to empower themselves and their communities. As more organizations and activists would join the fight, connections between both sides of this Black Atlantic insurgency would deepen. Their sacrifices would become bloodier, more personal, and more heartbreaking.

4

"Independence with Danger"
Indépendance avec Danger
الاستقلال مع الخطر
Uhuru na Hatari

WHILE SNCC ACTIVISTS were filling jails in the American South, the Congo joined the family of nations. The year 1960 had been declared the "Year of Africa" by the UN.[1] At that time, Congo's independence was particularly remarkable because its people had endured Belgian rule, which was more cruel and violent than France's colonization of Algeria and Guinea and Britain's colonization of Ghana.

Before the 1884–85 Berlin Conference, King Leopold II of Belgium privately acquired an African land mass (seventy-six times the size of his own country), which he organized as the Congo Free State.[2] Due to increased competition among European nations to seize and exploit as many African natural resources as possible (this bloody, ruthless effort is euphemistically taught as the "Scramble for Africa" in US schools), Germany called for the Berlin Conference to negotiate a treaty to avoid further escalating conflict. Attended by Austria-Hungary, Belgium, Denmark, France, Germany, Italy, the Netherlands, Turkey, Portugal, Russia, Spain,

Sweden, Norway, the United Kingdom, and the US, this notorious meeting produced the General Act of the Berlin Conference. The act prohibited slave trading on the continent by African and Islamic authorities (after nearly three centuries of the transatlantic slave trade, which enriched many of these nations), permitted free trade throughout the Congo Basin and through the Niger and Congo Rivers, and confirmed the Congo Free State as the private property of King Leopold II.

Following the conference, Leopold made himself even wealthier by granting private companies leases to large swaths of the territory so they could extract rubber, ivory, and other resources in a wholly deregulated environment. Although slave trading was forbidden by the Berlin Conference, forced labor practices by European-owned ventures were ignored. For example, the Anglo-Belgian India Rubber Company coerced Congolese men, women, and children into meeting quotas for rubber harvesting. Workers who failed to meet quotas were punished with beatings, imprisonment, and the amputations of loved ones' hands.[3] Leopold's army—the Force Publique—as well as the private militias of concessionaires meted out these vicious penalties and burned villages that resisted their tyranny.[4] During this period of unfettered capitalism between 1885 and 1908, the population of the Congo declined from an estimated 20 million to 8.5 million people due to violence, starvation, and illness.[5]

The human rights abuses in the Congo Free State created international pressure on Leopold because Christian missionaries from England and the US returned from the region with grisly tales and photographs of the suffering created by the military and private interests.[6] Public awareness about the issue also increased after Joseph Conrad published his semiautobiographical novella, *Heart of Darkness*, in 1902.[7] Later reimagined as the revered film *Apocalypse Now* and the "militainment"-critical video game *Spec Ops: The Line*, the story follows steamboat captain Charles Marlow as he journeys up the Congo River for an ivory trading company. He is charged with collecting goods from Mr. Kurtz, head of a far-flung yet significant trading post. Throughout his travels, Marlow discovers the impact Leopold's policies are having on the people of Congo. He witnesses hundreds of emaciated railway laborers who seem near death and the torture of a villager accused of arson. Eventually Marlow encounters Mr. Kurtz, who has embedded himself in the local culture and emerged as the leader of the local "natives." Kurtz is depicted as a mystical figure who gained astonishing spiritual insight from his time in the jungle. His awakened consciousness is distilled in the now iconic deathbed proclamation, "The horror! The horror!" Marlow returns to the United Kingdom forever changed by his trip. By the end of the story, he considers himself an outsider to the "civilized" world.[8]

Heart of Darkness became the paradigmatic representation of the Congo, sub-Saharan Africa, and White peoples' relationship to the developing world. This template story advances liberal racist ideology by asserting that the colonized environment—erroneously depicted as exotic, inscrutable, and savage—exists solely as a vehicle for the self-discovery of a White heterosexual male subject (whom Enlightenment discourse articulates as exclusively universal).[9] According to Nigerian novelist Chinua Achebe, the function of Africa and Africans in this trope is to be an objectified "Other," against which the normative humanity of White European subjects can be measured.[10] Acclaimed Cameroonian theorist Achille Mbembe explains in his work On the Postcolony that art like Heart of Darkness articulates Africa as "the absolute Other" and defines the continent solely in terms of what it lacks rather than what it has contributed to human history.[11] This framework allows the universal subject/character to express sympathy or concern about the dehumanizing conditions that exist on the continent but, as Achebe compellingly states, to "always . . . sidestep the ultimate question of equality between [W]hite people and [B]lack people."[12]

Although Heart of Darkness is discussed within the Western cultural canon as a critique of colonialism, the atrocities Conrad describes in the novella are scarcely noted in many discussions about the book.[13] The people of color who are directly impacted by colonialism and imperialism in the trope that Heart of Darkness helped popularize are never heroes or narrators. They are relegated to static scenery—supporting German philosopher Georg Wilhelm Friedrich Hegel's false argument that Africa lies "beyond . . . history" in "the dark mantle of Night."[14] The Congo, later known as Zaire and the Democratic Republic of Congo, has never overcome its stereotypical image as nonsensically and permanently dangerous and chaotic. In fact, negative conditions of the region can be traced directly to observable factors such as Belgium's colonial policies, internal conflicts during the early days of Congo's independence, and the international community's subsequent indifference to the ascent of the brutal, corrupt dictator Joseph Mobutu. The Congo's indisputable contributions to human culture are evident in Cubism, music, and literature.[15]

However, the liberal international outcry about human rights abuses in the Congo Free State did spur Leopold to relinquish the territory to the Belgian government in 1908. Belgium named its subsequent colonizing strategy "enlightened paternalism," which aimed to prevent Congolese rebellion by limiting education to the primary level, banning African political parties, and outlawing indigenous media.[16] As a result of these policies, mid-twentieth-century Congo was not populated with the class of *evolués*, or professionals, found in Ghana, Guinea, and Algeria. The country boasted only sixteen university graduates—none of whom were doctors or teachers.[17] Before independence, not one Congolese person was appointed to the top levels of civil administration within the colony or the Force Publique army.[18] Historians have argued that the lack of a colonial bourgeoisie in Congo may have increased the risk of instability following independence.[19] These observations ignore the fact that, at the time, the Belgian Congo had the third largest group of wage earners in Africa, which provided a vocal and committed base for a mass movement demanding independence.[20]

Another challenge to Congolese independence was the loose affiliation that the exceptionally mineral abundant Katanga Province had with the rest of the territory. The people of the Luba-Katanga kingdoms in Katanga fiercely resisted Leopold's reign between 1907 and 1917.[21] After the Congo became an official Belgian colony, foreign mining interests—including the Ryan and Guggenheim groups as well as the Rockefeller group—created political and economic autonomy in the Katanga region.[22] Both foreign investors and tribal leadership were resistant to compromises in their authority that a unified independent Congo presented.

AFRICAN CONSCIOUSNESS

By 1956, the nationalist fervor that had already erupted in Algeria and Ghana became evident in the Congo. Congolese activists published *Le manifeste conscience Africain* (African consciousness manifesto), which formally demanded independence from Belgium.[23] By 1958, the writers of the manifesto had organized into the Mouvement National Congolais (National Congolese Movement, MNC). Patrice Lumumba—a slender, bespectacled traveling salesman of the Polar beer brand—emerged as the organization's leader due in part to his inspiring speeches, affable demeanor, and ability to travel extensively throughout the colony to build a support base. This farmer's son, with a secondary school education and (like Guinean leader Sékou Touré) experience as a postal workers' union organizer, mastered the work of Enlightenment authors, including Jean-Jacques Rousseau.[24]

By the time he helped found the MNC in August 1958, Lumumba had published several anticolonial poems. For example, in "Dawn in the Heart of Africa," he wrote:

The moment when you break the chains, the heavy fetters,
The evil cruel times will go never to come again.
A free and gallant Congo will rise from black soil,
A free and gallant Congo-black blossom from black seed![25]

Although these words may be seem measured by twenty-first-century standards, Lumumba's work boldly challenged stereotypes advanced in Belgian-run churches, schools, and other cultural institutions. These misrepresentations indoctrinated the Congolese to believe that their country was a place of unending darkness that required the domination of Europeans. Lumumba's speeches and writings effectively mobilized the Congolese by framing Belgium as an oppressor and creating cognitive alternatives through which his countrymen could see themselves and their autonomy.[26]

Other independence-based political parties were also gaining followers in the Congo—including the Alliance des Bakongo (ABAKO), led by Joseph Kasavubu, and the Confédération des Associations Tribales du Katanga (CONAKAT), led by Moïse Tshombe. However, the MNC remained the only party that was not defined by region or tribal affiliation.[27] Although tribalism in Congo was more rampant than in Ghana or Guinea, under Lumumba's leadership, the MNC coalesced several key elements of the indigenous Congolese community, including wage workers, professionals, and rural farmers.[28]

In December 1958, a few months after Ghana's independence celebrations and shortly after the MNC elected Lumumba president of their organization, he traveled to Accra to attend the first All-African People's Conference (AAPC). The city's energy continued to crackle with the optimism and confidence of the early days of the Ghana nation. Building on the efforts of Kwame Nkrumah's Convention People's Party (CPP) to expand primary education for Ghanaians before independence, President Nkrumah had opened the Ghana Museum and the Arts Council of Ghana. However, his administration had also consolidated state control over the *Ghanaian Times* and the Ghana Broadcasting Service—limiting freedom of the press.[29] In addition, Nkrumah and his party had taken counterinsurgency measures to stave off political opposition that were reminiscent of the human rights violations committed by their British predecessors.[30] He passed the Avoidance of Discrimination Act, which banned political parties and organizations based on ethnic or tribal affiliation, as well as the Preventive Detention Act, which allowed incarceration for up to five years without charge or trial.

The eight African states that had achieved independence by 1958, including Ghana and Guinea, organized the gathering.[31] Lumumba joined approximately three hundred delegates from twenty-eight African countries and territories in this emancipated space.[32] Outside the conference venue, Ghanaian supporters held placards that proclaimed, "Welcome Africa's Freedom Fighters!" and "Hands Off Africa!"[33] Inside, attendees were seated beneath a banner with a quote from Kwame Nkrumah: "We prefer independence with danger to tranquility in servitude."[34] The conference's agenda included discussions about the use of violence in anticolonial struggles, the ongoing Algerian revolution, and on a lighter note, "what the well-dressed tribesman should wear."[35]

Occurring approximately fifty years before Facebook and fifteen years before color television was widely available on the continent, the AAPC was the first opportunity many attendees had to see, and build community with, independence activists and heads of state from other African countries. Witnessing the broad scope of African nationalism, and one's place in that unique historical moment, was likely to have been a profound and empowering personal experience for the participants. The AAPC demonstrated that African self-determination was more than a dream of any one organization or colony. It was an international and inevitable phenomenon.

During the conference, Lumumba connected with Frantz Fanon of Algeria's FLN, Guinea's president Sékou Touré, and Kwame Nkrumah.[36] Lumumba was inspired by his colleagues, and his time at the AAPC marked the beginning of his ideological commitment to pan-Africanism. (With a small "p," pan-Africanism is the belief that cooperation and solidarity between autonomous African nations are necessary to address the challenges posed by colonialism's legacy. Pan-Africanism with a big "P" includes communities in the African diaspora.) Nkrumah embodied this idea by hosting the AAPC and spearheading the formation of the United States of Africa (which would later become the Organization of African Unity and then the African Union). Touré demonstrated his support for pan-Africanism through his agreement to participate in the Ghana-Guinea Union, an early model for the OAU. Although the AAPC attendees were relatively unfamiliar with Lumumba and the MNC, his newfound inspiration impressed the audience during a speech on December 11, 1958: "In spite of the frontiers that separate us, in spite of our ethnic difference, we have the same conscience . . . the same wish to make the African continent . . . free of uncertainty [and] fear."[37] By the conclusion of the conference, Nkrumah and Lumumba developed a close mentoring relationship that lasted throughout Lumumba's lifetime.

Emboldened by the solidarity and success he experienced at the All-African People's Conference, in 1959 Lumumba led the Congolese people to escalate their activist critique of Belgian rule. In January, rebellions erupted in the capital city, Léopoldville (now named Kinshasa).[38] Dozens of people were killed. The African American newspaper the *Defender* reported that Congolese independence supporters shouted "We want independence now!" while attacking priests, "stoning" Europeans, and setting fire to shops, schools, and police headquarters.[39] Throughout the year, several regions of the country became ungovernable because their citizens refused to pay taxes, adhere to regulations, or participate in elections.[40]

Lumumba consolidated international support for the MNC as the leader of this nationalist surge by traveling to additional emancipated spaces, such as the International Seminar of the Congress for Freedom and Culture in Nigeria and a meeting of the permanent committee of the

All-African People's Conference.[41] Eventually, his militant opposition to Belgium's procrastination of independence fractured the fragile leadership coalition within the MNC. In October 1959, as members of the Force Publique attempted to arrest Lumumba in the city of Kisangani, community members responded by attacking property and White residents.[42] The rebellion lasted for two days and caused at least twenty deaths.

As a result of the resistance, Lumumba was taken into custody, tried, and found guilty of inciting violence in January 1960. His sentence— six months of hard labor—was to be carried out at the Likasi subterranean prison. But Lumumba's arrest only buttressed his popularity. Protesters greeted Belgium's King Baudouin throughout his visit to Brazzaville with silently raised fists or "thunderous shouts of 'Indépendance!'"[43] Fearful of descending into a protracted unpopular conflict—as France had done with the Algerian Revolution—Belgian citizens popularized the slogan "Not One Soldier for the Congo."[44] In response to these international and domestic pressures, the Belgian government chose the path of compromise.

INDEPENDENCE CHA-CHA

Just four days into his prison sentence, Lumumba was released so that he could join his colleagues in Brussels for the Round Table Conference. He was still bandaged from wounds caused by restraints (see figure 4.1). Despite the infighting within the MNC and among the various regionally affiliated nationalist groups, Lumumba, Kasavubu, and others maintained a united front and refused to accept anything from Belgium but immediate and total autonomy. Belgium set June 30, 1960, as Congolese Independence Day. The Congo's new constitutional principles and governance structure were also established by the conference.

The fraternity of these anticolonial activists (all participants in the talks were men) was celebrated by the Congolese pop anthem "Indépendance Cha-Cha." Emerging from Havana in the 1950s, the cha-cha (or cha-cha-chá) is an internationally popular music and dance sensation inspired by Afro-Cuban spiritual traditions. The choreography of the dance is a simple sensual three step, in which two partners mirror or anticipate each other's movement in unison. In the twenty-first century,

4.1. Patrice Lumumba reveals his wounds in Brussels, 1960. Photograph by Herbert Behrens. Courtesy Nationaal Archief, ANEFO Photo Collection.

the cha-cha continues in the mainstream interpretations of Latin American cultures found, for example, in *Dancing with the Stars* and Zumba. During the 1950s and 1960s, youths throughout the Americas, Europe, and Africa took up the sweetly sensual partner dance as well as the hip swivels needed to keep up with the syncretized African rhythms. By combining two cultural phenomena, songwriter and performer Le Grand Kallé (née Joseph Kabasele) created what some argue was the first Pan-African hit in 1960. The lyrics proclaimed, "Oh Liberty . . . we've conquered . . . United as One."

The Congolese people voted in parliamentary elections in May 1960 to begin the process of returning to self-governance. The MNC and its allies won 29 percent of the seats.[45] Subsequently, Lumumba was able to assemble a coalition consisting of twelve nationalist parties to become prime minister. As Congolese independence organizations prepared to transition from social movement to government, Belgian leaders began a public relations campaign that would allow them to bow out of colonialism gracefully while maintaining control over privately held resources.

Leopold's descendant King Baudouin attended the independence celebrations with the expectation that Kasavubu (who held the ceremonial role of president), Lumumba, and other incoming state leaders would thank him and Belgium for their hard work developing the Congo from the alleged darkness of their savagery. During a parliamentary address, the king framed the granting of independence as the final victory of Belgium's civilizing mission. "The independence of Congo is the result of the . . . genius of King Leopold II," said Baudouin. "A task taken by him with courage and tenacity and furthered by Belgium's own perseverance."[46] Baudouin also warned the new Congolese Parliament that "it is up to you to show we were right to trust you" with autonomy. The Parliament applauded enthusiastically while Lumumba, Kasavubu, and other representatives looked on.

A twenty-first-century perspective can see how the king's comments foreshadow neocolonialism. Although self-determination is recognized by the United Nations' Declaration of Human Rights, in the latter half of the twentieth century, former colonizers reconsolidated their external control of many African states using financial and geopolitical levers of power. These levers had of course been strengthened by the surplus of resources extracted by force from areas such as the Congo. Like colonialism, neocolonialism continued a vicious, racist lie: the chaos that the Congo and other African countries experienced was due primarily to a lack of personal responsibility by these citizens and their leaders. Of course, all adults should accept consequences for their mistakes. However, neocolonialism disappears the West's accountability for genocide, slavery, and theft, while it dismisses any discussion of colonialism's impoverishing legacy for Africa as excuse-making.

By placing the burden on the Congolese to prove they're deserving of a basic human right that is freely given to Whites in Europe and settlers in Africa, Baudouin engaged in "color-blind racism."[47] With this kind of racism, elites complicit in White supremacist acts mobilize the language of seemingly neutral political liberalism and its focus on meritocracy.[48] This willful blindness disappears the historical context that has shaped the actions of communities of color, thus absolving elites of any responsibility. Since independence, this discourse has trapped the people of Congo in an oppressive loop. They live in chaos because they have not had full autonomy. They are deemed by the international community to be undeserving of full autonomy because they live in chaos.

During Baudouin's speech, and Kasavubu's polite comments that followed, Lumumba sat in the front row, quickly scribbling notes. His prepared statements were no longer sufficient given Belgium's articulation of the day's meaning. Just six months after Belgium had tried to physically and historically bury him alive in a prison, he approached the lectern and microphone as the nation's prime minister to address parliament and, via radio, the people of Congo and the world.

Wearing his trademark spectacles, a black suit with bow tie, and a red ceremonial sash, Lumumba calmly began his speech with a direct refutation of the king's claim that Congo's independence was a gift. He stated:

> For this independence of the Congo, even as it is celebrated today with Belgium, a friendly country with whom we deal as *equal to equal*, no Congolese worthy of the name will ever be able to forget that it was by fighting that it has been won, a day-to-day fight, an ardent and idealistic fight, a fight in which we were spared neither privation nor suffering, and for which we gave our strength and our blood. We are proud of this struggle, of tears, of fire, and of blood, to the depths of our being, for it was a noble and just struggle, and indispensable to put an end to the humiliating slavery which was imposed upon us by force.[49]

Lumumba continued by reminding his constituency and the world that Belgium's colonization of Congo was also an overtly racist regime. Congolese had endured de jure segregation of public space as well as exclusion from political participation and most economic opportunities.[50] He then turned his attention to the Congo's future: "Together, we are going to establish social justice and make sure everyone has just remuneration for [their] labor. . . . We will count not only on our enormous strength and immense riches, but on the assistance of numerous foreign countries whose collaboration we will accept if it is offered freely and with no attempt to impose on us an alien culture." Throughout the Congo, the continent, and the African diaspora, Lumumba's speech was greeted with praise.

His account of the atrocities of Belgian colonialism was factual and, some might argue, generous. For example, he refrained from mentioning genocide and severed hands. His recognition of the sacrifice independence activists of all parties had made and his impassioned plea for unity were typical of inaugural speeches designed to heal past wounds and turn a constituency's gaze optimistically forward. Lumumba touched on several critical challenges that all new African nations faced: recovering from the degraded community self-image created by colonialism, coalescing indigenous ethnic factions that had been forced together by arbitrary colonial borders, autonomously building prosperity, and negotiating with former colonizing nations as equals.

IMAGINARY MONKEYS AND NONALIGNMENT

The mainstream international community's response to Lumumba's address presaged that the relationship between Black leaders who promoted self-determination and dominant (predominately White) elites would not be a sensual cha-cha. The integrity Lumumba displayed during his address and the speech's diasporic popularity confirmed the fears of Belgium and her Western allies.[51] He would not be easily intimidated or controlled. A Congolese leader's compliance with Western interests was critical to NATO's success in the African arena against the Soviet Union in the intensifying Cold War. Extensive private investment—particularly in resource rich Katanga—was also imperiled by Lumumba's vision of economic autonomy.

Lumumba's address was broadcast using the technology available at the time—live radio and newspaper reporting. Many who did not hear Lumumba live read in mainstream newspapers, such as the *Guardian*, that his address was "offensive" and likely turned off Belgian authorities.[52]

Media distortions were so rampant that a Léopoldville bishop alleged "such propaganda . . . was designed to enslave the Congolese people."[53] The *Amsterdam News* reported to its African American readership that White settlers in still-colonized African countries were frightened by Lumumba's speech.[54]

A persistent rumor emerged that Lumumba was so defiant in his address that he proclaimed to King Baudouin, "Nous ne sommes plus vous singes." (We are no longer your monkeys.) Although a variety of texts continue to attribute this quote to Lumumba, there is no evidence that he ever uttered these words. Independence activists throughout Africa, and increasingly strident antiracist activists in the US, may have spread this rumor to lovingly transform Lumumba into a symbol of their rebellious spirit. Private investors and members of the Belgian king's entourage, who perhaps had never heard a Black person speak so candidly about the suffering caused by segregation and economic hardship, may have mischaracterized Lumumba's address rather than confront uncomfortable feelings about their complicity with colonialism.

In the months that followed, the fragile coalition led by the MNC crumbled. Aided by Belgian troops and claiming he was blocking communist influence in the region, Moïse Tshombe led Katanga's secession from the new Congo republic in July 1961.[55] Mutiny and panic spread throughout the country. Both the US and the Soviet Union supported UN intervention as a means of curtailing each other's influence and restoring order.

Lumumba continued to enjoy support from independence leaders and the African American press as he struggled to maintain democracy in the Congo. The *Amsterdam News* reported that at the UN, developing nations that were nonaligned (with the Soviet Union or the US) heavily supported Lumumba as head of the troubled nation's "legitimate government."[56] The *Amsterdam* also reported that Lumumba's ally and mentor Kwame Nkrumah led the nonaligned bloc in the Congo solidarity effort. The Ghanaian president stated there was "a real danger" that Congo would become "a pawn in a worldwide politics struggle for power between the great states of the world."[57] Nkrumah continued, "The policy of my government is to keep the Cold War out of Africa, to condemn and resist the re-introduction of colonialism in any form, and to see that the Congo Republic maintains its . . . national independence."

Nkrumah and Lumumba were key figures in the nonaligned movement, which would later influence Black Power organizations through this diaspora underground. Disillusioned by the North and West–centrism of the Cold War conflict, the nonaligned states sought to construct a geopolitical order that centered their specific interests and needs as new nations. Similarly, after years of witnessing federal, state, and local agencies fail to respond to nonviolent petitions for equality, Black Power organizations would later reject the civil rights movement's strategy of seeking remedies for racial injustice from dominant institutions. Strongly influenced by the writings and examples of Nkrumah, Fanon, Touré, Lumumba, and other African independence leaders, Black Power strategy centered on mobilizing the Black community's autonomous resources to resolve their own problems—while working in coalition with allies from different backgrounds and other countries in the diaspora.

Just six weeks after Lumumba's inaugural address, an all-White UN peacekeeping force arrived, but it did nothing about the Katanga secession or the presence of Belgian troops in the Congo.[58] From Lumumba's perspective, the UN's intervention seemed a pretext to undermine the autonomy of his government. Although it was supposedly neutral, the UN force failed to support this nonaligned nation. Suspicious and enraged at the UN's inaction, Lumumba issued an ultimatum stating his government would request Soviet aid if the UN did not remove all Belgian troops. When the UN refused to leave, Lumumba felt he had no choice but to request military assistance from the Soviet Union. The USSR obliged.

PAPERING A CRISIS

The increasing pressures on Lumumba's authority and the unified Congo Republic became known as the "Congo crisis" in the African American press. African Americans had witnessed White intransigence to racial progress as SNCC activists were spat on and assaulted while attempting to desegregate lunch counters. As the Congo crisis unfolded and was covered extensively by Black newspapers, the community began to identify the West's lack of support for Congo's self-determination with the US's indifference to racial inequality.

The African American press responded to the Congo crisis by amplifying support for Lumumba among their readers as well as highlighting similarities between experiences of discrimination in the two countries. For example, an article described Congolese official Joseph Okito's "surprise visit to Harlem," during which he stopped at a well-known location for stepladder speakers on 125th Street.[59] The United Nations drew diplomats and their staff from recently independent African nations to New York—and often north to Harlem. The street corners in Harlem located at the intersections of Lenox Avenue—which is now called Malcolm X Boulevard—and 116th, 125th, and 135th Streets were a significant site of political discourse because of the tradition of stepladder speakers. As the title suggests, stepladder speakers would appeal to passersby in this historically African American neighborhood while perched on an ordinary stepladder.[60] If they were effective, a crowd would draw around.[61] According to *Amsterdam News*, after being introduced to the crowd on such a stepladder, Okito was greeted with "thunderous applause and cries of 'Viva la Congo!' 'Viva Lumumba!'" as the throng pressed to shake the diplomat's hand.[62]

The *Amsterdam* also praised a report by the Associated Press that quoted a Congolese soldier: "Belgian officers [raped] our women all the time. But we could never sleep with theirs."[63] The editorial continued, "It is obvious that the White man in Africa has acted the same way as the White man first acted in America." By drawing parallels between the abuses Congolese women suffered during colonialism and the violence African American women suffered during slavery and Jim Crow, the author encouraged readers to consider themselves on the same side of the same fight as Lumumba's constituents.

When a number of enthusiastic segregationists, including Mississippi senator James Eastland and South Carolina senator Strom Thurmond, sought to undermine the MNC government by forming the American Committee for Aid to Katanga Freedom Fighters, the Black press provided a venue for critique of these leaders' hypocrisy. In the *Amsterdam*, NAACP leader Roy Wilkins wrote about the committee, "Here in the US they want the Federal Government to let the Jim Crow states run civil rights matters as they please. . . . Over in the Congo, they want the UN to let colonial mining . . . handle matters as it pleases. They are battling for freedom all right—for the freedom of those on top."[64] Once again, African American newspapers—as indigenous institutions—channeled information to their readers about African independence in a manner that fostered the mutual identification between groups across borders that facilitates a diaspora underground.

The supportive coverage Lumumba and the MNC received in the Black press diverged greatly from mainstream news about the Congo crisis.[65] Once again, the region was portrayed as senselessly violent and chaotic. White Europeans were routinely depicted as being endangered by the lack of order and Lumumba's supporters. Amid this narrative of growing panic, UN, Belgian, and US officials—including the Central Intelligence Agency (CIA)—came to the consensus that Lumumba should be removed, according to a Senate Committee investigation led by Senator Frank Church between 1975 and 1976.[66] CIA station chief Lawrence Devlin proceeded to work with Colonel Mobutu, who led the Congolese Army, and Katangan leader Tshombe to achieve this goal.

Katanga's secession was a brutal blow to the Congo Republic's economic prospects because of its abundant mineral resources, including copper and cobalt.[67] The region's wealth and support from the West provided Tshombe incentive to persist in his balkanization effort. Similarly, Mobutu, now sanctioned as a reliable US ally, stood to gain complete power over Congolese society. In September 1960, just two months after independence, Mobutu seized governing authority in the name of the military, expelled the Soviet and Czechoslovakian embassies from Congo, and pledged to "neutralize" Lumumba as prime minister and Kasavubu as president.[68] In October, Mobutu's troops surrounded the cordon of UN protection around Lumumba's home in Léopoldville, in essence placing him under house arrest without due process.

By November, Lumumba concluded that the only way he could regain power and restore democracy to Congo was to escape and lead an armed struggle against Mobutu's army.[69] Under the cover of night, he fled his home with the hope of reaching Kisangani, where he remained popular among the leadership. US and Belgian intelligence agencies aided Mobutu in the nationwide hunt for Lumumba. In less than a year, he had gone from prisoner to prime minister to fugitive.

On December 1, 1960, Lumumba was captured. After being paraded in front of the international press in Léopoldville with his hands bound behind his back and soldiers attempting to gag him, Lumumba was taken to an armored camp in the Lower Congo. Detained and tortured with Lumumba were Youth and Sports Minister Maurice Mpolo and Senate Vice President Joseph Okito, who was cheered by Harlem crowds a few months earlier.

While Lumumba, Mpolo, and Okito endured severe beatings and illegal imprisonment, their supporters in Kisangani expanded their control of the eastern region of the Congo. Nationally, pro-Lumumba forces demanded his release. Fear mounted that a countercoup would attempt to reinstall Lumumba. Senior Belgian and Congolese officials—including Mobutu—devised a plot to remove Lumumba permanently with US approval and UN cooperation. On January 17, 1961, Lumumba, Mpolo, and Okito were physically assaulted on a plane ride to Katanga. A few kilometers from the center of the region's capital, Lumumbashi, they were beaten so brutally by Katanga leaders and Belgian officers that blood spattered on the assailants.[70] Finally, they were fatally shot by a firing squad. Several months later, Lumumba's body was sawed apart and doused with sulfuric acid. Physically, he was reduced to dust. The year of Africa was over.

GRIEF

To the progressive African American community, Patrice Lumumba's death became symbolic of the peril that resulted from the Black community's misplaced confidence in dominant institutions.[71] The UN's failure to effectively intervene in the Congo crisis was eerily similar to the US federal government's reluctance to penalize Southern segregationists on behalf of civil rights workers in Mississippi. The vilification of Lumumba as a communist was similar to the red-baiting aimed at Bayard Rustin, Martin Luther King Jr., and other prominent American antiracist activists by some mainstream press outlets, as well as local and federal authorities. Lumumba's defeat was particularly galling to increasingly politicized African American youths—including those participating in SNCC—because, according to author/activist James Baldwin, African independence was "a great antidote to the poison of self-hatred" provoked by American racism.[72] These activists' skepticism of the benevolence of mainstream institutions contrasted sharply with the "hearts and minds" approach of the civil rights movement, which utilized the emotional impact of nonviolent civil disobedience to pressure dominant institutions into taking action.

In response to Lumumba's death, a coalition of progressive Black groups demonstrated at the United Nations during a meeting of the Security Council to discuss the Congo crisis. These groups included the Cultural Association for the Women of African Heritage—led by jazz singer/actress Abbey Lincoln, who was also a pioneer in the 1960s natural hair movement.[73] Over two hundred smartly dressed demonstrators marched in front of the iconic UN building and along 42nd Street from the UN toward Times Square, carrying signs that read "Congo for the Congolese!" and "Belgian butchers, we accuse YOU."[74] They refused to halt when ordered by the New York Police Department. In response, the police charged the crowd of peaceful protesters. Meanwhile, inside the UN visitors' gallery a group of African American protesters erupted in a "riotous outburst" of "white hot indignation" about the UN's failure to save Lumumba's life and Congolese democracy.[75] The UN building closed for two days following this action.

The Black press highlighted the perspective of this increasingly visible community, which would in a few years coalesce into the Black Power movement. For example, the *Defender* discredited claims that pro-Lumumba demonstrators were communists. According to this indigenous institution, these lies were "a studied exaggeration, designed to smear all those who are in sympathy with . . . African freedom."[76] The *Amsterdam* reported that another stepladder speech rally—this one held by the NAACP—was heckled and booed by youths carrying placards with the now martyred Lumumba's photo on it. The group chanted in support of Robert F. Williams, the controversial leader of the Monroe, North Carolina, chapter of the NAACP who had encouraged members to literally arm themselves against White supremacy. Williams, who was in the crowd, took the microphone and declared he would continue to advocate for Black self-defense. According to the *Amsterdam*, Williams "sympathized with the Muslims" and denounced "those who 'turn the other cheek.'" The group also called to the mic a quietly observant, bespectacled Nation of Islam minister in the audience named Malcolm X.[77]

By relating Lumumba's courage—as well as the failure of mainstream institutions to support African democracy—to their own struggle for equality, African American youths began to articulate their own frustrations with US elites' lack of responsiveness to their nonviolent direct action.[78] They also began synthesizing the information about African independence that they received from indigenous institutions, such as the Black press and historically Black colleges and universities, into innovative ideas and tactics for internationalizing their struggle for racial equality. For example, Atlanta University Center students, who were also part of SNCC and had participated in sit-ins throughout the city, released *An Appeal for Human Rights*. The document declared, "We . . . have joined . . . our bodies in the cause of gaining those rights which are inherently ours as members of the human race. . . . Every normal human being wants to walk the earth with dignity."[79] As the frustrations of SNCC leaders grew, so would their engagement with African independence movements through this diaspora underground.

MONOPOLY

While the Congolese people's dream of autonomy crumbled, the Algerian Front de Libération Nationale surged from their headquarters in Tunis with the help of Frantz Fanon's activism and Ahmed Ben Bella's leadership, as well as support from a diaspora underground and the broader international community. After the UN recognized Algeria's right to self-determination, a cease-fire was declared. Both sides negotiated a peace agreement in Evian, France. On July 1, 1962—a year after Lumumba's inaugural address—six million people cast their ballots for an *"Algérie algérienne,"* or Algerian Algeria.[80]

The "unlimited revolution" for Algeria's independence to which *les neuf historiques* (the historic nine) had committed was won. It had cost Ali LaPointe, Petit Omar, and hundreds of thousands of other Algerians, *pieds-noirs*, and French soldiers their lives. It had required Zohra Drif, Saadi Yacef, and hundreds of other Algerians to sacrifice their freedom. After the end of the war, the *Afro-American* reported that, during a thousand-kilometer soldiers' march home, veterans of the revolution showed the sacrifices they had made for self-determination: "Armless coat sleeves, a legless pants leg, one or no eyes, faces bearing huge scars, shaven heads with skull depressions—all earmarks of combat, but all [the soldiers] had laughter and light-heartedness in their voices. Surely this was their 'hour of triumph.'"[81] The wounds these veterans bore further encouraged African Americans to identify with the Algerian struggle. They also signaled the profound trauma independence movement organizations had to heal in order to enjoy prosperity in freedom.

Although some African independence movements were winning, and the antiracist movement in the US continued to gain momentum, the collapse of Lumumba's Congo foreshadowed the formidable obstacles that activists and communities desiring full autonomy would face in the coming years. On the continent, forging strong democratic states would remain challenging for most and impossible for some.[82] The benefits of living in a strong state include physical security and consistent access to public goods such as education, clean air, water, and transportation infrastructure such as roads, bridges, and public transit. Access to these goods are directly relevant to citizens' ability to survive and have a foundation for the core elements of human advancement: scientific and artistic innovation, entrepreneurship, sustainable work, and wealth building. The inability of independence movement organizations—such as Nkrumah's Convention People's Party in Ghana, Touré's Parti Démocratique de Guinée, and Ben Bella's FLN—to transform into effective governing political parties would almost guarantee that their constituencies lived with "poverty in freedom" or in "independence with danger."

According to political theorist Max Weber, a government or state is a group of individuals working in concert to exercise a "monopoly of force" that controls the people, organizations, and economic activities within their borders.[83] In the late twentieth century, the interventions of the West in the Congo—and both sides of the Cold War in African politics—inhibited the people of most African countries from creating such an autonomous monopoly of force over their own resources and decision-making. In the US, the intervention of police and the FBI would similarly inhibit Black Power organizations and their supporters from exercising full control of their communities. In fact, African independence and Black Power leaders who did not align themselves with elites would be consistently treated as pieces of property on the board game Monopoly. Things that could be acquired and exploited at will.

Lumumba's demise revealed that African independence and Black Power would never be in a fair fight with geopolitical elites. It also indicated that their reasonable demands to enjoy human rights would be treated as unfettered aggression. These pressures would ultimately stifle both movements' direct engagement in this diaspora underground.

5

"Our Problem Is Your Problem"
Notre Problème Est
Votre Problème
مشكلتنا مشكلتك
Shida Yetu ni Shida Yako

SHORTLY AFTER THE UN rebellion that protested Patrice Lumumba's murder, the young dancer/writer/activist Maya Angelou, who was also a leader of the Cultural Association for Women of African Heritage, reached out to Malcolm X. By 1961, the Harlem mosque minister had gained an international reputation for his confrontational, unapologetic oratory, which reflected the Nation of Islam's candid discussions about the complicity of White people with racial terror, slavery, and segregation. Years before the Black Power movement, Black studies, and the Voting Rights Act, Malcolm flouted his era's expectation that African American men in public space would be deferential to the mainstream's perspective about "race relations." For example, during an appearance on the news program *Open Mind*, he corrected a fellow commentator: "When you say the 'power structure,' I know you mean the White power structure because that's all we have in America today."[1] Like Patrice Lumumba, Malcolm refused to wear what W. E. B. Du Bois famously described as "the veil." The veil is a metaphor for the public face of complicity and contentment that elites expect Black people to present to the world in order to cover the anguish and rage that White supremacy engenders.[2] There was no distinction between the cultural critique and political commentary Malcolm offered on a Harlem street corner, at Yale University, or on CBS.

Following the UN protest of Lumumba's assassination, New York City's police commissioner alleged that Malcolm X and the NOI were partly responsible for the violence that broke out during the demonstration. In response to the accusation, Malcolm said, "We don't involve ourselves in any politics, whether local, national or international." He also added, "I refuse to condemn the demonstrations . . . because I am not Moïse Tshombe, and will permit no one to use me against the nationalists."[3] The contradictory nature of this statement—we're apolitical but not anti–African independence—illustrated the growing internal conflict between the Harlem-based phenomena of Malcolm X and his Mosque No. 7 and the national leadership of the Nation of Islam, which was headquartered in Chicago and headed by the Honorable Elijah Muhammad.

With all of its militant pro-Black theology, NOI remained a strictly religious organization that mobilized its followers purely for the benefit of its own advancement and prosperity. Although participation in the NOI required acknowledging the consequences of anti-Black racism, members and ministers were actively dissuaded from working to change it on a systemic level. Malcolm's personal journey of enlightenment—which brought him through a Garveyite household in Nebraska, street life in Roxbury and Harlem, prison, and conversion to Islam—was now awakening a passion for social change that was at odds with his clerical obligations.[4] Because of his passionate antiracist rhetoric and subtly expressed sympathy for Lumumba, young Maya Angelou was optimistic that Malcolm would endorse the Cultural Association's protest.[5] However, while she met with him in the back of an NOI restaurant, Malcolm chided Angelou's strategy by saying, "Carrying placards will not win freedom for anyone." But he also pledged to make a press statement that the UN demonstrations were "symbolic of the anger in this country." Ideologically, he vacillated between the NOI's nihilistic view of politics and his personal human rights–centered ethos.

DREAM

After over two years of battle in the Deep South, the consortium of organizations leading the civil rights movement decided to organize the March on Washington for Jobs and Freedom, to occur in August of 1963. Coordinated in cooperation with the Kennedy administration, the March aimed to build momentum and galvanize public support for Kennedy's proposed Civil Rights Act. This legislation aimed to ban segregation in public places; employment discrimination based on race, color, religion, sex, or national origin; and extensive voting requirements, which had disproportionately excluded Black voters in the South.[6]

While movement veteran Bayard Rustin coordinated the nuts and bolts of the march, political strategy was also directed by what was known as the "Big Six," the leadership of the most influential antiracist organizations during this period. These included Reverend King of the SCLC (who would eventually win a Nobel Peace Prize for his activism) and John Lewis, who had risen from Freedom Rider to executive director of SNCC. The consortium represented the movement's interest in joining concerns about the injustice of racial segregation with proposed solutions for the economic inequality that disproportionately impacted African Americans. Rustin and labor leader A. Phillip Randolph (head of the Brotherhood of Sleeping Car Porters) had first envisioned a march on Washington for civil rights in 1941.

The Big Six efforts in organizing the March highlighted SNCC's diverging perspective about the best route forward to racial justice. Unlike King and other leaders, Lewis and his fellow SNCC workers did not possess a steady confidence in the goodwill of the Kennedys or the Democratic Party. From the youth perspective, President Kennedy and Attorney General Robert F. Kennedy had seen SNCC activists beaten, fire-hosed, and shot on the television news and in *Life* magazine. Yet, they consistently refused activist pleas for federal intervention.[7] SNCC workers had grown exasperated by JFK's lack of responsiveness to their objectives and to the aspirations and sacrifices of the economically impoverished, human rights–deprived, but courage- and self-respect-rich African American families who had welcomed these committed students into their homes during the previous two years. Due to their firsthand experience of the brutal lengths that Southern elites were willing to go to preserve their White privilege, SNCC perceived Kennedy's legislation as "too little, too late."[8] Their slogan was "Freedom Now!" and SNCC activists believed that goal was imminently possible.

Lewis, along with other Big Six leaders, was invited to address March attendees. In the original draft of his speech, he did not confine his critique to what became the safe, vague scapegoats for American racism to which civil rights leaders often pointed: Southern racists and those who opposed civil rights legislation.[9] Instead, he pointed to the Kennedy brothers' silence in the South and called for more robust action against poverty. Other members of the Big Six worried Lewis's speech was too confrontational and would alienate the allies needed to give the movement a major legislative victory with the passing of the Civil Rights Act. He intended to say, "Segregation is evil and . . . must be destroyed in all forms." In addition, he had written, "All of us must get in the revolution."[10] While the tone and content of Lewis's planned speech was commonplace in SNCC offices and mass meetings throughout the South, it was too radical for African American elites and their allies at the time. Lewis conceded and revised his speech, though in the end it contained much of his original criticism as well as a description of the police brutality endured by protesters.[11]

The march itself became one of the most iconic events in the civil rights movement and American history. Over 250,000 people attended. Luminaries who participated included actor Marlon Brando, singer/dancer Josephine Baker (the only woman to speak at the march), actor Ossie Davis, James Baldwin, and actor/singer/activist Harry Belafonte.[12] However, SNCC was frustrated not only with domestic elites such as White police officers, politicians, and business owners. They were also at their wits' end with members of the older clerical Black establishment, who were more focused, in these young activists' opinions, on negotiation instead of revolution. While Reverend King and Mrs. Coretta Scott King continued to present themselves in suits and press-and-curl hairstyles, according to Lewis, "You could see more identification with heritage and race among [SNCC] members, more [African] dress and hairstyles. Racial integration remained our focus, but there was a growing sense of separation . . . of [pride in] racial identity."[13]

These frustrations would also lead SNCC to increased engagement in this diaspora underground. By the spring of 1964, Lewis observed that both SNCC workers and local community members were increasingly expressing their solidarity with African movements: "I think people are searching for a sense of identity," he recalled.[14] "And they're finding it."

PILGRIMAGE

Between 1961 and 1964, Malcolm X continued to refine his oratory skills and political ideology, often on the streets of Harlem. With these stepladder speeches, Malcolm electrified crowds of people who were becoming increasingly vexed with dominant institutions' refusal to respond to the civil rights movement in the North or the South. Before Peter Bailey became editor of *Blacklash*, newsletter of the OAAU (Organization of Afro-American Unity), he witnessed Malcolm's rhetorical appeal at the corner of Lenox Avenue and 116th Street: "The image that was generally projected of him by the [mainstream] press [was his] talking about Black folks going out and beating up and brutalizing White folks . . . so [my friend and I] decided to see what he had to say." Bailey continued, "We stood there for three hours as he spoke, and for me it was like a complete eye opener. I had never heard anyone discuss and present the racist situation in this country with such truthfulness and forcefulness and clarity. . . . Malcolm said Black people in society are not up against individuals; we're up against a system of White supremacy."[15] Sylvester Leaks, who would help Malcolm found the OAAU, described having a similar experience when he first met the magnetic leader at the corner of 125th Street and Lenox in front of the National Memorial Bookstore: "He spoke with such intelligence. I would say even profundity."[16] Maya Angelou eloquently expounded on Malcolm's unique charisma: "His aura was too bright. . . . A hot desert storm eddied around him and rushed to me. . . . His hair was the color of burning embers and his eyes pierced."[17] Malcolm's oratory, along with Robert F. Williams's classic text, *Negroes with Guns*, is credited by the founders of the Black Panther Party and leaders of SNCC with inspiring their focus on self-defense and autonomy.[18]

Malcolm became unbearably dismayed by Elijah Muhammad's indifference to effecting social change. Because of Muhammad, he found himself in the extraordinary position of being an internationally celebrated critic of racial injustice who was sidelined from the African American and African social movements that were creating observable political progress. Conversely, Muhammad could no longer tolerate Malcolm's ever escalating popularity and the widespread perception that he was the de facto leader of the Nation of Islam.

On November 22, 1963, President John F. Kennedy was assassinated in Dallas. Several days later, during a press conference following a lecture in New York City, Malcolm X flagrantly defied Muhammad's order to refrain from commenting about Kennedy. Malcolm not only stated that Kennedy's assassination was an instance of "the chickens coming home to roost."[19] He also added, "Being an old farm boy myself, chickens coming home to roost never did make me sad. They've always made me glad."[20] Muhammad seized the opportunity to "silence" his former protégé by suspending him for ninety days. The suspension was the first in a series of maneuvers that framed Malcolm as an enemy to the NOI and financially cut him off from the organization.[21] On March 8, 1964, Malcolm announced via an interview with a New York Times reporter that he resigned from the Nation of Islam: "It is going to be different now. I'm going to join in the fight wherever Negroes ask for my help."[22]

The next day, Malcolm and a few followers established the Muslim Mosque, Inc. (MMI), whose aim was to offer a Muslim African American alternative to the NOI. The following month, he traveled to Mecca in order to make the hajj—the holy pilgrimage that all physically and financially capable Muslims are required to make in their lifetime. This six-day community ritual includes extensive prayer and repentance. From Mecca on April 25, 1964, he wrote to his friend, Amsterdam News reporter James Booker, "Here in the Muslim world . . . one ceases to be looked at as '[W]hite' or as 'Negro.'" Malcolm continued, "If White Americans would accept . . . the Oneness of God (Allah), then they could also sincerely accept the Oneness of Man, and cease to measure [men] in terms of their difference in color."[23]

The two most iconic articulations of Malcolm X's life story—his auto-biography and the Spike Lee film *Malcolm X*—depict this pilgrimage as a catalyst for an extraordinary political transformation. In these versions of Malcolm's life, he has a few days of intense reflection after enduring harassment, threats of violence, and probably unjust exile from his spiritual and professional home in the NOI. Then, Malcolm emerges from the politically ambivalent Black supremacist ideology of the Honorable Elijah Muhammad and steps into the light as a passionate advocate of international human rights.

However, Malcolm's political evolution was much longer in the making and also involved extensive travel to emancipated spaces in postcolonial Africa. As historian William Sales points out, Mosque No. 7's minister was a well-known fixture at street corner speeches and neighborhood events about African independence.[24] Malcolm had traveled to Cairo in the late 1950s and was impressed by the experience of being in a majority Black country. He was as amicable to the efforts of the Cultural Association for Women of African Heritage to highlight the injustice of Patrice Lumumba's death as his NOI post would allow. After his pilgrimage to Mecca, Malcolm would explore the emancipated spaces of Accra and Algiers and become further committed to a transnational solution to racial inequality. His experiences in this diaspora underground made a steady contribution over time to his articulation of anti-Black racism as "a world problem."[25]

REVOLUTION BY COMMITTEE

After leaving Mecca, Malcolm traveled to Accra. A group of African Americans living in Ghana, mentored by Shirley Graham Du Bois, named themselves the Malcolm X Committee and organized an itinerary for him.[26] This group was part of a larger community of hundreds of Black American expatriates who emigrated to Ghana due to Kwame Nkrumah's Pan-Africanist ideology in order to contribute their skills to the new nation.[27] By 1964, the Convention People's Party, which Nkrumah continued to lead, had fully transformed from a social movement for African independence to a one-party state apparatus that had little tolerance for dissent.[28] However, since Lumumba and Fanon attended the All-African People's

Conference in Accra a few years earlier, the capital had evolved into an emancipated space for antiracist and anticolonial activists.

One of the members of the Malcolm X Committee was Vicki Garvin, who had been in Ghana for several years to work with Dr. W. E. B. Du Bois on the *Encyclopedia Africana*. According to Ms. Garvin, the committee formed during a get-together at the home of playwright Julian Mayfield due to the expatriate community's excitement about Malcolm's visit.[29] Several committee members had known Malcolm in Harlem, including Garvin, who befriended him during his street life days at the neighborhood bar Small's Paradise.[30] Another participant was Maya Angelou. Since meeting Malcolm about the UN protest, she'd moved to Ghana with her son and worked in various capacities for Radio Ghana and the University of Ghana.[31]

The committee agreed to supplement Malcolm's government-sponsored itinerary with visits to historic sites, meetings with "important personages and contacts," and personal accompaniment "wherever he needed it."[32] In his autobiography, Malcolm X uncritically remembered that much of the organizing work of the committee was done by women, including dentist Sara Lee, Alice Windom, and Julian Mayfield's "pretty Puerto Rican wife," Ana Livia, who was also in charge of Accra's health program. When Malcolm arrived, Julian and Ana Livia Mayfield hosted a reception in their home, during which he was "plied with questions" about the antiracist movement in the US.[33]

Throughout his time in Accra, Malcolm urged people to be mindful of the African American struggle. He was also impressed by Ghanaians' warm response to him. At a dinner party in his honor at the Press Club in Accra, he exclaimed, "Now, dance! Sing! But as you do . . . remember Lumumba in his grave! . . . You wonder why I don't dance? Because I want you to remember twenty-two million Afro-Americans in the US!"[34] In a letter to *Amsterdam News* reporter James Booker, Malcolm observed, "[Ghanaians] opened their hearts and their arms to me when they learned that I was an African American." He continued, "I must confess that their joy and respect was greater still when they discovered I was 'Malcolm X' of the Militant American Muslims. Africans in general and Muslims in particular everywhere love militancy."[35] As a result of his time in this emancipated space, Malcolm deepened his understanding of the parallels between African independence and what would become Black Power.

Later during the visit, he addressed Ghanaian parliament and met privately with Kwame Nkrumah in his home. Malcolm was aware that, like his deceased father, Earl Little, Nkrumah was strongly influenced by Marcus Garvey. He described their conversation's personal and political impact in his memoir: "We agreed that Pan Africanism was the key also to the problems of those of African heritage." Malcolm remembered, "I could feel the warm, likable and very down-to-earth qualities of Dr. Nkrumah. . . . I promised faithfully that when I returned to the United States, I would relay to Afro-Americans his personal warm regards."[36] After the meeting, Malcolm wrote to his wife, Mrs. Betty Shabazz. Months earlier, she had warned her husband of the possibility that, because of Elijah Muhammad's indiscretions, he needed to envision a professional future without the Nation of Islam.[37] Malcolm indicated that through his time in the emancipated space of Accra, he had perhaps found it. "Unity between the Africans of the West and the Africans of the fatherland will well change the course of history," he wrote.[38]

After Accra, Malcolm headed to Algeria, where Ahmed Ben Bella had recently become the nation's first postindependence president in 1963. Although he'd been sidelined by his arrest during the Battle of Algiers, Ben Bella had emerged as an adept politician who was able to balance two core factions of the new government: veteran independence-war guerrillas and the new FLN army.[39] However, his popular support could not compensate for the heated conflicts his autocratic demeanor and arrogance often caused. During his Ghana visit, Malcolm had met with the Algerian ambassador and was impressed by his dedication "to solve the problems of the world's masses."[40] He observed that the ambassador was attuned to the issues confronting people of African descent throughout the world. The ambassador's perspective reflected the objectives of Ben Bella's administration, which would initiate agrarian land reforms and espouse socialist beliefs.[41]

Once in Algiers for his thirty-ninth birthday on May 19, 1964, Malcolm learned about the lingering effects of the Algerian Revolution. As he walked around the ancient city, he heard what he described as "expressions of hatred for America" because the US supported the French. He described postwar Algerians as "true revolutionists, not afraid of death."[42] Being in this emancipated space helped Malcolm understand the sacrifices that would be necessary in the next phase of his activist life.

ORGANIZATION OF AFRO-AMERICAN UNITY

When Malcolm returned to New York from his pilgrimage in Mecca, Accra, and Algiers in June 1964, he had gained a clarity of purpose that he was eager to share with his community and the world. At a press conference when he first landed in the US at the John F. Kennedy International Airport, he exclaimed, "The non-White peoples of the world are sick of the condescending White man! Can you imagine . . . what would certainly happen if all of those African-heritage peoples ever realize blood bonds, if they ever realize they all have a common goal—if they ever unite?"[43]

The FBI, under the leadership of J. Edgar Hoover, previously branded the former NOI minister as a threat to national security. Malcolm's expanding international profile drew heightened surveillance of his political activities, according to government documents. Astonishingly, much of this classified, taxpayer-funded intelligence consisted of information that was easily available through the *Amsterdam News* or fliers posted throughout Harlem. For example, an agent placed Malcolm's public statement about the founding of the OAAU in Malcolm's secret FBI file with a note that the former minister was inspired by Nkrumah's Organization of African Unity. According to the agent, and freely available OAAU literature, Malcolm's new entity intended to "transcend all superficial, man-made divisions between the Afro-American people of this country who are working for human rights."[44]

The OAAU launched as a membership organization with a rally and informal reception on June 28, 1964, at the Audubon Ballroom in the Manhattan neighborhood of Washington Heights, just north of Harlem. Perhaps to the dismay and concern of his wife, Mrs. Betty Shabazz, Malcolm X continued to be an open book despite ongoing death threats and ire from the NOI. Noted historian John Henrik Clarke and former SNCC activist Gloria Richardson were among the intellectuals and activists who helped Malcolm X crystallize his diasporic perspective into this new organization.[45] Unlike the founding of Muslim Mosque, Inc. two months earlier, OAAU's charter—cowritten by Clarke—illustrated how Malcolm would continue to divert ideologically and strategically from Elijah Muhammad's influence. In addition to stating its intentions to support environmental sustainability, economic justice, educational opportunity, and Black culture, the OAAU's charter affirmed it would mobilize African Americans as an independent voting bloc and promote community organizing. The OAAU resolved to "reinforce the common bond of purpose between our people" and establish "a non-religious and non-sectarian constructive program for human rights."[46] An FBI informant claimed that Malcolm was disappointed by the initial number of members in the OAAU who signed up at the organization's debut.[47]

Shortly after founding the OAAU, Malcolm X embarked on a second tour of Africa. He explained to the second OAAU rally that he aimed to persuade African leaders to bring the issue of anti-Black racism in the US to the floor of the United Nations.[48] He journeyed to Cairo for the Organization of African Unity's Summit Conference of Heads of State. Malcolm was housed with conference delegates from a variety of African independence organizations on *Isis*, a yacht docked on the Nile. He felt fortunate to be residing with these leaders as a designated representative of "Afro-American freedom fighters." He recalled to journalist Milton Henry that his time in this emancipated space "opened my eyes to many things. And I think I was able to steal a few ideas that they used, and tactics and strategy that will be most effective in your and my freedom struggle."[49]

HEADS OF STATE AND THE HOPE OF MILLIONS

Initially, there was some debate among the organizers as to whether Malcolm should be credentialed as an "official observer" at the conference. He did not allow the credentials issue to inhibit him from engaging with attendees, including Abdulrahman Muhammad (referred to as "Babu," a Tanzanian term of endearment meaning grandfather).[50] Babu had led the socialist revolution in Zanzibar, which allowed Tanzania and the island to unite under the leadership of President Julius Nyerere. By 1964, he served as Tanzania's minister of economic planning. Babu shared Malcolm's critique of US foreign and domestic policy. The US was a threat to the socialist vision his government had for Tanzania.[51]

Malcolm was ultimately credentialed as an observer to the conference, which enabled him to submit a memo that provided some context to the passage of the Civil Rights Act of 1964. It also explained the background of that summer's Harlem "riots," which were a rebellion against police misconduct that caused millions of dollars of property damage and hundreds of arrests. The Civil Rights Act was called for by President Kennedy in 1963 before the March on Washington for Jobs and Freedom, co-organized by SNCC. It was ultimately signed into law by President Lyndon B. Johnson after Kennedy was assassinated. To recently emerged African states, US intelligence agencies promoted the Civil Rights Act as an example of the US government's goodwill toward Black people. In an era before social media empowered activists to provide their own news reporting and analysis directly to the public, African independence leaders had few alternative sources of rapidly disseminated information about the Black freedom struggle. Not all of the conference attendees were aware of the grisly events that motivated American support for the Civil Rights Act and provided kindling to the rage expressed in the Harlem riots.

In the South, SNCC's relentless campaigns of nonviolent civil disobedience had effectively mobilized widespread antipathy for Jim Crow. The now well-known images of women assaulted by armed police officers in riot gear, child protesters attacked by German shepherds and fire hoses, and the grieving families of martyrs like Medgar Evers, as well as the Four Little Girls killed in the bombing of a Black church in Birmingham—Addie Mae Collins, Cynthia Wesley, Carole Robertson, and Carol Denise McNair—forced the nation into confronting the consequences of its White supremacist practices. The perseverance of HBCU students turned movement leaders John Lewis, Diane Nash, Stokely Carmichael, and Ruby Doris Smith, as well as SNCC's increasing capacity to acquire new recruits from all walks of life, demanded federal lawmakers take action. While messengers of the Johnson administration portrayed the passage of the Civil Rights Act as America kindly doing the right thing, antiracist activists were aware the legislation was metaphorically signed with the blood and bone of everyday people who put their bodies on the front line for racial justice.

Malcolm believed that the "freedom fighters" in Cairo needed to understand the brutal reality of Black life in the US that continued in spite of the good intentions of the Civil Rights Act.[52] By this point in the summer of 1964, African American communities had endured White supremacists' violent backlash against civil rights protesters in St. Augustine, Florida, and Nashville, as well as police suppression of uprisings in

Rochester and Harlem. In his speech at the conference, "Appeal to African Heads of State," he lobbied the attendees for a resolution in support of African Americans to be passed.[53] "Our problem is your problem," Malcolm said. "No matter how much independence Africans get here on the mother continent," he further explained, "when you visit America, you may be mistaken for one of us." Malcolm asserted, "[Racism] is not a problem of civil rights but a problem of human rights."[54]

Impressed with Malcolm's request for solidarity with the African American community, Babu persuaded President Julius Nyerere to suggest that the conference agenda include a discussion of his resolution "thoroughly condemning the mistreatment of Afro-Americans in America."[55] The proposed resolution urged the US government "to intensify their efforts to ensure the total elimination of all forms of discrimination based on race, colour, or ethnic origin." In the OAAU's newsletter, *Blacklash*, the resolution was described in an article entitled "Racist America Blasted by Africa."[56]

Ultimately, the resolution did not pass. However, Malcolm considered his presence on the conference floor a success because he felt it dispelled the myth that African Americans and Africans did not have mutual interests. He also discovered that within the OAU, there were differences about how to achieve continental unification, especially between Nkrumah and Nyerere.[57]

Encouraged by Nyerere's support of his resolution, Malcolm traveled to Tanzania, which was ruled by Nyerere's Tanganyika African National Union (TANU). TANU had led the fight for independence and was now transforming into a one-party socialist state.[58] Malcolm's visit was organized, as it was in Ghana, by a small group of African American expatriates who had emigrated to support Nyerere's postcolonial vision. In between meetings with independence leaders, including Bibi Titi Muhammad—cofounder of TANU and head of the women's wing of the party—Malcolm took the opportunity to encourage solidarity between Tanzanians and Black Americans. He proclaimed to the Black press publication *Tanganyikan Standard*, "American Negroes are beginning to see that their relationship to Africa is something which cannot be denied."[59]

With some persistence, Babu was able to persuade Nyerere to meet face-to-face with Malcolm X in Tanzania's capital, Dar es Salaam. The president's reluctance was rooted in his commitment to nonviolent civil disobedience, which had led TANU to victory. It was also connected to the international mainstream media's misrepresentations of Malcolm X as violent and anti-White.[60] Although Nyerere agreed to a brief three-minute meet and greet, Malcolm's charm and earnestness transformed the event into a three-hour-long dialogue. For both parties, the meeting enabled the breaking down of image barriers created by American intelligence and dominant media sources. Just as Nyerere expected a loose cannon, Malcolm expected a docile US lackey. He was surprised to learn of the president's commitment to African socialism.

FROM PEACE TO PURPOSE

Once Malcolm returned to the US from Dar es Salaam, he dedicated himself to developing the OAAU. Every Sunday at the Audubon Ballroom, the organization held public gatherings that attempted to reproduce his experiences in the emancipated spaces of postcolonial Africa for Harlem community members. Malcolm described Nyerere to his constituents as "thoroughly supporting the freedom struggle for the human rights of our people in this country." During one meeting, he shared the similarities between the divide and conquer tactics used in Africa and the United States that he had observed: "One thing I noticed was the twenty-four-hour-a-day effort being made in East Africa to turn the African against the Asian; and in West Africa to turn the African against the Arab." Malcolm concluded, "You can see that . . . it's not a divisive situation that's indigenous to the African himself . . . [the system] does the same thing with you and me right here in Harlem."[61]

Blacklash editor Peter Bailey explained that the presence of diplomats from Congo, Tanzania, and other countries at OAAU events was part of an ongoing transnational dialogue. For example, Babu was a guest speaker at an OAAU gathering a few months later.[62] He informed the crowd, "Imperialist countries just don't understand that the African countries are determined to plan their own destinies."[63] Bailey also noted, "The African UN missions would [regularly] invite Brother Malcolm down to receptions."[64] Scholar and activist George Breitman observed that the relationships Malcolm developed with African UN representatives heightened their public support of the African American freedom struggle.[65]

The size of the audiences at the OAAU's weekly meetings in the winter of 1964–65 never matched the hundreds or thousands of people he routinely addressed as a Nation of Islam minister. As Pulitzer Prize winning historian Manning Marable points out in his thorough biography, *Malcolm X: A Life of Reinvention*, Malcolm's prior reach and influence was in part due to the robust financing and administrative infrastructure the NOI provided.[66] However, the gatherings did create an emancipated space in the US, through which activists could connect the OAAU's African American constituency with the ideas and tactics of African anticolonial movements. With only a few months left in his life's journey of enlightenment, Malcolm affirmed, "I . . . would like to impress, especially upon those who call themselves leaders, the importance of realizing the direct connection between the struggle of the Afro-American in this country and the struggle of our people all over the world."[67]

Similar to Malcolm's first tour of Africa, his experiences connecting with independence leaders in Cairo and Dar es Salaam show how emancipated spaces in a diaspora underground help break down barriers between activists. His engagement in these spaces highlights how the face-to-face connections that can be cultivated in emancipated spaces break down misinformation propagated by elites, allow for deeper transnational connections between organizations, and facilitate attribution of similarities between groups across national boundaries. Malcolm's engagement in emancipated spaces invigorated his commitment to a transnational solution to anti-Black racism and helped him innovate ideas about how the OAAU could foster further collaboration between Africans and African Americans.

The transnationalism of Malcolm X and the OAAU captured the imagination of a younger generation of burgeoning activists who witnessed the success of African independence and the limitations of the civil rights movement. From Oakland, California, a young community college student sent Malcolm a letter and money order donation via the OAAU's offices.[68] His name was Bobby Seale.

6

"Mississippi Eyes"
Les Yeux du Mississippi
عيون المسيسيبي
Macho ya Mississippi

IN THE NORTH, Malcolm X was exploring how to expand the OAAU's reach from a small but devoted circle of supporters and how to best achieve the organization's goal of transnational antiracist action. In the South, members of the Student Nonviolent Coordinating Committee sought to escalate their impact on federal legislation, which they felt was too slow in coming and too timid in its challenge of Southern segregation and economic injustice. SNCC organizers zeroed in on the worst offending Confederate states when it came to blocking the African American vote and flouting the federal bans on public segregation. These were Mississippi, Alabama, and Georgia.

Among the SNCC organizers in Mississippi was brooding intellectual James Forman, who joined the civil rights movement because of Ghana's success using nonviolent direct action to gain independence.[1] Forman was joined by Ruby Doris Robinson, who was incarcerated at the notorious Parchman Farm after the Freedom Rides; John Lewis, who gave a fiery, yet slightly censored speech on behalf of SNCC at the March on Washington; and soft-spoken Bob Moses, a close protégé of SNCC facilitator Ella Baker. Although as a leader of the voter registration effort in Greenwood, Mississippi, Moses had endured beatings, shootings, and imprisonment, he became convinced Black people in Mississippi "would vote in huge numbers, if given the chance."[2] Howard University student, Nonviolent Action Group (NAG) member, Freedom Rider, and former Parchman inmate Stokely Carmichael was also involved in the campaign.

Like all of the most effective community organizers, SNCC workers understood that the marginalization their constituencies experienced was intersectional in nature. Due to practices such as literacy tests and poll taxes, in Mississippi only 5 percent of Black people were registered to vote and 0 percent held political office.[3] From largely middle-class backgrounds in major cities, SNCC workers came to towns like McComb, Hattiesburg, and Greenwood to discover most African Americans living in tar paper shacks and chicken coop–like wooden boxes without toilets, bathtubs, or running water.[4] Field Organizer Ivanhoe Donaldson wrote to the organization's Atlanta headquarters from LeFlore County: "Mr. Meeks [and his wife] . . . have eleven children . . . they have no money, no food, no clothes, and no wood to keep warm by, and they now want to go register [to vote]."[5] Historian and Spelman College professor Howard Zinn observed that the more SNCC workers addressed community members' economic scarcity, the more eager Black Mississippians were to participate in electoral politics.[6]

Through its efforts to integrate public facilities and dismantle electoral exclusion, SNCC arguably made the largest contribution to inventing the period of social movement activity referred to as the '60s.[7] Their signature repertoire of mass mobilization; direct nonviolent confrontations with authorities; coalescing of youths, clergy, and labor; and provision of hands-on protest training evolved into a model that influenced the second-wave feminist movement, the United Farm Workers union, and a variety of activism today—including Black Lives Matter.[8] During the voting registration campaigns in Mississippi and Alabama, SNCC activities contained five elements:

1. canvassing community members;
2. recruiting and developing youths;

3. organizing and attending mass meetings (usually held at churches) to provide information to community members who might be too intimidated for one-on-one contact with organizers;

4. teaching in Citizenship Schools with curricula about politics, problem solving, Black history, and social movements; and

5. distributing food and clothing to address the urgent economic needs of the community.[9]

Despite the group's adherence to a philosophy of nonviolence, at the core of SNCC's approach was an unwillingness to be intimidated or concede its moral high ground. Bob Moses explained, "It seemed to be the only way to answer this kind of violence: instead of letting up, to pour it on. Instead of giving any signs of fear, to show them that for once the Negro was not going to turn around and it was not possible to shoot them out."[10]

In order to show respect for the rural Black communities in which they were working, the organization's rules for "staff decorum" prohibited alcohol consumption, mixed-gender housing, and regular absences from church.[11] SNCC developed a dress code of denim and Afros—quite distinct from the ties and crew cuts for men, gloves and hot-combed bobs for ladies, which they wore during sit-ins. John Lewis remembered, "Overalls became the standard outfit for our Black volunteers. . . . It fit our lifestyle of sleeping on sofas and floors and walking miles and miles of dusty back roads."[12] In the countryside, away from the media's glare, SNCC workers were no longer focused on impressing mainstream elites to prove they deserved a seat at the lunch counter or in the front of the bus. Bob Moses observed that Black people "in Mississippi haven't the money to eat in [lunch counters] anyway. They don't still dare go to the White half of the integrated bus terminals—they just weigh that against having their houses bombed or losing their jobs."[13] SNCC participants were done with their good-kid image. They were focused on winning the confidence of everyday African Americans.

For students who were not originally from the Deep South, living the everyday humiliation and terror of Jim Crow was both a traumatizing and an enlightening experience. A state trooper assaulted Field Secretary Lawrence Guyot and then turned him over to members of a Citizens' Council, a White supremacist organization that worked in unison with the Ku Klux Klan. They beat him until his eyes were swollen shut. His crime? Refusing to respond to the officer with "Yes, sir."[14] While driving a truckload of aid to address the severe poverty in which families were living, Ivanhoe Donaldson was accosted by police, who put a gun in his mouth and threatened to pull the trigger.[15] The *Amsterdam News* reported that Greenwood's SNCC office was set on fire and a worker was machine-gunned outside of town.[16]

However, the activists were emboldened and inspired by the psychological fortitude of the families with whom they organized. Ella Baker encouraged students to connect with indigenous leadership within their new communities.[17] This concept was later reflected in the Black Power slogan "Power to the People."[18] Rather than focus on a single charismatic figure (no matter how well-meaning), Baker advocated for a decision-making structure that centered the community members who were most impacted by the problems an organization aimed to solve. She insisted that indigenous leaders be empowered to direct the movement as well as the new institutions that evolved from it.[19]

Indigenous leaders are community members who are already respected and actively contributing but may be doing so outside of a social movement context. In Greenwood, Lowndes, and other towns, SNCC workers found leaders within families that were the nuclei of Black life. Stokely Carmichael remembered, "The core of the movement community was really a particular group of strong families, grandparents, and children." Part of why their neighbors and fellow congregants held these families in high esteem was that, according to Carmichael, they "had never surrendered. Had never accepted the limitations racism tried to impose" and "instilled self-respect, no matter how materially poor their circumstances." In the Deep South, which Moses described as the "heart of the iceberg," these indigenous leaders had been touched by the spirit of the movement long before SNCC arrived on their doorsteps.[20]

BELIEVING IN FREEDOM

Inspired by the resilience of the community members with whom they were collaborating, Bob Moses suggested SNCC "pour it on" and discredit White supremacy even more between May and August 1964 with Freedom

Summer. The campaign drew over a thousand predominately White, Northern college student volunteers to the South. Freedom Summer built upon years of strategizing and nonviolent civil disobedience experience acquired by this cadre of youths who started out at lunch counters in 1960, endured the Freedom Rides and subsequent incarceration in 1961, and persevered with mass demonstrations and voter registration throughout Mississippi, Alabama, and Georgia—in spite of the violently racist backlash against their efforts. Bob Moses became executive field secretary of this massive endeavor.

The most prominent local activist that summer was the petite, curvaceous, and charismatic Mrs. Fannie Lou Hamer. The youngest of twenty sharecropper's children in Sunflower, Mississippi, who had been forcibly sterilized at age sixteen, Mrs. Hamer was also married to a sharecropper and worked as a plantation record keeper. She learned about SNCC's voter registration drive at a mass meeting hosted by her church. As soon as she heard people explaining what voting meant, she recalled, "I could just see myself votin' people out of office that I know was wrong."[21] Like many rural community members who worked with SNCC during this period, Mrs. Hamer was not found by the movement. She had been searching for it.[22]

Freedom Summer's goals, including "the elimination of racial oppression," were warm and idealistic. But the strategy was cold political genius. The organization's prospectus for the project observed, "As the winds of change grow stronger, the threatened political elite of Mississippi becomes more intransigent and fanatical. . . . Negro efforts to win the right to vote cannot succeed against the extensive legal weapons and police powers of local and state officials without a nationwide mobilization of support."[23] Historian Charles Payne noted that Freedom Summer was "self-consciously an attempt to use the nation's racism, its tendency to react only when White life was endangered, as a point of leverage."[24] Bob Moses, Lawrence Guyot, Mrs. Hamer, and other activists were aware that national support for the civil rights movement would involve a significant number of White youths, and therefore challenge the federal government to take action and prove it believed all lives mattered.

Hundreds of young people from the most prestigious universities in the nation—Black and White, legacy and scholarship, Jewish and Christian—volunteered to join the front lines of one of their generation's defining political issues. Perhaps after JFK's assassination the previous November, these volunteers felt they needed to heed that president's call to "ask what you could do for your country." Historian Howard Zinn observed that both Black and White students were drawn to Freedom Summer for similar reasons. "When we talk about growing up in a . . . new world . . . we mean changing the world into a better place," nineteen-year-old African American Cordell Reagan explained. A White student told Zinn, "I intend to fight that society, which lied to me and mothered me for so long. . . . I believe in freedom, and must take the jump; I must take the chance of action."[25]

At the Freedom Summer orientation in Oxford, Ohio (see figure 6.1), volunteers were trained in the SNCC political philosophy of empowerment and offered a candid picture of the opposition students would confront. An official memo, written by organizer Annell Ponder, offered guidelines for interacting with Mississippi community members: "Let local people speak for and with you. Whenever possible get some good, strong local person (and there are many around) sold on your [voter registration] program. . . . Remember that they are adults, though many . . . will be overdependent because of this repressive culture."[26] Bob Moses encouraged organizers to provide support that would make community members feel capable in a culture that bamboozled them into believing they were inferior.[27] He advised volunteers, "Our goals are limited. If we can go and come back alive, that is something."[28]

In addition to continuing the established activities of canvassing and mass meetings, Freedom Summer volunteers helped create an empowering popular education program called the Freedom Schools for students of all ages. In proposing the program, SNCC field secretary and former Howard NAG member Charles Cobb explained why education was critical for the political mobilization of African American Mississippi communities. "People in the South, essentially Black people, are beginning to build their own life," Cobb wrote.[29] Education "is not the development of intellectual skills, but a preparation for participation in living." Unfortunately, the staff of the schools were predominately women because SNCC adhered to gendered labor practices.[30] Canvassing was considered more suitable for men. Classes were held in buildings that were as dilapidated as most community members' housing. However—similar to most popular education efforts in

6.1. Mrs. Fannie Lou Hamer and other Freedom Summer volunteers during orientation in Oxford, Ohio, 1964. Photograph by George R. Hoxie. Courtesy of the Ohio History Connection, AR 87-0319.

low-income communities—the demand in Black Mississippi for knowledge that was directly relevant to its social conditions and delivered in an engaging, culturally inclusive manner was overwhelming.

This rigorous diasporic curriculum was a forerunner to Paulo Freire's theory about the pedagogy of the oppressed.[31] A "Power Structure" unit created "an awareness that some people profit by the pain of others or by misleading them."[32] There were also units about the marginalization of lower income Whites, critiques of materialism, and the philosophy of nonviolence.[33] By the end of the summer, a statewide conference of Freedom

Schools called for economic sanctions against apartheid South Africa, affordable housing, a universal public health care system, and the elimination of the poll tax.[34] Through the Freedom Schools, SNCC provided African Americans in the South information about African independence movements that encouraged their constituents to identify with Black communities across borders. This creation of an alternative institution, which was by and for the community to solve social problems created by racial injustice, anticipated SNCC's work with the Mississippi Freedom Democratic Party and its adoption of Black Power philosophy.

SUPER-AMERICA

From the perspective of Mississippi elites, Freedom Summer was yet another Northern incursion into the Confederacy's sovereignty. Inexpensive Black labor, the exclusion of African Americans from public space and educational opportunity, and the pushing out of the near majority Black population from the voting bloc had all helped the South rise again after its defeat in the Civil War and the end of legal slavery.[35] Significant outflows of African Americans during the two waves of the Great Migration in the early twentieth century had already placed pressure on the South's socioeconomic stability.[36] Further threats to the racial order were threats to Southern prosperity as these political and social elites knew it.

The backlash against activists and Freedom Summer volunteers was immediate and severe. Early in the ten-week project, James Chaney, Andrew Goodman, and Michael Schwerner were arrested in Philadelphia, Mississippi, by a deputy sheriff and member of the Ku Klux Klan (KKK).[37] After they were released that night, they disappeared. After a few days of SNCC's petitioning the federal government for intervention, Attorney General Robert F. Kennedy ordered an investigation. For weeks their case was reported in the national news. During the search for Chaney, Goodman, and Schwerner, the macabre nature of Mississippi's countermovement strategy came to light. The remains of eight other Black activists were discovered in and around Philadelphia. Nearly two months after their disappearance, on August 4, 1964, the bodies of Chaney, Goodman, and Schwerner were found. The three young men had been ambushed by Klansmen who executed Goodman and Schwerner (who were White, Jewish, and from New York City). The mob then chased Chaney (who was African American from Mississippi) and brutally assaulted him before shooting him.

This horrifying violation of human rights was one of many incidents of violence and intimidation waged by the consortium of power in local Mississippi towns, which included the police, Citizens' Councils, and Ku Klux Klan. During Freedom Summer, volunteers and the local Black families that worked with them were subjected to drive-by shootings, evictions, and firing from employment. Sociologist Doug McAdam documented that over one thousand people were arrested, beaten, or murdered during Freedom Summer. Thirty-seven African American churches and thirty homes were bombed or burned. The viciousness of these attacks was ameliorated somewhat due to SNCC's adept national media strategy. Lewis remembered, "We used that weapon [the media] in every way we could."[38] Consistent reporting of the gruesome events in Mississippi, and the victimization of White participants, pushed the racial justice issue even further onto the national stage.

While pouring it on helped SNCC achieve some of the summer project's goals, repeatedly enduring White supremacist violence and intimidation took a toll on the young participants. Harvard psychiatrist Dr. Robert Coles conducted a study after the conclusion of the campaign. He found the students displayed posttraumatic stress disorder (PTSD) symptoms, including, "depression, "battle fatigue" similar to that of shell-shocked soldiers, exhaustion, weariness, despair, frustration, and rage."[39]

By feeling the chill of racism in the "heart of the iceberg," Freedom Summer volunteers came to understand that Mississippi was not the exception to systemic inequality in America. It was the most earnest expression of it. "The South is not some odd, unique corner of this nation," explained Stokely Carmichael, who had been beaten, gassed, arrested, and incarcerated because of his activism. "It is super-America."[40] Decades after their weeks in the South, Freedom Summer volunteers would speak of having "Mississippi Eyes." One participant who would later become involved in the United Farm Workers union stated, "Once you witness that injustice and then you go to Harlem or Salinas, and you see the same injustice there, you realize a lot of places are just like Mississippi."[41]

By August 1964, SNCC had the political wind at its back. Although the backlash against their efforts by local elites had been brutal and extensive, Moses, Mrs. Hamer, Carmichael, and other leaders continued to have confidence in federal political institutions. They decided to use the upcoming Democratic National Convention (DNC) in Atlantic City to attack the legitimacy of the all-White Mississippi delegation in particular—and the state's electoral process in general. The core question of their challenge was, How can the Mississippi delegates, who were all White, claim to represent the people of Mississippi, when not all the people in the state are allowed to vote?

As an alternative to the official Mississippi Democratic Party, SNCC founded the Mississippi Freedom Democratic Party (MFDP). The MFDP held caucuses and a state convention, which used national Democratic Party rules to legitimately elect its own delegates to the DNC. The MFDP asserted that its delegates were the only ones from Mississippi who should decide on the Democratic Party's nomination that year, which was favored to be incumbent president Lyndon B. Johnson. Over a few months during Freedom Summer, the MFDP emerged with eighty thousand members as an integrated and viable alternative to the state's official Democratic Party. Stokely Carmichael played a key role in this effort.

On the top of the MFDP ticket were Mrs. Fannie Lou Hamer (who was the party's vice chairperson) and Aaron Henry. Since becoming involved with SNCC in 1962, Hamer had become one of the organization's most powerful organizers. Her straightforward, persuasive, and charismatic oratory appealed equally to African American sharecroppers and Ivy League college students. "Whether you have a PhD or no D, we're in this bag together," she once said.[42] With a booming voice, Mrs. Hamer led volunteers in the singing of African American spirituals that she learned from her mother, such as "Woke Up This Morning," which inspired SNCC members to remain resilient despite the beatings, bombings, evictions, and loss of employment they faced at the hands of violent local elites.

One of Hamer's colleagues in the MFDP was Aaron Henry, a World War II veteran and pharmacist who had helped organize a boycott and voter registration campaigns in Clarksdale, Mississippi. In the face of economic and legal retaliation by local authorities, Henry persisted in his activism.[43] Similar to his movement colleagues Bayard Rustin and James Baldwin, Henry was not heterosexual. He fell victim to Mississippi's criminalization of homosexuality in 1962 and 1972.[44] Hamer's and Henry's fierce courage and passionate dedication propelled them into the MFDP's leadership.

In buses and automobiles, an MFDP caravan including Henry, Mrs. Hamer, and Carmichael headed to the convention in Atlantic City. They carried documentation of the "systemic oppression of Mississippi's Blacks" to support their demand to be seated at the convention, including notarized depositions from discrimination victims, pictures of the deplorable conditions in which African Americans were forced to live, and a list of the churches that had been bombed and burned.[45] By bringing Black Mississippi's suffering face-to-face with the Democratic Party, they aimed to undermine the power of the Dixiecrats (Southern White Democrats), who at the time controlled over 75 percent of the influential committees in Congress.[46]

In an attempt to appease these activists, President Johnson offered the sixty-four-person MFDP delegation two at-large seats to the convention, one of which would be assigned to Aaron Henry. Neither seat would hold any voting power. At this point, the MFDP had two options: accept this small victory as the finale to the ordeal of Freedom Summer or follow party rules and take their dispute to the DNC's Credentials Committee. If only eleven committee members voted to send the issue to the convention floor, a convention-wide roll call vote could decide the issue. Given the overwhelming support and moral authority the MFDP had mobilized, many delegates thought if they could make it to the convention floor, they would win the vote in a landslide.[47]

During a meeting that was broadcast on live television to discuss the proposed compromise, Rev. Dr. Martin Luther King Jr., the NAACP's Roy Wilkins, and Bayard Rustin persuaded some delegates to take the deal.[48] Mrs. Hamer objected, "We didn't come all this way for no two seats."[49] Henry humorously explained, "Lyndon made the typical White man's mistake. Not only did he say, 'You've got two votes,' which was too little, but he told us to whom the two votes would go. But, you see, he didn't realize that sixty-four of us came up from Mississippi on a Greyhound bus, eating cheese and crackers and bologna. . . . Suffering the same way. Now you say . . . 'Aaron can get in but the other sixty-two can't.' This is typical White man picking Black folks' leaders, and that day is just gone."[50]

Mrs. Hamer, who was vice chair of the MFDP, made a candid and compelling speech to the Credentials Committee explaining why she disagreed with the compromise. She described an incident of police misconduct that occurred after she and several other volunteers were arrested in Mississippi for attempting to register to vote. "[The state highway patrolman] said, 'We're going make you wish you was dead.'" Hamer then described a harrowing scene in which state patrolmen ordered two of her fellow African American prisoners to beat her with a club until they were exhausted: "I began to scream and one White man got up and began to beat me in my head and tell me to hush."[51] Hamer continued, "If the Freedom Democratic Party is not seated now, I question America."[52] The Credentials Committee refused to send the issue to the convention floor.

Mrs. Hamer, Henry, Carmichael, Moses, and their supporters were disgusted and disappointed. Bob Moses reflected that the Democratic Party's failure to recognize the MFDP, and the civil rights movement's support of compromise over confrontation with the Dixiecrats, eroded SNCC's trust in American institutions. "The idea that we would move and work through the system . . . got really severely challenged," Moses said.[53] "We thought the way to change [was] . . . to get rid of the Dixiecrats . . . excise the party [of] the most virulent, backward racists."[54] John Lewis agreed that Atlantic City was a "cruel lesson. We'd made our way to the very center of the system . . . had arrived at the doorstep, and found the door slammed in our face."[55] For the first time since the sit-ins and wade-ins sparked the youth movement in early 1960, the bitterness of defeat did not inspire SNCC leaders to pour it on. They began questioning themselves and each other. According to Moses, "I think that pushed Stokely . . . into what eventually flowered in 1966 as Black Power."[56] This frustration with dominant elites also encouraged SNCC activists to seek transnational alternatives in this diaspora underground.

After the bologna at the 1964 Democratic National Convention, longtime supporters of SNCC—including actor/musician/activist Harry Belafonte—became concerned about the abysmal morale and emotional exhaustion among the organization's most dedicated veterans.[57] Belafonte, a Harlem native born to parents from Jamaica and Martinique, had helped fund the March on Washington for Jobs and Freedom the previous year. At this time, he was an international sex symbol best known for the calypso crossover sensation "The Banana Boat Song (Day-O)" and the hit movie musical *Carmen Jones*. As a close friend of Dr. King's, Belafonte utilized his celebrity, talent, and connections to raise hundreds of thousands of dollars to support SNCC and King's SCLC. "I had become sensitive to the fact that many of the people in SNCC were on burn out," he later said in an interview for the documentary *Eyes on the Prize II*. "They had really been on the front line for so long doing so much and had been beaten and battered and . . . intimidated and still held the line. . . . What became very clear to me was that they really needed a hiatus. They needed to get away."[58]

Belafonte had become friends with Sékou Touré, who, with his wife, Hadja Andrée, had made a strong impression on African Americans through the Black press's coverage of their US tour in 1959. However, the progressive ideals Touré espoused internationally contradicted his silencing of opposition at home. In the five years since their triumphant visit, Touré and the PDG had established one-party socialist rule in Guinea and nationalized land. Through an election in which he had run unopposed in 1961, Touré was named president. Although Guinea enjoyed economic relations and support from the US, Soviet Union, and China, the economy had not fully recovered from France's punitive withdrawal of investment after independence. Touré continued to be a close ally of Ghanaian leader Kwame Nkrumah's since cohosting the All-African People's Conference in 1958, which was attended by Congolese leader Patrice Lumumba and FLN activist Frantz Fanon. Although Touré had a constructive relationship with President John F. Kennedy, relations between Guinea and the US began to deteriorate after Lyndon B. Johnson took office in 1963.

During Freedom Summer, Belafonte and President Touré had discussed the respect Touré gained for SNCC after learning about their determination and courage in news reports.[59] Touré proposed hosting a group from SNCC to engage in an exchange with young Guineans. After the disappointment of Atlantic City, Belafonte thought it was very important for SNCC leaders to directly experience the emancipated space of Conakry, Guinea. "Many people talked about the emerging Black leadership of Africa, hoping that America would fall in place with the . . . Kwame Nkrumahs and the Sekou Tourés and the Julius Nyereres," Belafonte recalled. "I felt that . . . the African environment . . . removed from certain aspects of White pressure . . . would be a very different place. It would be a chance to get out of self."[60] He raised $10,000 to fund a SNCC delegation to this independent African nation. An itinerary was planned for September 11–October 4, 1964.

The eleven-person group included James Forman, a veteran of the voter registration campaigns in Mississippi, as well as Freedom Riders and field organizers Ruby Doris Robinson (formerly Smith) and John Lewis. Bob Moses, who innovated Freedom Summer, Dona Moses (formerly Dona Richards), and Atlanta sit-in veteran and SNCC communications secretary Julian Bond were also part of the group. They were all joined by Mrs. Hamer, who had recently proclaimed her exhaustion with White supremacy and its defenders at the Democratic National Convention. "I am sick and tired of being sick and tired," she said.[61]

Lewis considered the opportunity "the chance of a lifetime."[62] From the moment the delegates boarded their Air Guinea flight, they felt as if they were traveling to an alternate universe. These organizers had been embedded in "super-America," the ultrasegregated South, for several years. A place where Black people were routinely assaulted, arrested, and killed for attempting to vote, eat at a lunch counter, or go to school. Forman noted that in the emancipated space of Conakry, "there were no sheriffs to dread, no Klan breathing down our neck, no climate of constant repression. We had come from years of living as Blacks in an enemy White world to this land of Black people with Black socialist rulers. We could relax at last."[63]

Touré set the tone for the delegation's experience when he paid an unexpected visit on their first day in his country. After being silenced and shut out of the Democratic National Convention a few weeks earlier, Mrs. Hamer burst into tears when she was introduced to Guinea's head of state.[64] "Imagine the president [of the United States] coming to see us," she said to her colleagues. Touré explained to the group, "It is fundamental that you see the problem as exploitation."[65] He continued, "While you should speak to Black people first of all, it is the entire community that must be liberated."[66] His statements echoed the themes of Ella Baker's speech at SNCC's founding conference, when she encouraged Moses, Lewis, and others to consider their fight to be about something "bigger than a hamburger." Forman would be heavily influenced by Touré's emphasis on the need for organizers to thoroughly and candidly evaluate their leadership.

In Conakry, SNCC delegates were astonished to be surrounded by Black leadership and success. "This was the first time I'd ever seen Black pilots," John Lewis remembered. "I was struck by the sight of Black police officers, Black men behind the desks in banks . . . Black people in charge. Black people doing for themselves."[67] Mrs. Hamer, a former cotton picker and police brutality survivor, was impressed by the positive psychological impact of seeing people who looked like her "just doing everything I was used to seeing White people do."[68] She later told Stokely Carmichael, with whom she organized the Mississippi Freedom Democratic Party, "It was *ordinary* people like me, who were running *everything*. The ones who were left back and never had no chance. Now they have the chance to run they own country."[69] To the delegates, Guineans appeared to enjoy the opportunities and equal citizenship that African Americans had been fighting to achieve since emancipation.

Women members of the delegation had strong feelings of cultural identification with Guinean women during the trip because they noticed different cultural forms that were retained from West Africa by African Americans.[70] Mrs. Hamer explained, "Most of the African people wear their heads tied up. My mother would do the same thing. She . . . could have two pails in her hand and a pail on her head and could go for miles and wouldn't drop them."[71] For the first time, the delegation saw women wearing cornrows in their hair. In 1964, the natural hair movement was still burgeoning in the US, although SNCC women—including Ruby Doris Robinson—embraced the Afro. Jazz singer and movie star Abbey Lincoln of the Lumumba-supporting Cultural Association for Women of African Heritage had first modeled the look years earlier. The trend's slow start was due in part to the fact that, in this pre-YouTube and pre–Black Power era, there were few resources available for Black women who did not want to straighten their hair. Inspired, Ruby Doris Robinson had a local woman braid her hair into cornrows.[72] Dona Moses remembered that participating in these Guinean customs helped the SNCC women feel "a kind of belonging that most of use never felt" in America.[73]

The contrast between SNCC activists' affirming experiences in Guinea and the brutality they endured at home was heightened when they discovered how the conflict at the Democratic National Convention was being publicized in Africa by the US government. Efforts were made to downplay the racial inequality in America, which these young activists had sacrificed so much to transform. Julian Bond remembered, "There were all these pictures of [African American] . . . judges, policemen." "If you didn't know anything about America, like Africans would not, you would think that these were really commonplace things," he continued. "That's the worst kind of deceit."[74] Bob Moses was gobsmacked to see a photo of Mrs. Hamer and himself in a magazine published by the US Information Agency. It had the misleading caption, "Moses and Hamer leading delegates of the MFDP to their seats [on the floor of] the Democratic Party convention."[75] Although the federal government was unwilling to appear racist in Africa because it would lead to a disadvantage in the Cold War, it was still willing to perpetuate racism at home. While in this emancipated space in a diaspora underground, the delegates were validated in their frustration with US political elites.

According to the journey's benefactor, Harry Belafonte, the trip achieved its goals. "I don't think anybody who was on that trip ever saw themselves in quite the same way again," he recalled. SNCC activists experienced Guinea as an emancipated space that showed that their political aspirations were reasonable and achievable. "In a hundred ways Guinea represented to us the antithesis of everything to which we had been exposed in the United States," Forman observed.[76] Of course, Touré's government insulated the delegates from the harsher realities of rural Guinean poverty and suppressed political opposition. On this voyage through a carefully curated emancipated space, the Mississippi Eyes of SNCC activists witnessed only the possibilities of antiracist activism and transnational solidarity.

After leaving Guinea shortly before Lyndon B. Johnson's election to the presidency, participants in the delegation possessed a renewed vigor for their activism and a desire to advance their newfound diasporic perspective. Dona Richards encouraged all of SNCC to "expand our borrowed cry of 'one man, one vote' to 'self-determination and dignity throughout the world!!!'"[77] Forman, who would soon become SNCC's International Affairs director, recalled returning to the US "full of ideas and enthusiasm for formalizing and expanding" connections between "Black resistance in the United States and the African struggle for total independence."[78] SNCC's engagement with the emancipated space of Conakry led to immediate ideational and tactical innovations.

The leaders also held a self-reflective meeting about the vulnerabilities of the organization. They identified their weaknesses as the pervasiveness of American liberalism, rapid growth without restructuring decision-making processes, and conflict between predominately White, Northern, middle-class volunteers and SNCC's predominately Black, Southern, rural, and low-income constituency. Ruby Doris Robinson suggested establishing Friends of SNCC groups in Africa.[79] Dona Richards proposed an African Affairs department for SNCC that would directly address the myth of pathological Black culture that lay at the core of Johnson's proposed welfare reforms.[80] She wrote, "Through identification with . . . African heritage we can find the strength with which to fight Johnson's plan, and we can find out what it really means to be [African] American . . . in the positive sense."[81] Their time in Conakry apparently led the SNCC leadership to take a transnational approach to nearly every organizational challenge.

However, the reinvigorated leaders were not clear about how diasporic engagement would address SNCC's core fragilities. This disconnect would prove to be a stumbling block to their sustained existence and transnational exchanges. In December 1964, Mrs. Fannie Lou Hamer and the SNCC Freedom Singers accepted an invitation to speak at one of Malcolm X's OAAU gatherings at the Audubon Ballroom. The OAAU was also struggling with how to take what Malcolm had learned during his journeys through emancipated spaces in this diaspora underground into a concrete, community organizing reality.

7

"Love Our Community"
Aimons Notre Communauté
أحب مجتمعنا
Penda Jumwiya Yetu

IN HARLEM AFTER New Year's in 1965, Malcolm X revealed his political philosophy had evolved into a version of Black Marxism.[1] The time he spent during the previous year with Kwame Nkrumah and Julius Nyerere—and in the emancipated spaces of Cairo and Algiers—buoyed Malcolm's belief that African Americans needed to consider socialist solutions to their problems and avoid internal divisions. When he introduced Mrs. Fannie Lou Hamer (still invigorated from her voyage to Guinea) to OAAU supporters in the Audubon Ballroom, Malcolm asserted, "Almost every one of the countries that has gotten independence has devised some kind of socialistic system, and this is no accident."[2] In an interview at New York's public radio station, WBAI-FM, Malcolm explained that he wanted to show his constituency how socialism was directly relevant to their struggle against racism.

Malcolm commented that he now wanted to do more than "stand on the sidelines and make militant-sounding declarations."[3] However, the bulk of his professional experience was as a numbers runner, burglar, and orthodox minister of an unconventional branch of Islam. Unlike SNCC veterans, he had no background as a community organizer. His childhood friend recalled that Malcolm earnestly wanted to live up to his community's expectations that he could lead the entire Black nationalist movement.[4] "It was a task of frightening dimensions," he observed.[5]

Meanwhile, the Nation of Islam continued to treat Malcolm X as a threat. As he juggled his responsibilities to the OAAU, his work with Alex Haley to complete *The Autobiography of Malcolm X*, and his appearances and speeches, the NOI targeted Malcolm and his supporters with violence and intimidation.[6] Malcolm continued to publicly criticize NOI leader Elijah Muhammad. "There was no God in him," he said during an interview.[7] It was not uncommon for Malcolm's appearances to conclude with brawls between his security and Nation of Islam supporters. "My death has been ordered by higher-ups" in the NOI, he stated to the *Amsterdam News*.[8]

By February 1965, the extraordinary burden of being Malcolm X—the radical, earnest, relentless, pious human rights activist/political theorist/international celebrity—who was invented by Malcolm Little, a penniless orphan from Nebraska, was palpable. His associates noticed that he no longer cared to present a meticulous image by dressing in a starched suit, bleached white shirt, tie, and shined shoes. A depressed fatalism clouded his conversations. Alluding to the mysterious circumstances surrounding his Garveyite father's demise, Malcolm noted to a friend that "the males in his family didn't die a natural death."[9]

A visit to Selma, Alabama, in support of SNCC's voter registration campaign (led by Nashville sit-in veteran Diane Nash and recent Guinea travelers James Forman and John Lewis) provided some relief. However, when he returned to New York on February 14, the home in Queens that he shared with his wife, Mrs. Betty Shabazz, and their four little girls was firebombed with two Molotov cocktails.[10] He managed to help his wife and daughters escape as flames engulfed the building. Years later, NOI member Edward X was confirmed as the leader of the group who committed this arson.[11]

Absurdly, according to his wife, or heroically, according to his OAAU followers, Malcolm barreled forward with a busy itinerary after the bombing.[12] "I live like I am already dead," thirty-nine-year-old Malcolm told the

New York Times.[13] At a security briefing, Malcolm overruled decisions to search all future attendees to OAAU meetings at the Audubon and to arm his security from the Muslim Mosque, Inc.[14] Both organizations were still finding their financial and administrative footing, so his associates were still primarily "Malcolmites" more than OAAU or MMI members. Although they varied in enthusiasm about his new inclusive humanist message, they united in concern about his life. Malcolm refused offers for him and his family to have political asylum in Ethiopia, or to live as guests of the state in Saudi Arabia or Accra.[15] It is unclear if Malcolm's indifference to his safety was a result of a death wish caused by his depression or a resignation to martyrdom.[16]

For Malcolm, February 21, 1965, began as ordinarily as Sundays did for him. He was staying at the New York Hilton, while Mrs. Shabazz and his daughters stayed with a family friend in Queens.[17] He invited his wife and children to attend that afternoon's OAAU rally at the Audubon. When he arrived at the venue, he reviewed some copies of the OAAU's newsletter, *Blacklash*, with Peter Bailey. By the time Malcolm arrived backstage, Malcolm's staff noticed he was irritated about last-minute changes in the day's program. It was finally time to announce the OAAU's political platform publicly. When introducing his mentor to the crowd, Benjamin 2X exclaimed, "Men like this don't come every day." Malcolm "cares nothing about the consequences, cares only for the people," he continued. The Audubon crowd of about four hundred, including Betty and his children, applauded vigorously.

Shortly after Malcolm greeted OAAU members from the podium with *"as-salaam alaikum"* and the audience responded with *"wa alaikum salaam,"* an odd commotion erupted in the back of the room that drew the attention of his security. A smoke bomb ignited in the ballroom, creating panic and confusion. Then Willie Bradley of the Nation of Islam stood, walked quickly to the stage, raised a sawed-off shotgun from beneath his coat, and fired at Malcolm X. Betty grabbed her children, pulled them to the floor, and shielded them with her own body. "They're killing my husband!" she screamed. The gunfire blew a hole around Malcolm's heart. While Bradley escaped through a side entrance, two other gunmen who created the commotion were apprehended and beaten by the infuriated crowd.

On the stage, OAAU member Yuri Kochiyama leaned over Malcolm and wishfully exclaimed, "He's still alive!" Betty ran toward Malcolm in hysterics. CPR was attempted but unsuccessful. "Are they going to kill everyone?" one of Malcolm's daughters asked. While waiting for Malcolmites to bring a gurney from nearby Columbia-Presbyterian hospital, a group of his supporters surrounded his body, begging him, praying him, willing him back to life. Roughly an hour later, an emergency room doctor declared their hope futile. "The man you know as Malcolm X is dead," he proclaimed.

The *Amsterdam News* reported that over thirty thousand people "from all walks of life" paid their respects to Malcolm while he lay in state at the Unity Funeral Home, just one block from where he used to give memorable street corner speeches on 125th Street.[18] The funeral service at Faith Temple was filled to capacity. Three thousand additional mourners listened from the sidewalk. John Lewis and James Forman of SNCC as well as Bayard Rustin attended the funeral. Actress Ruby Dee read several messages of condolence.[19] One was from Kwame Nkrumah. Dee's husband, actor Ossie Davis, gave a devastating eulogy. "If you know him you would know why we must honor him," Davis said. "And we will know him then for what he was and is . . . our own Black shining prince—who didn't hesitate to die, because he loved us so."[20] Davis quoted Malcolm's words from his final tour in Africa: "The main thing is that we keep a united front wherein our most valuable time and energy will not be wasted fighting each other."

For months after his death, Malcolm's sister Ella Collins and the most devoted Malcolmites worked to continue the efforts of the OAAU and Muslim Mosque, Inc.[21] However, the projects lost momentum without their founder's zeal and charisma. SNCC leader Bob Moses recalled, "Malcolm's assassination . . . left a vacuum." "As soon as you are most of the time out giving speeches but, at the same time, telling people the most important work is the organizing," he explained, "it's oil and water . . . the organizing issue can't be . . . theoretical, it really has to grow."[22]

BLOODY

While Malcolm was struggling to build OAAU before his death, the SNCC leadership returned from their empowering trip to Guinea to pour it on in

Selma and Lowndes County, Alabama. Diane Nash had been on the ground for months working with the people of Selma to dismantle their disenfranchisement by coordinating mass meetings, voter registration drives, and demonstrations. James Forman and John Lewis were also organizing there.

Soon after Malcolm's assassination, the Selma campaign escalated into one of the most violent events in the civil rights movement: "Bloody Sunday." On March 7, 1965, organizers engaged in a peaceful march across the Edmund Pettus Bridge in an attempt to march to Montgomery. Montgomery, Alabama, was where Martin Luther King Jr., Rosa Parks, Claudette Colvin, and hundreds of others had helped wage the successful bus boycott that had sparked this cycle of the civil rights movement ten years earlier. The Pettus Bridge demonstration protested the slaughter of a young African American man, Jimmy Lee Jackson, by White state trooper James Bonard Fowler.

On the bridge, Alabama state highway patrolmen teargassed, clubbed, and whipped the unarmed civilians, among them John Lewis.[23] As the event was reported by the national and international news, Bloody Sunday victims drew widespread sympathy and support, which culminated in a march of twenty-five thousand people from Selma to Montgomery later that month. Among the marchers were Harry Belafonte, funder of SNCC's Guinea delegation, and King.

After the celebrities and charismatic leaders left Selma following the march, SNCC workers, including Freedom Summer veterans Stokely Carmichael and James Forman, "moved into the hard core areas [of Alabama], where the percentage of Negroes is as high as the terror and intimidation."[24] As historian Hasan Kwame Jeffries documented in the book *Bloody Lowndes*, Alabama's corrupt political culture enabled economic and physical retaliation against rural African Americans citizens when they attempted to exercise their human rights.[25] This was the case in Lowndes County, where SNCC workers and local organizers founded the Lowndes County Freedom Organization (LCFO) and encouraged African American community members to register to vote.[26]

The LCFO was inspired by SNCC's success with the Mississippi Freedom Democratic Party. The Lowndes campaign was supported with funds raised by SNCC's New York City office, whose staff included Barnard student and diplomat's daughter Kathleen Neal. Neal grew up near Fisk and had eagerly waited as a teenager to become involved with the civil rights movement. When Neal came to SNCC, she discovered the organization was struggling to stay in front of the change it helped create and to fully include women's leadership. Soon, she would be drawn to the energy and rebelliousness of another youth-led antiracist organization in Oakland, California.

The LCFO logo was a black panther. Organizers chose this logo for a few reasons: The state of Alabama required every political party to have an emblem, perhaps to assist less than literate White voters with decision-making at the ballot box. Second, from their perspective, a black panther symbolized "the strength and dignity of Black people." The logo was also an icon of the principle of self-defense. A panther "never strikes back until he's back so far into the wall, he's got nothing to do but spring out," Carmichael observed. "And when he springs he does not stop."[27] Due to the emblem, some people began referring to the LCFO as the Black Panther Party.

Using organizing techniques they had refined for several years, SNCC field secretaries in Lowndes—including former Howard University student, Nonviolent Action Group member, and Freedom Rider Courtland Cox—helped create political workshops and door-to-door outreach campaigns. Also among the organizers were HBCU alumni Jennifer Lawson and Charlie Cobb, who helped establish Freedom Schools in Mississippi. They accompanied African American residents to the registrar's office and were routinely turned away. White landowners in Lowndes began evicting Black tenant farmers en masse. Under the cover of night, Klansmen fired shotguns into organizers' homes. On August 20, 1965, White seminary student and SNCC volunteer Jonathan Daniels was murdered as he defended African American teenager Ruby Sales during an attack by sheriff's deputy Tom L. Coleman. The violence that characterized Freedom Summer followed SNCC to what became known as "Bloody Lowndes." This continued intransigence of racist elites, the lingering disappointment over the 1964 Democratic National Convention, and what SNCC perceived as the federal government's ambivalence toward the plight of Southern African Americans continued to build organizers' frustrations.

During this backlash, SNCC organizers turned to the example of the Front de Libération Nationale (FLN) and the work of Frantz Fanon for inspiration. Jennifer Lawson remembered, "The most influential [book] to me [in] 1965 and later was . . . Fanon [*The Wretched of the Earth*]. . . . As students we would go over and over [this] and have many discussions."[28] Since leaving his post as a psychiatrist in 1955, Fanon was immersed in the war for Algerian independence. In addition to writing for the FLN's official publication, he was an ambassador for the movement at emancipated spaces, including the All-African People's Conference in Accra (where he met with Patrice Lumumba in 1958). Since the FLN won its war against the French in 1962, Fanon's writing and the FLN's triumphs were slowly becoming legend among antiracist activists in the US.

Fanon originally published the book *Wretched of the Earth* in French as *Les damnés de la terre* in 1961. In some ways, the book is a synthesis of the ideas he put forth in previous work, such as *Black Skin, White Masks*; *A Dying Colonialism*; and his essays in the FLN's newspaper *El Moudjahid* (later anthologized in *Toward the African Revolution*). *Wretched* contained two theories that were particularly impactful on this generation of antiracist activists. First, in the chapter "Concerning Violence," he asserts that violence is a cathartic resolution to the longtime conflict between the colonizer and the colonized. Second, in the chapter "On National Culture," Fanon describes the psychological impact of colonialism on the "colonial bourgeoisie." Fanon asserts that colonial institutions—such as schools, churches, and mainstream culture—train the colonized middle class to identify so much more with their colonizers than with their indigenous group that they have a "colonized mind." According to Fanon, the colonization of the mind is perhaps the most effective weapon of domination because it trains the subjected to discipline themselves and their community members without intervention from the oppressor.

By the time Fanon's work was available in English in 1963, his ideas about violence and the colonized mind were particularly salient to SNCC workers. Cleveland Sellers, a Freedom Summer veteran, observed that SNCC activists "spent a lot of time studying . . . revolutionaries in . . . Africa" and that Frantz Fanon's work "helped us understand many things that had been puzzling us since [the Democratic National Convention in] Atlantic City."[29] Having witnessed the frustrations endured by the non-violent civil rights movement, SNCC organizers now embraced the principles of self-defense. They'd also recently become aware—due in part to their engagement with and learning about African independence—that much of what they'd been taught in schools, churches, museums, and mainstream media about African and African American history, politics, and culture was inaccurate and tailored to legitimize White supremacist ideas. Through the Freedom Schools in Mississippi, their journey to Guinea, and the Lowndes County political workshops, SNCC organizers experienced how broadening constituents' knowledge about Black history empowered political participation and healing from racial trauma. They were able to see Fanon's articulation of the African's path to cognitive liberation as a prescription for how their movement in the US should move forward.

Fanon did not have the opportunity to engage directly with SNCC organizers or other Black Power activists about his work. He dictated *Les damnés de la terre* from his sickbed on the Tunisian front during the final months of the Algerian revolution, four years before the Lowndes County campaign. He had been diagnosed with leukemia. At age thirty-six, the middle-class Martinican who became disillusioned in France as a medical student and then transformed into a revolutionary in Algeria died in Bethesda, Maryland, while receiving treatment from the National Institutes of Health in 1961. His FLN comrades buried him with full military honors in Aïn Kerma, Algeria, a small village by the sea.

Although it is a work of fiction, the gritty, documentary-style depiction of Ali LaPointe and others in the FLN by the Gillo Pontecorvo film *The Battle of Algiers* also had an impact on SNCC activists.[30] Charles Cobb recalled that learning about the Algerian independence movement expanded activists' conception of power and the possibilities beyond local Southern governments. "It became clear that you needed allies," Cobb stated. "It was fascinating to think about the world of Africa. . . . If you added yourself into that world, you were no longer a minority . . . you suddenly became part of a majority world."[31] The allure to SNCC organizers of being part of a diaspora underground, and being part of a transnational majority-Black alliance, was heightened by their belief America was failing to significantly advance toward equality and the relentless aggression of Southern elites.

ENGINEERED FROM THE OUTSIDE?

Ultimately, SNCC's partnership with the people of Lowndes increased the number of African American registered voters from one to approximately nine hundred in just a few months.[32] However, SNCC's effectiveness during the Alabama campaign obscured growing discord among its members about the way forward and the organization's "open-door policy" to White organizers.[33] Tensions had been growing since Freedom Summer. Some field staff claimed Whites alienated local Black community members and further inflamed tensions between the organization and local White communities. One of the consequences of segregation was that few SNCC workers, volunteers, or local organizers—regardless of their backgrounds—had ever worked as equals or partners in a racially integrated environment. Some White volunteers were unaware of how their implicit bias shaped their interactions with Black staff members or how they used the educational opportunities and skills training to which they had disproportionate access to wield influence in meetings and decision-making. This dynamic reinforced the racist structures of inequality SNCC sought to dismantle.

John Lewis, who had participated in SNCC's delegation to Guinea and had been assaulted during Bloody Sunday in Selma, explained in a staff meeting that it was essential for White SNCC staff to "recognize the fact that we are caught up with a sense of destiny with the vast majority of colored people all over the world who are becoming conscious of their power."[34] Awareness of and engagement with African independence through this diaspora underground was helping African Americans redefine their identity, which had been subjugated and dehumanized by mainstream American discourse in schools and popular culture for hundreds of years. "If the movement and SNCC are going to be effective in attempting to liberate the Black masses," Lewis continued, "the civil rights movement must be Black-controlled, dominated, and led."[35] Following Fanon's thesis in *The Wretched of the Earth*, some SNCC leaders believed that decolonizing the African American mind was essential to liberating the African American body.

Another faction held that the diversity of participation and leadership within SNCC allowed the organization to serve as a model for the society they were working to build. It was also an opportunity for African American participants to have more empowered expectations of how they could interact as equals with Whites. An organizer observed that given the history that African Americans in Mississippi and Alabama had lived through, "they had pretty low expectations of White people, and by those standards the volunteers looked pretty good."[36] The hindrance to fundraising that forging a Black-only organization would create was also a consideration. Harry Belafonte, one of SNCC's most effective fundraisers, recalled, "The people who were White and supportive of our cause, who saw it in non-racial terms . . . began to take a position that this became a little too sectarian, too alienating."[37]

Still another percolating issue was the tension between SNCC's commitment to racial equality and the patriarchal culture that permeated the organization. Although Ella Baker, Ruby Doris Smith Robinson, Fannie Lou Hamer, and other women had taken impactful leadership roles, the gendered expectations about responsibilities, compensation, and respect in the workplace that existed in mainstream society also existed within SNCC. Due to fear of retaliation, two women anonymously circulated a memo after Freedom Summer that urged SNCC men to take sexism as seriously as racism. Just as "the average White person doesn't realize that *he assumes he is superior,*" the memo's authors claimed, "so too the average SNCC worker finds it difficult to discuss the woman problem because of the assumptions of male superiority."[38] The memo described the everyday hostilities, or microaggressions, that women in the organization faced. For example, "Any women in SNCC, no matter what her position or experience, has been asked to take minutes in a meeting when she . . . is outnumbered by men."[39]

These divisions within SNCC were insignificant compared to the escalating conflicts in Algeria's FLN and Ghana's CPP. In the emancipated spaces of Algiers and Accra the previous year, Malcolm X experienced unity, progressive politics, and cultural pride. However, behind the scenes of these large public presentations were deep-seated tensions between party factions about how to transform from a social movement organization to a governing political party. As agitating protesters, OAAU and SNCC retained the luxury of representing the interests of a small number of communities coalesced around a common goal. Political parties in power are charged with unifying a variety of competing interests in order to administer a functioning state. Scarcity of public resources, residual trauma from recent conflicts, or a lack of strong support during the electoral process can all make this unifying task more difficult. In a diaspora underground, an emancipated space for activists engaging across national borders may occur in a political context that is far from democratic or liberated for all its constituents.

In Algeria, President Ahmed Ben Bella's presidency became threatened due to his deteriorating relationships within the FLN. His rise to political power was predicated on his ability to balance the interests of the government's new National Liberation Army, veterans of the Algerian Revolution, and government administrators. Ben Bella adapted some socialist policies; however, the more power he consolidated, the more self-centered his behavior and decision-making reportedly became. The success of the FLN relied on a firm commitment to collective leadership, which Ben Bella and others in the first nine (*les neuf historiques*) made to each other and the people of Algeria at the start of the independence war. The president's obsession with his own image as a star freedom fighter who hobnobbed with the radical guerrilla elite (such as Cuban minister of industry Ernesto "Che" Guevara) directly conflicted with the original FLN vision of democracy.[40]

By 1965, Ben Bella's increasing interest in international affairs drew criticism from competing factions in the government. According to his detractors, his foreign policy work interfered with his dedication to domestic concerns. He was increasingly paranoid about being overthrown. The Associated Press reported that at a luncheon, he turned to his close friend, former FLN comrade and Algeria's defense minister Houari Boumédiène, and asked half jokingly, "How are your intrigues going?" Boumédiène, who was well-known for his avoidance of cameras and deadpan communication style, responded, "Very well, thank you."[41] Under Boumédiène's leadership, the Algerian army deposed Ben Bella in a bloodless coup on

June 21, 1965. His friend placed Ben Bella under house arrest in Algiers with his wife, Mrs. Zohra Sellami, where he remained until 1979.[42] Boumédiène would be president of Algeria until 1976.

In Ghana, the success and Pan-Africanist optimism of Nkrumah and his Convention People's Party had inspired King during his visit to the nation's independence celebration in 1957. Later, its success would also encourage James Forman and other young activists to participate in SNCC. When Malcolm met the Ghanaian president in Accra in 1964, he was so enthralled by Nkrumah's leadership of the Organization of African Unity that he named his new organization the Organization of Afro-American Unity. However, Nkrumah's popularity with the diaspora underground did not warm the hearts of Ghana's economic elite.

President Kwame Nkrumah could no longer fend off critics with his administration's control of the media and its censorship of dissent. Since independence, at least five attempts had been made on Nkrumah's life in public, which left thirty Ghanaians dead and three hundred wounded.[43] In February 1966, officers and soldiers of the Ghanaian army, now organized as the National Liberation Council, invaded the presidential palace while Nkrumah was on a state visit to Asia and seized control of the government. Officially, this coup d'état was motivated by a Republican Party–like opposition to the national budget deficit. The *Amsterdam News* reported that according to the Ghanaian army officer who led the coup, "Nkrumah wasted the country's resources in prestige projects that did not help the people but mainly boosted his own image." The officer continued, "The $560,000,000 foreign reserve that Ghana had at independence in 1957 vanished completely, being replaced by a foreign debt of over $1,120,000,000."[44]

Although Nkrumah's fiscal mismanagement was a legitimate cause for concern, his administration was also threatened by its increasing tensions with Ghana's professional class. Essayist Charles Howard noted the anti-Nkrumahists "feel themselves a privileged group" and had hoped after independence they would "substitute themselves for the colonial masters."[45] In contrast, Nkrumah had "slept in subways in Harlem" during his time as a student in America and envisioned a postcolonial Ghana, Africa, and African diaspora that would have greater economic and social equality. He had become so attached to his reverie, he could not see the perilous nature of the political situation on the ground. Ironically Nkrumah, an internationally impactful advocate of Pan-African unity, could not coalesce his most influential constituents to support his vision. Several months after the coup, a general election was held that, according to the *Amsterdam*, seemed to indicate the people wanted no more of their president.[46] The new regime led Ghana into an alliance with the International Monetary Fund and the West in the Cold War.

Nkrumah and his supporters remained convinced that in spite of the internal conflicts, the success of the coup was "engineered from the outside."[47] In a letter to Guinean president Sékou Touré, Nkrumah asserted, "This plot is by the imperialists, neo-colonialists, and their agents in Africa."[48] His government had strengthened ties with the Eastern bloc, which would have caused concern in the US State Department and Pentagon at the time. Conflicting and disputed reports claim that the CIA was involved in the coup against Nkrumah and that the KGB deceived him into believing the US was responsible in order to rally his and Touré's support.[49]

While the coup may not have been technically plotted or funded by external authorities, it certainly was furthered by outer pressures. Like many African nations, Ghana was left with the bill for decades of underdevelopment by its colonizers. Physical infrastructure, human capital, and a national culture (comprised of several indigenous tribal cultures) all required investment and planning. The escalation of the Cold War made it nearly impossible for African nations to remain nonaligned and truly autonomous on the international stage. Major international cultural, political, and business institutions continued to stigmatize Africans as subhuman and inferior, placing an additional burden on international partnerships and trade.

Despite the devastation of being exiled from a country he had served for more than twenty years, Nkrumah seemed to have remained committed to his politics. He wrote, "As these imperialist forces grow more militant and insidious, using traitors to the African cause against the freedom and independence . . . we must strengthen our resolution and fight for the dignity of our people."[50] After the coup, Nkrumah settled in Conakry, where he was granted political asylum by his ally Sékou Touré. His wife, Fathia, and children fled to her hometown in Egypt. Touré's own escalating intolerance of dissent may have been impacted by his friend's misfortune and Ben Bella's fall in Algiers. By the mid-1960s, the backlash against progressive socialist administrations, which began with Lumumba's assassination, had gained significant momentum. This emerging political reality would make it increasingly difficult for African independence organizations that had transformed into governing political parties to fully engage in a diaspora underground.

POWER AGAINST FEAR

As Nkrumah's government collapsed in Accra, the faith of SNCC veterans in the civil rights movement's "hearts and minds" approach continued to wane. Leaders of the movement had committed to nonviolent civil disobedience with two goals in mind: First, to disrupt the everyday practice of segregation in the South until change became necessary. Second, to perform African Americans' deservedness of equal treatment under the law in a manner that dismantled prevailing White supremacist stereotypes.

In many high school American history textbooks, the heroic actions of King, Parks, Lewis, Hamer, and others are depicted as somewhat spontaneous or anchored purely in religious conviction. The reality was that the entire civil rights movement—including the mass mobilizations in Montgomery, Birmingham, and Selma—was a result of incessant strategizing and planning that accounted for the specific political climate of the time. For some, accurately describing the work of the movement's brilliant political theorists and community organizers (e.g., Bayard Rustin and Diane Nash) as performance and dramaturgy diminishes the romance of this period.[51] Romance alone cannot actualize the progress toward racial justice that the world desperately needs.

Since they engaged in a wave of sit-ins throughout the South in 1960, SNCC activists had done their part to disrupt the everyday life of Jim Crow. Whether they wore knee-length skirts or denim overalls, at lunch counter stools, bus stations, and courthouse steps these young people demonstrated patience and resilience, as well as their adherence to mainstream American values, such as freedom and democracy. John Lewis, Ruby Doris Smith Robinson, Stokely Carmichael, Mrs. Fannie Lou Hamer, and hundreds of other activists had eviscerated racist stereotypes with articulate, compelling oratory and brazen acts of courage, discipline, and sacrifice. SNCC participants had taken the beatings, threats, gunshots, arrests, and verbal abuse that civil rights movement leadership demanded of them.

With the 1964 Voting Rights Act, Civil Rights Act, and establishment of the Equal Employment Commission, some changes were made. But the longtime activism of SNCC leadership made them see America's racial justice crisis with Mississippi Eyes. It was not only "bigger than a hamburger," as their mentor Ella Baker had advised years earlier. The problem was intrinsic to the structure of inequality in America.

After the march from Selma to Montgomery—and during the Lowndes County voter registration effort in June 1966—activist James Meredith launched a protest he called the "March against Fear" from Memphis to Jackson. Meredith desegregated the University of Mississippi after the Kennedy administration intervened. He shared SNCC leadership's frustrations with the pace of change. With the objective of highlighting the continued segregation and lack of voting rights in Mississippi, Meredith invited only Black men to join him and hoped to avoid any participation by more well-known leaders such as King, Lewis, or Carmichael. On the second day of the 220-mile walk, he was shot three times at close range by a White sniper named James Aubrey Norvell. Meredith was seriously injured, but he survived.

SNCC and the SCLC joined to continue Meredith's march in response to the violence. Stokely Carmichael had been elected as chair of SNCC, replacing John Lewis, and was a leader of a growing faction within SNCC that was interested in bringing economic concerns to the forefront of the organization's agenda.[52] In the context of the Cold War, part of the "hearts and minds" strategy was to avoid any appearance of allegiance with the communist Eastern bloc.

Along the route, organizers registered thousands of African American voters. The Deacons for Defense and Justice signed on to act as a security for marchers. The Deacons continued in the spirit of former Monroe, North Carolina, NAACP chapter leader Robert F. Williams, who years earlier argued that African American self-defense was necessary in the Jim Crow South, where there was no rule of law. Mississippi's governor also publicly committed to keeping the marchers safe.

Once King began marching alongside Carmichael, thousands more joined the effort. National media covered the protest daily. Celebrities including Harry Belafonte and Nina Simone, who performed her protest anthem "Mississippi Goddam" for marchers, participated in the event. Local churches provided food and tents along the route. Although the goals of the march remained murky, the goodwill of participants from diverse backgrounds throughout the US was abundant and clear. The vitriol of White supremacists, who launched insults and threats to the Black and White participants, was also unambiguous. Each evening, leaders of the march would give inspirational speeches. The press noted that SNCC field secretary Willie Ricks would engage the crowd in a call-and-response of "Black Power!" during these events.[53]

The March against Fear arrived in Greenwood, Mississippi, where SNCC and local community members had a widespread base of support. State troopers declared protesters could not erect tents for shelter at a local Black high school, although organizers had previously secured permission. Carmichael balked at the troopers' orders and was arrested.[54] He returned to that evening's rally from jail. Carmichael survived sit-ins, the Freedom Rides, notorious Parchman Farm, Freedom Summer, and Bloody Lowndes. This was the twenty-seventh political arrest he had endured in the six years since he arrived at Howard University from Bronx High School of Science as a bright eyed teenager in a starched suit.

Three thousand people were scattered among tents and makeshift canopies in the thick, hot Mississippi night. Wearing a light blue denim shirt and dark jeans, twenty-four-year-old Stokely Carmichael saluted the enthusiastic crowd with a raised arm and clenched fist before taking the microphone. "I ain't going to jail no more!" he said.[55] The crowd exploded into applause. He continued, "The only way to stop White men from whuppin' us is to take over." Then Carmichael alluded to SNCC's original slogan, "Freedom Now." "We have been saying freedom for six years and we ain't got nothin," he asserted. "What we gonna start saying now is BLACK POWER!" SNCC field secretary Cleveland Sellers, who, like Carmichael, had been part of the Nonviolent Action Group at Howard University and had participated in Freedom Summer, recalled that the crowd roared in response, "BLACK POWER!" Willie Ricks, who had introduced marchers to the catchphrase days earlier, led the crowd once again in a call-and-response:

"What do you want?"
"BLACK POWER!"
"What do you want?"
"BLACK POWER!"
"What do you want?"
"BLACK POWER! BLACK POWER! BLACK POWER!"

Initially, James Meredith conceived the March against Fear as a protest of the climate of intimidation, violence, and marginalization that controlled Black Mississippian lives. At a Black institution in the "heart of the iceberg," for a few moments Carmichael helped his audience transform their racial terror into Black desire.

What one sees at the sight of three thousand mostly African American people shouting "BLACK POWER!" in unison depends a great deal on the perspective of the person holding the gaze. From the point of view of the mainstream journalists present (most of whom were White because America's newsrooms remained segregated until the early 1970s), the protesters seemed like a "mob" or a "throng" that was on the brink of rioting. From the platform where Carmichael, Ricks, Sellers, and other activists stood, the moment may have seemed like years of community organizing and political education work finally bearing fruit. Backstage among the SCLC leaders (King was not in attendance that evening), there may have been visions of the scatological hitting the fan. For someone standing within the crowd on the school grounds looking left and right, the sight may have been one of perennially frustrated, frightened, yet still faithful people finally allowing themselves an earnest cry for relief.

The March against Fear concluded ten days later in Jackson. By that time, it had swelled to a mass of fifteen thousand people, which included music pioneer James Brown and Oscar winner Marlon Brando. The buoyant spirit of the protesters remained. But the tolerance for what SNCC perceived as American indifference to segregation, economic inequality, and disenfranchisement had evaporated. Their frustration with US elites was no longer simply palpable. It was overwhelming. And it would encourage SNCC leaders to seek more transnational engagement in this diaspora underground.

WHAT WE WANT

The national media latched onto Carmichael and his catchphrase. "Black Power!" created a news cycle that lasted for months. Carmichael's impromptu speech left SNCC with no preparation for the fallout. SNCC staff spent a great deal of time clarifying the meaning of the "Black Power philosophy," although the press coverage seemed to overstate the newness and "militant" nature of the idea. In a speech in Greenwood during Freedom Summer, Carmichael stated, "We have to stop being ashamed of being Black. . . . We have to move into a position where we can define terms of what we want to be, not what racist White society wants us to be."[56] In the summer of 1966, the organization fielded many requests for interviews and appearances by the person whom SNCC veterans began to refer to as "Stokely Starmichael."

Carmichael's frustrations with the pace of change in the US drove him to explore emancipated spaces throughout Africa in 1967. In May of that year, he stepped down as chair of SNCC. He followed in the footsteps that his fellow Freedom Riders and Freedom Summer veterans made in 1964 and visited Guinea. There he was deeply inspired by the time he spent with President Sékou Touré, who continued to consolidate his power in the country. Carmichael also formed a mentor relationship with deposed Ghanaian leader Kwame Nkrumah, who remained in Conakry in exile. During their conversations, Carmichael became even more convinced that Nkrumah's version of Pan-Africanism was the best way forward for African Americans.[57] For example, in an interview with *El Djeich*, the magazine of the People's National Army of Algeria (formerly the FLN), he stated, "Black Power means that all people who are Black should come together, organize themselves, and form a power base to fight for their liberation."[58] This concept that the force for racial justice should generate from a coalesced and radicalized transnational community of African descent—rather than a multiracial cadre of liberal Americans—was a profound shift in ideological direction for SNCC and the broader civil rights movement.

The multiracial coalition that had been SNCC's backbone through the Freedom Rides and Freedom Summer could not withstand the brutally frank conversations about allyship and alienation that the popularity of "Black Power" required. Black and White activists who had risked their lives together on the front lines of confrontations with Jim Crow struggled to have productive dialogue about the impact of what we now know as White privilege on the internal dynamics of SNCC. White students from affluent backgrounds had come to the movement with, in some cases, vastly more skill sets and cultural capital than other SNCC activists because they (and their parents and grandparents) had not been subjected to segregated educational, employment, and housing opportunities. Mainstream press outlets and elected outlets responded to campaigns more compassionately when White people were involved. On one hand, the presence of White people enhanced the effectiveness of SNCC's work. On the other hand, the manner in which their presence advanced the work perpetuated notions of White supremacy.

Seasoned African American SNCC activists sought to center Black leadership and decision-making within the organization as a solution to this paradox. They viewed this not as an act of hostility toward White people but as an act of self-affirmation that would help their community break through the limitations imposed by the racist backlash against their work. A Harlem-based SNCC activist explained, "We love our community very much . . . through unity, block by block, store by store, we can achieve political victory and self determination."[59] In the US, SNCC staff members followed Carmichael's internationalism and further committed to linking the African American struggle for equality with successful efforts at African independence abroad. They also decided to become an exclusively Black organization.

In a position paper, the leadership contextualized its decision within the political thought of Frantz Fanon and other independence leaders. "SNCC, and the Civil Rights Movement in general, is in many aspects similar to the anti-colonial situations," they wrote. "We have the Whites in the movement corresponding to the White civil servants and missionaries in the colonial countries who . . . have developed a paternalistic attitude." According to SNCC leaders, "the whole myth of 'Negro citizenship' perpetuated by the White elite" leads African Americans to react to society in "the same manner as colonial peoples react to the West in Africa," as "the colonized toward the colonizer."[60] Carmichael began to describe the African American community as an "internal colony," which needed to develop autonomous institutions and resources in order to enjoy freedom.[61] SNCC's engagement with a diaspora underground led them to new ideas and tactics with which to advance their activism.

Although SNCC's new post–Black Power language was commonplace within this diaspora underground, American mainstream media and police authorities used it to frame the organization as filled with "radical separatists." According to the *Amsterdam News*, SNCC's continued emphasis on Black autonomy as the solution to the cultural, economic, and political challenges created by Jim Crow in the South and racial oppression in the North had "shaken" the White liberal hearts and minds that sympathized with the cause of integration and voting rights.[62] The organization's declining popularity emboldened police authorities to increasingly target SNCC activists. After returning to the US, Carmichael wrote to Nkrumah that "one-fourth of our staff throughout the country is in jail. Over one half who are out on bond will soon be rearrested."[63] Many White members and large foundations abandoned the organization.

SNCC's ideological focus on Black Power also disrupted the cohort of leaders that had steered the organization since the sit-ins six years earlier. James Forman and Ruby Doris Smith Robinson—who traveled to Guinea in 1964—as well as Freedom Schools innovator Charles Cobb and Freedom Summer veteran Cleveland Sellers struggled with how to transmute the transnational ideology of a diaspora underground into a concrete program for political action. (This struggle paralleled that of Malcolm X and his OAAU.) Suggestions abounded, such as the establishment of a Bureau of Third World Affairs and a seminar in revolutionary ethics led by African independence leaders.

However, these ideas veered significantly from SNCC's tried-and-true community organizing tactics. For example, building interpersonal relationships over time, cultivating indigenous leaders in a community, and using consensus decision-making to commit to achievable short-term goals were extremely effective movement building techniques introduced to SNCC by the organization's mentor Ella Baker. In a pre-Twitter era, these methods were also difficult to quickly operationalize across nation-state boundaries or in the more fragmented social environments of large Northern cities.

Some SNCC staff members became too vexed with these new challenges to continue. Communications director Julian Bond, veteran of the Atlanta sit-ins, resigned in frustration about what he felt was the prioritization of ideology over action.[64] Former chairman and Nashville sit-in veteran John Lewis resigned due to his concerns about what he perceived as the increasingly violent rhetoric used by Carmichael and his supporters.[65] On the other side of their declaration of Black Power, the remaining SNCC survivors committed to the possibilities they witnessed in this diaspora underground. They could not turn back. But they were unsure of the way forward.

8

"We Have Come Back"
Nous Sommes Revenus

لقد عدنا

Tumerudi Tena

AS SNCC BEGAN to splinter in 1966, a small group coalesced in Oakland, California. Bobby Seale—who had previously sent a letter and donation to Malcolm X's OAAU—became friends with Huey P. Newton, his classmate at Lake Merritt Community College. They were both members of the Bay Area's Afro-American Association, which was inspired by SNCC's sit-ins in the South, as well as the racial microaggressions its Black participants were experiencing at San Francisco State University (SFSU) and other predominately White campuses.[1] Eventually led by Howard alumnus Donald Warden, who was studying law at UC Berkeley, the Afro-American Association utilized study groups, rallies, and street-corner speaking to heighten awareness about Black history and political thought, which were not taught in mainstream classrooms.[2] According to historian Donna Murch, participating in this study group helped Newton and Seale understand their Oakland community's experiences of race, class, and migration from the South.[3]

Newton's avarice for Black studies knowledge was likely due to the miseducation he received. He was the youngest of seven children, born to a Louisiana sharecropper who fled Jim Crow and arrived in Oakland when Newton was seven years old. "During those long years in Oakland public schools," Newton would later write, "I did not have one teacher who taught me anything relevant to my own life. . . . All they did was try to rob me of the sense of my own uniqueness and worth."[4] A victim of school push-out and the criminalization of Black boys in schools, Newton was suspended thirty times. Ultimately, he was given a diploma so that he would leave high school. When he graduated, he was illiterate. He taught himself how to read before attending college using a classic work of political theory: *The Republic* by Plato.

Newton and Seale worked together directing youth programs at the North Oakland Neighborhood Anti-Poverty Center. By October 1966, they had an extensive education in radical political theory and experience providing social services, as well as palpable dissatisfaction with local activists' failure to mobilize young Black working-class and underemployed men. Newton and Seale referred to this constituency, people like themselves, as "brothers on the block."[5]

Seale and Newton founded the Black Panther Party for Self-Defense (BPP) after Matthew Johnson, a young Black man in San Francisco, was killed by police officers. Seale was chair and Newton was minister of defense. Newton was inspired by the self-defense philosophy of Robert F. Williams—the Monroe, North Carolina, NAACP chapter leader who wrote the incendiary memoir *Negroes with Guns*. (Williams also spoke in support of the Congolese people after Lumumba's assassination to an audience in Harlem that included Malcolm X.) Newton and Seale believed that, like the KKK, rogue police officers were a terrorizing force in African American communities. The original concept of the BPP was to patrol police while legally armed. They raised funds for weapons by selling copies of the *Little Red Book* by Chinese communist party leader Mao Zedong at UC Berkeley.

By November, the duo expanded to a six-member group, which included Elbert "Big Man" Howard, Sherman Forte, Reggie Forte, and Lil' Bobby Hutton. Hutton was treasurer. Newton was twenty-four years old, Seale thirty, and Hutton sixteen. They adopted the Black Panther logo from the Lowndes County Freedom Organization, which SNCC organized in Alabama. They also developed a signature uniform to appeal to the brothers on the block: blue shirts, black pants, black leather jackets, black berets, and Afros. Their first police patrols began in early 1967.

Later that year, the BPP manifesto, the *Ten-Point Program: What We Want, What We Believe*, was published in the organization's newspaper, the *Black Panther*. The program accomplished what OAAU and SNCC could not. In a concise, accessible document, it articulated the desired outcomes of the Black Power movement. Each want—for example: "freedom," "an end to the robbery by the capitalists of our Black Community," "decent housing"—preceded a brief explanation of how that outcome was the solution to problems caused by anti-Black racism. The program did not initially address intersectionality as it impacts Black women and members of the LGBTQ community. However, it did provide a compelling articulation of the relationship between race and class as it was experienced by Black people living in cities.

The *Ten-Point Program* also made the connection between race, economic injustice, and colonialism. The program described the African American community as a "Black colony" and demanded "a United Nations–supervised plebiscite . . . for the purpose of determining the will of Black people as to their national destiny." Clearly influenced by Malcolm X and the OAAU's program, Seale explained in an interview that the plebiscite would deal "politically with all the racist atrocities that have been committed in the nation."[6] However, similar to the OAAU and SNCC, the Black Panther Party did not put forward a specific plan of how it would achieve its goals of transnational Black liberation.

SURVIVAL

In the early months of the Black Panther Party, SNCC reached out to Newton and Seale with hopes of forging a long-term collaboration. Stokely Carmichael met with the group on several occasions. Once the upstart Panthers began framing their relationship with the more established and well-known SNCC as a "merger," rather than a collaboration, friction between the leaders arose. The alliance between SNCC and the BPP promised to unite a generation of progressive young activists in the East, West, and South who had a nuanced analysis of systemic inequality as well as developing international networks in this diaspora underground. However, external pressures on both organizations would prevent that union from flourishing.

James Forman, who was working in SNCC's Brooklyn office, recalled being initially keen on what he described as a "working alliance" between SNCC and the BPP.[7] Due primarily to the efforts of the Guinean and Tanzanian UN delegations, Forman was invited to the UN Conference on Racism, Colonialism, and Apartheid in Kitara, Zambia, in 1967. Echoing Malcolm's speech at the All-African People's Conference in Cairo a few years earlier, in a press release the SNCC delegation asserted, "No matter what the experts and the United States Government may say, there is an indivisible nature to the struggle against *apartheid*, colonialism, and racism throughout the world."[8] Just three years after Malcolm's "Appeal to African Heads of State" was rejected, independence leaders were fully welcoming the voices and participation of Black Power.

Just a year after Newton and Seale founded the Black Panther Party for Self-Defense, their national popularity soared, with chapters in Chicago, New York, Kansas City, Los Angeles, and other cities. Their legal brandishing of rifles, candid confrontational rhetoric, and bereted, leather jacketed cool also made the Panthers a media sensation. With both men and women at the forefront of the party's leadership and image, they came to represent some people's worst trepidations about—and some people's greatest aspirations for—a post–civil rights movement America.

The BPP's brashness, which was sympathetically covered in the Black press, reminded African Americans of the unapologetic style of sorely missed Malcolm X. It provided a stark contrast to portrayals of African Americans as subservient, foolish, or restrained, which were still popular in mainstream media. The BPP continued SNCC's departure from the performance of piety and respectability that had been an astute strategy with the sit-ins and Freedom Rides. SNCC staff member Kathleen Neal found herself attracted to this brashness when she met Eldridge Cleaver, the party's minister of information, during a conference she organized at the HBCU Fisk University. After she and Cleaver began a romantic relationship, she moved to Oakland.

Neal appointed herself as the BPP's communications secretary in the mold of her former SNCC colleague Julian Bond. "We were so young," remembered Neal, who became a fashion icon because of her trademark voluminous Afro, sunglasses, hoop earrings, and knee-high boots. "We did not realize how shocking [our style] was."[9] Neal was one of many SNCC workers who left to join the BPP or were too burned-out to continue organizing. As the Panthers grew in popularity in the late 1960s, SNCC continued to decline.

With the BPP's increasing impact came heightened attention from the FBI and local police authorities. In October 1967, Newton was arrested and charged with the voluntary manslaughter of Oakland police officer John Frey. Newton, who was shot during an encounter with Frey and Officer Herbert Heanes when he was pulled over, maintained his innocence. While he was in solitary confinement at the Alameda County Jail in Oakland, the Black Panther Party began the "Free Huey" campaign.

As described by historian Peniel Joseph, in addition to raising funds for Newton's defense, "Free Huey" mobilized thousands of new recruits to the party and readership of the *Black Panther* newspaper.[10] Lined up in formation on the steps of the Alameda County courthouse in black leather jackets and minidresses, young Panthers shouted "Off the Pigs!" Members of the Panther leadership attempted to change the frustration and outrage about police persecution into grassroots collective action. "The Man doesn't have us outnumbered," Seale asserted to an audience of allies in Berkeley. "He has us out-organized. C'mon now! Come up to the surface."[11]

New York City Panthers were also targeted by the police between 1969 and 1971. Some who became known as the "Panther 21" included Afeni Shakur (mother of rapper/actor Tupac Shakur) and Joan Byrd. The twenty-one activists were arrested for allegedly coordinating the bombing and shooting of two police stations and the Queens Board of Education office. Collectively, the Panther 21 received 156 charges, including conspiracy to murder a police officer.

The young, earnest defendants electrified people from all walks of life (including a teenage musician named Nile Rodgers, who would go on to produce classics for Chic, David Bowie, and Madonna). Crowds lined Centre Street outside of the Manhattan Criminal Court building during the trial. The *Amsterdam* reported that when Joan Byrd was released on bail, she stood across the street from the Queens House of Detention. "She raised her fist and shouted 'Power!' to the mass of impassioned women [prisoners] pressed against the windows of jail," the article reported. "They answered her with a shouted 'Power!' which carried for several blocks."[12]

The prosecution played *The Battle of Algiers*, the hyperrealistic drama about the Algerian Revolution that influenced so many SNCC activists, as evidence.[13] The FLN and the work of Frantz Fanon had also impacted Black Panther Party members. The prosecution argued this influence pushed Party members to make violent attacks against authorities. Apparently, authorities were aware of this diaspora underground and the threat it posed to the status quo. After nearly two years and the most expensive trial in New York City, all of the Panther 21 were acquitted.

While the BPP had multiple battles on the criminal justice front, it also advanced social service efforts, which helped bolster its popularity within African American communities. As sociologist Alondra Nelson observes in *Body and Soul*, local chapters administered health-care initiatives, such as sickle-cell anemia testing.[14] BPP chapters organized the school breakfast program, clothing drives, and food drives in coalition with local churches and peers, such as the National Welfare Rights Organization and the Young Lords Party.[15] The BPP referred to these efforts as "survival programs." They were designed initially not as a substitute for community organizing but to build trust with constituents and highlight the possibilities of self-determination. Black people providing themselves with health care, education, and food—essential public goods that were denied by colonization—was a key element of African independence philosophy, which the BPP fully embraced and turned into action.

BLACK STUDIES FOR EVERYBODY

The rise of the Black Panther Party occurred as African American college students and their allies began organizing to establish Black studies programs throughout the US. Historian William Van Deburg observes that throughout the late 1960s, in response to civil rights legislation, historically White colleges and universities began admitting students of African descent at an unprecedented pace.[16] Their presence led to the establishment of Black student unions (BSUs), such as the Bay Area Afro-American Association, where Newton and Seale met, which were led by and attractive to this generation of students. The Classes of '68, '69, and '70, for example, had benefited from decades of civil rights advocacy by African American elites and, yet, questioned the value of these elites' aspirations to full participation in American capitalism and citizenship. Arriving at college with the examples of the sit-in movement, Freedom Summer, and the BPP preceding them, these young people were part of a radical Black youth culture that was searching for alternatives to the politics of respectability.[17]

After finally being physically included en masse at predominately White institutions (PWIs), Black students in the late 1960s quickly discovered that their community's history, contributions, and cultures were invisible in the academic canon. The movement for Black studies that arose from BSUs charged that this disappearance undermined the academic performance of students of color. For example, the Black student union at San Francisco State had a ten-point program that its members believed would democratize the university's curriculum. They explained they wanted an education "for our people that exposes the true nature of this decadent American society . . . that teaches us our true history . . . that will give our people a knowledge of self."[18] These organizations powerfully articulated that when someone is not allowed to see themselves as a valued part of history, they will struggle to understand themselves as fully human.[19]

Although Black students were only 6 percent of American collegians in 1969, they were involved in over half of campus protest incidents that year.[20] The demands and tactics of BSUs seemed directly influenced by the Black Power movement. Members of organizations such as Columbia University's Black Student Congress and City College's Onyx Society displayed Malcolm X's image on their dormitory room walls and organized cultural festivals on his birthday, May 19.[21] They used nonviolent direct action methods, including boycotting classes, marches, and burning Confederate flags. Blown out Afros and raised fists became the uniform for barricading buildings and enduring arrests. Sometimes the student-activists brandished graffiti on campuses. For example, at the City College of New York, a wall was tagged, "HONKIES: ATTENTION/YOUR TIME HAS COME."[22]

While BSU students agitated for Black studies programs and curricula, they filled the perceived void with reading groups and other forms of self-directed study. They discovered Africa's influence on African American culture as well as how African history, culture, and politics counterbalanced stereotypical representations of Blackness found in the ivory tower.[23] For example, a course at an Ivy League university in Antiquity would focus exclusively on ancient Greece and Rome. However, readings about Nefertiti or Muhammad's travels to Ethiopia illuminate how people of African descent were also establishing a foundation for human civilization during this period. While these learning experiences had been routinely available to HBCU students, Black students at historically White campuses were discovering this kind of curriculum for the first time on a large scale.

By the late 1960s, community-centered studies by Black student unions and the Black Panther Party's political education classes emerged as indigenous institutions through which African American youths learned to identify their concerns with the African independence movement. A frequently used text in the BSU movement and the BPP's political education classes was *The Wretched of the Earth* by the FLN'S Frantz Fanon. Barbara Easley, a San Francisco State University student, remembered, "*The Wretched of the Earth* . . . was mandatory for BSU students . . . that was how you learned about Algiers and that struggle with the French. . . . There was always some dialogue [about African independence]."[24] "It was the first time I started hearing positive things about Africa," Easley remembered.[25] "Not about slavery, not about the Middle Passage . . . so when I read that . . . I wanted to be a good representative of African Americans," Easley affirmed. After her participation in the BSU movement at SFSU, Easley joined the Oakland chapter of the Black Panther Party. Just as HBCUs had been one of the indigenous institutions chiefly responsible for disseminating information about African independence to current and potential SNCC activists, BSUs were providing information to current and potential Panthers.

BPP political education classes were required for members, including the leadership. In Oakland, they were facilitated by George Murray, Wendell Wade, and Bobby Seale until 1972. Lil' Bobby Hutton, one of the earliest members of the party, was illiterate when he joined.[26] Like Newton, Hutton was a product of segregated Oakland public schools. Within months, he could discuss complicated political texts, including *The*

Wretched of the Earth and *The Handbook of Revolutionary Warfare* by deposed Ghanaian leader Kwame Nkrumah.

The classes' review of African independence philosophy encouraged BPP members to consider the relationship between capitalism and racial inequality. This curriculum mirrored African independence by asserting that systemic changes to distribution of power were the key to achieving social justice. Bobby Seale proclaimed in a session, "All of us are laboring people—employed or unemployed. . . . Dashikis don't free nobody and pork chops don't oppress nobody."[27] The BPP's interest in African independence was not simply about attributing cultural similarities. Panthers were absorbing the fact that they shared common goals with activists and organizations in this diaspora underground.

As SNCC's organizational structure continued to fray in 1968, a group of activists who were also Howard University alums returned to Washington, DC, and began a community-centered education project. This group included Courtland Cox and Freedom Schools founder Charlie Cobb, and former Nonviolent Action Group members, Freedom Riders, and Bloody Lowndes campaigners. Cobb in particular was interested in continuing the radical pedagogical work he began during the Freedom Summer and Lowndes voter registration drives. In 1968, Cobb and his colleagues founded the Drum and Spear bookstore and the Drum and Spear Press near Howard University's U Street corridor (which was then a predominately Black neighborhood). The collective also founded the Center for Black Education as an independent Black studies institution.

Courtland Cox recalled that their goal was to "create a sense of consciousness" about how the degrading representations of Black life often propagated by dominant institutions (such as schools and mainstream media) were racist myths, not reality.[28] "Within the country there was a whole negation of the Black community," Cox said. "There was a sense that Black people didn't have . . . mental capacity." This concept of psychological destruction was articulated powerfully to SNCC activists through *The Wretched of the Earth* and writings by Tanzanian independence leader Julius Nyerere, who had also influenced Malcolm X.

The Drum and Spear project included Jennifer Lawson and SNCC veteran Daphne Mews, who wrote and illustrated a children's book called *Children of Africa*. Drum and Spear worker and Howard student Geri

Augusto had grown up with parents who welcomed African exchange students from HBCUs and weary SNCC organizers into her home in Dayton, Ohio.[29] She started college the year Stokely Carmichael made his Black Power speech at the March against Fear in Mississippi. Augusto recalled, "You could walk into Drum & Spear Bookstore, which many people did from right off the street, and ready yourself into an international consciousness."[30] The collective inspired a new generation of Howard University students to engage with African independence movements in a diaspora underground.

These educational efforts evolved into indigenous institutions that communicated information across national boundaries, nurtured critical thinking skills and improved technical capacities among community members. Augusto recalled, "The notion was to create education that was IN-DE-PEND-ENT not just an alternative."[31] "The big giant energy" moving Black Power organizations and activists to connect with African independence "was . . . an assertion that 1. Black is beautiful and 2. We are an African people," Drum and Spear Collective coleader Courtland Cox stated.[32] "We began to define ourselves in ways that did not allow other people to define us." Cox continued, "We began to see and search for different relationships that we could have." The influence of African independence inspired Black Power–informed education projects to define Blackness as an international identity and liberation project.

AWAKENING

The branding of the Black Panther Party was led in part by Minister of Information Eldridge Cleaver. He grew up in a home marred by domestic violence, was abandoned by his father, and had been incarcerated repeatedly since he was a teenager. Before joining the BPP, Cleaver's most recent time in prison was for a series of rapes he committed of Black and White women, which he described in the viciously sexist yet critically acclaimed memoir *Soul on Ice*. In his book, Cleaver theorized that his acts of misogynist violence were a cathartic expression of his rage against White supremacy. He strongly identified with the FLN's willingness to take armed revolutionary action as explained by Fanon in *The Wretched of the Earth*.

Shortly after Newton, Seale, and Lil' Bobby Hutton began expanding the party, Cleaver joined the group. His experience as a writer with progressive *Ramparts* magazine, oratory skills, and leather jacketed, shades-wearing cool were all helpful to the Panthers' becoming a media sensation and mobilizing widespread support for the "Free Huey" campaign. In fact, he conceived of the iconic fundraising poster featuring Huey P. Newton sitting in a wicker chair, brandishing a spear and a rifle.

The rebellious, unapologetic politics and style of the BPP contrasted sharply with the starched shirt dignity of the Reverend Dr. Martin Luther King. During the eleven years since the triumph of Kwame Nkrumah and the Convention People's Party had so impressed King in Accra in 1957, King had committed totally to the goal of equality for African Americans through the March on Washington, campaign in Selma, and a myriad of other actions and negotiations with federal legislators. Although his style contrasted significantly to that of the Panthers, King and his Southern Christian Leadership Conference also illuminated the relationship between economic and racial justice. His speech at the March on Washington for Jobs and Freedom in 1963—during which he proclaimed, "I have a dream!"—had already become one of the most memorable moments in the African American freedom struggle and in human history. However, King's focus on economic equality had not fully caught on with the mainstream.

In April 1968, King traveled to Memphis to support a strike by the city's sanitation workers, who were predominately Black. Although he was emotionally and physically exhausted from over a decade of movement leadership, and threats against his life were escalating, King continued to appear publicly at marches, speeches, and press conferences. Much like Malcolm X, it is unclear whether his actions reflected a suppressed death wish brought on by the extraordinary pressure of his work or a resignation to martyrdom. On April 5, while standing on a balcony at the Lorraine Motel, the Reverend Dr. Martin Luther King Jr. was assassinated by a sniper. Some witnesses described the murderer as "a well-dressed White man." According to news reports, a bystander observed that when King was shot, "the bullet exploded in his face."[33]

To many African Americans and Black Power activists, on that day the dream of peaceful racial reconciliation and faith in mainstream American institutions died along with Dr. King. The frustrations with dominant elites that had been percolating for years simply boiled over. Rebellions erupted in African American neighborhoods in cities throughout the US, including Chicago; Washington, DC; Baltimore; and Pittsburgh.

A clearly bereaved Stokely Carmichael, who had been subjected to increased police harassment since his "Black Power" speech in Mississippi, explained this collective outrage in a press conference: "When White America got rid of . . . Malcolm X, they said he was crazy, he deserved what he got." Carmichael continued, "But . . . Martin Luther King was the one man who was trying to teach our people how to have love, compassion, and mercy for what White people have done." He continued, "When White America killed Dr. King last night, they declared war on us."[34]

Carmichael's grief due to King's death overlaid fear for his own life. By this time, FBI head J. Edgar Hoover felt Carmichael "had the necessary charisma" to become a Black "messiah" who could lead a revolution in the US.[35] As a result, Carmichael was a target of the bureau's unlawful, yet effective Counterintelligence Program. Known as COINTELPRO, the initiative borrowed from counterinsurgency techniques developed by the CIA to suppress the wave of dissent that emerged in the late 1960s and early 1970s. In addition to the Black Panther Party and SNCC, the Students for Democratic Society, American Indian Movement, and the Puerto Rican Young Lords Party were also impacted. Among COINTELPRO's repertoire of attack was a divide-and-conquer strategy that involved disseminating false information to organizational leadership that turned them against one another. This tactic embroiled activists in bitter interpersonal disputes—distracting them from their organization's broader mission. In Carmichael's case, he was "bad-jacketed" with false rumors that he was a CIA agent and subjected to police surveillance and numerous death threats.[36]

Kathleen Neal, who had left SNCC to join her partner, Eldridge, and help lead the work of the BPP, was now married and known as Kathleen Cleaver. She recalled that Eldridge was both outraged by King's murder and convinced that a preemptive armed strike against police authorities was the best strategy of self-defense for African Americans.[37] Two days after King was murdered, he recruited several Panthers, including Lil'

Bobby Hutton, to ambush Oakland police officers.[38] Hutton, who was the first treasurer of the Black Panther Party, was seventeen years old.

The BPP attack led to a shootout in which two officers were critically wounded. Cleaver was shot by police during the conflict. He and Hutton ran during the melee and found themselves surrounded in the basement of a home in West Oakland. Police teargassed the building. Eldridge and Hutton agreed to surrender, stripping down to their underwear to show the squadron of officers with weapons aimed at the building that they were unarmed. Two years prior, Hutton had joined the party as an illiterate high school dropout.[39] Since then, he had become an astute analyst of Nkrumah, Fanon, and other African independence theorists through the BPP's political education classes. Before Cleaver, Lil' Bobby, so nicknamed because of his slight frame, emerged from the building in his underwear with his hands up—the international signal for "Don't Shoot." This signal did not help Lil' Bobby any more than it helped eighteen-year-old Mike Brown in Ferguson, Missouri, nearly five decades later. Police officers fatally shot Hutton more than twelve times.[40]

FUGITIVES

The shootout brought even more attention to the Panthers in general, and the Cleavers in particular. While Newton languished in solitary confinement, Eldridge deftly courted the press and college campus audiences while he was out on bail. At over six feet tall with his signature Ray-Ban wayfarer sunglasses, goatee, and provocative oratory, Eldridge confirmed dominant stereotypes about African American hypermasculinity but also challenged unreasonable expectations of Black docility in the face of White supremacist aggression. With sophisticated, stylish, and intelligent Kathleen at Eldridge's side in photographs and interviews (and behind the scenes coordinating strategy), the couple enchanted the countercultural imagination as a contemporary Bonnie and Clyde.

The campaign Kathleen organized to free Eldridge united BPP members with White student activists, Mexican American Panther counterparts the Brown Berets, and other progressive allies. Eldridge, Kathleen, and others expressed fear that he would be unlawfully murdered in police custody. Kathleen presented a courageous public image. The organization was kept alive despite this barrage of police attacks because of the deft stewardship of women. However, behind closed doors, Kathleen and other women Panther leaders battled sexism in the form of microaggressions and gaslighting. "Things I suggested myself were always implemented," she remembered. "But if I suggested them [they] might be rejected; if they were suggested by a man . . . [they] would be implemented. . . . The fact that the suggestion came from a woman gave it some lesser value. And it seemed that it had something to do with the egos of the men involved."[41] The visibility and impactful work of BPP women—which historian Robyn Ceanne Spencer explores in her work *The Revolution Has Come*—perhaps made the organization's male leadership appear more feminist than they were in practice.[42] As Elaine Brown powerfully describes in her memoir, sexual favors, secretarial work, and other gendered burdens were routinely placed on women.[43] Some accepted this dynamic, begrudgingly, as a pink tax on their service to the community they loved.

Once his bail was revoked in fall 1968, Cleaver decided to go underground. He resurfaced in Cuba, where he met two fellow African Americans: Byron Vaughn Booth and Clinton Robert Smith Jr. (who went by the nickname "Rahim"). After escaping from a maximum security penitentiary in Chino, California, Booth and Smith arrived in Havana via a plane bound for Miami, which they hijacked by brandishing a pistol and four sticks of dynamite.[44] Although they were initially detained by Cuban authorities, Eldridge intervened on their behalf to get them released.

Eldridge sent word to a very pregnant Kathleen to rendezvous with him in exile in Algiers. "I didn't know anything about Algeria," Kathleen remembered. "I'd read *Wretched of the Earth*, seen *The Battle of Algiers*, but that was about it."[45] This quick change in Eldridge's asylum was brought about by push factors in Cuba and pull factors in Algeria. Eldridge became increasingly uncomfortable with Cuba's color-blind approach to advancing racial equality. Prior to the success of the Cuban revolution, which was led by a coalition of activists and armed guerrillas named the July 26th Movement, Cuba functioned as a racially segregated society, much like the US. After the revolution in 1959, leaders (including Fidel Castro, Juan Almeida, and Celia Sanchez) implemented changes that legally dismantled race-based discrimination and prohibited discussions about race.[46] While this strategy suppressed White power groups similar to the Ku Klux Klan in Cuba, it also inhibited antiracist groups like SNCC and the Black Panther Party from advocating against the forms of structural racism that continued after the revolution.[47] The obvious limitations to the color-blind approach, and Cleaver's need to speak frankly about racial inequality, caused increasing friction between him and Cuban officials.

Meanwhile, the Algerian government was planning the first Pan-African Cultural Festival. Since staging a breezy coup and placing his FLN comrade Ben Bella under house arrest, former defense minister and current president Hoauri Boumédiène had helped Algiers become a haven for liberation movements throughout the developing world, including Palestine, Guinea-Bissau, Mozambique, and Rhodesia (now Zimbabwe). Kathleen remembered, "Fugitives from all over Africa and other parts of the world lived peacefully."[48] Revolutionaries enjoyed this seaside Mediterranean capital as an emancipated space similar to those built in Accra by Kwame Nkrumah and in Conakry by Sékou Touré.

Much like the All-African People's Conferences, which Malcolm X, Frantz Fanon, and Patrice Lumumba attended in the previous decade, the Pan-African Cultural Festival aimed to heighten the visibility and affirmation of African culture, while encouraging unity and collaboration throughout the diaspora. The Black Panther Party was invited to join the festivities through the leadership in Oakland and Eldridge Cleaver in Havana. Once Eldridge agreed to attend, Boumédiène's government worked with Cuba to arrange his and Kathleen's relocation to Algiers. Ministry of Information official Elaine Klein (later Mokhtefi), a White American who began working with the FLN in Paris, was assigned as their foreign liaison and translator. Eldridge, who had slipped through the grasp of Bay Area authorities a few months earlier, emerged from hiding in Algiers on July 15, 1969, during an international press conference arranged by the state's Algerian Press Service. Kathleen, who was nine months pregnant, stood with him.

Sponsored by the Organization of African Unity, the first Pan-African Cultural Festival occurred in Algiers between July 21 and August 1, 1969. Over ten years after Nkrumah and his Convention People's Party colleagues appeared at the Accra Polo Grounds to declare Ghana independent, the festival sought to coalesce independence movements for a discussion about the cultural, economic, and political future of African self-determination. Thirty-one independent African nations and six liberation movements were represented.[49] In addition, an African American contingent, which included members of the Black Panther Party; Stokely Carmichael (now going by his African name, Kwame Ture), Charles Cobb, and Courtland Cox from SNCC; student activists from San Francisco State (who had helped establish the first ethnic studies programs in the US); Don L. Lee (later Haki R. Madhubuti) and other poets from the Black Arts Movement; and Julia Wright Hervé, chair of the Paris Friends of SNCC and daughter of *Native Son* author Richard Wright.[50]

The triumphant spirit and buoyant energy of Algerians who had fought so long for independence were visible in the enthusiastic crowds that turned out in support of the event.[51] Approximately four thousand activists, artists, and intellectuals attended from throughout Africa, the Middle East, Europe, and the US.[52] Delegates from newly independent nations wearing indigenous clothing paraded past a cheering multitude in the same Casbah where Ali LaPointe, Zohra Drif, and other FLN members waged the Battle of Algiers eleven years earlier.[53] The ideas of Frantz Fanon, whose name adorned streets and government buildings throughout Algiers, saturated the gathering. He was quoted in the festival's literature and discussed at length during plenary sessions in the Palace of Nations.[54]

The Pan-African Cultural Festival was also a radical diasporic predecessor to Made in America and AFROPUNK in that it featured folkloric performances as well as concerts by several international stars committed to activism. Headliners included singer Miriam Makeba, who was exiled from South Africa due to her opposition to apartheid and would eventually be exiled from the US because of her marriage to Kwame Ture. Nina Simone, who raised awareness about the movement with her iconic protest song, "Mississippi Goddam," sang a poignant version of the French classic "Ne me quitte pas" while wearing her trademark cornrow updo. Avant-garde jazz saxophonist Archie Shepp performed an experimental set with Don L. Lee, Ted Joans, and dozens of Algerian musicians from the country's different ethnic groups. During one song, Joans proclaimed, *"Nous sommes revenus. We have come back. Jazz is a Black power! Jazz is an African power!"*[55]

In addition to the Cleavers, the Black Panther Party delegation to the festival included the slim and somber chief of staff David Hilliard and

Minister of Culture Emory Douglas. Hijackers and prison escapees Byron Vaughn Booth and Clinton Robert "Rahim" Smith accompanied Eldridge from Havana and were now also part of the BPP contingent. The Panthers' presence at the festival underscored that the organization belonged to the exclusive and dangerous club of liberation movements that populated this diaspora underground at the time. The Panthers earned their stripes through articulating how African Americans were a colonized people who endured cultural imperialism and economic oppression, the clear influences of Frantz Fanon and Kwame Nkrumah on their political philosophy, and FBI director J. Edgar Hoover defining them as the "biggest threat to internal security in the United States."[56] All the activists present, including SNCC veterans Ture, Cobb, and Cox, were grappling with frustrations over the difficulty of participating as equals within mainstream institutions.

Muhammad Yaya, Algeria's minister of information, gave BPP members a space to set up their own exhibition as part of the festival. Eldridge and Kathleen called it the "Afro-American Center" (see figure 8.1) and, with assistance from their government liaison Elaine Klein, filled the gallery with the art of fellow Panther Emory Douglas, images of Huey P. Newton, and informational pamphlets about the BPP.[57] Douglas's bright and bold portraits of Black revolutionary men, women, and children fighting for their liberated future were an intriguing contrast to the landscape of downtown Algiers, with its bombed out buildings from the independence war and ancient North African architecture.[58] The festival crowd and international press enthusiastically converged on the Panther exhibition.[59] With their backstory of being in love and on the run from American police, Eldridge and Kathleen entertained throngs at the center and pulled focus away from the somber symposia at the Palace of Nations. Kathleen gave birth to their son, Ahmad Maceo Eldridge Cleaver, toward the end of the festivities on July 29, 1969.

REVOLUTION'S EMBASSY

Following the Panthers' warm reception at the Pan-African Cultural Festival, between 1969 and 1970 the group in long-term residency in Algiers expanded from the Cleavers, Byron Vaughn Booth, and Clinton Robert

8.1. The Black Panther Party's Afro-American Center at the Pan-African Cultural Festival in Algiers, 1969. Copyright © Robert Wade.

"Rahim" Smith Jr. to include Michael Cetewayo Tabor—well-known within the BPP for his pamphlet *Capitalism = Dope + Genocide*—as well as Tabor's wife, Connie Matthews, who had previously coordinated BPP relations with European governments. Participants also included Julia Wright Hervé, Don Cox (a.k.a. DC), and Barbara Easley (now Barbara Easely-Cox) from the Oakland chapter.[60] Don was a widely respected Panther organizer—featured in Tom Wolfe's controversial article about "Radical Chic"—who fled the US after being charged with the murder of a police informant (throughout his life, he maintained his innocence).[61] Barbara committed to the Black Panther Party after her participation in the Third World Strike for ethnic studies at San Francisco State.

Between 1969 and 1970, Eldridge sought to build a diplomatic relationship between the BPP and North Korea's government by attending a journalism conference in Pyongyang. Booth recalls that while Eldridge was in North Korea, Smith and Kathleen were seen flirting and dancing with each other in public in Algiers.[62] In her memoir, BPP liaison Elaine Klein recalls hearing rumors that the two were seen appearing intimate.[63]

According to Booth, when Eldridge returned from North Korea, he also heard these rumors and became outraged. Booth claims one evening he and Smith went to the Cleavers' home at Eldridge's invitation. After accusing Smith of having an affair with Kathleen, Eldridge lowered an AK-47 to Rahim's heart and murdered him.[64] Booth also remembers that he helped Eldridge dispose of the body in a shallow grave near the International Section's villa. Booth left Algeria after burying Smith. "I didn't sign up to kill other Panthers," he said.

Klein, who claims to have had a close working friendship with Eldridge, recalls that Eldridge casually confessed the crime to her. "He drew up a chair, sat down at the side of my desk, lowered his eyelids and murmured: 'I have something to tell you. Something happened last night. I killed Rahim . . . Byron was there," Klein writes in her memoir.[65] "'The two of us took the body up into hills behind Pointe Pescade and buried him.' All this in whispers. Then he got up, put on his shades . . . with no hint of a conscience disturbed." Klein alleges Algerian authorities discovered Rahim's body but did not investigate the circumstances surrounding his death. Don Cox wrote to her that the other Panthers in Algiers confronted

Eldridge about the killing and he did not deny it. "What's mine is no one else's," Eldridge allegedly told the group.[66]

With assistance from Klein and Algeria's former UN representative Muhammad Yazid, in May 1970 the BPP received official recognition from the Algerian government as a revolutionary organization in exile. This honor came with concrete material benefits, including a seaside government villa, a monthly stipend, car, telephone, telex (the email of this period), and the ability to obtain visas for guests and organization members.[67] These government resources supplemented the royalties Eldridge received from his best-selling memoir, *Soul on Ice*, which were also used to support the group. BPP members in Algiers named themselves the International Section of the Black Panther Party. Although the section began as "a kind of embassy of the American revolution," through producing a newsletter, audio documentaries (the podcasts of the day), and nonfiction films for US audiences, the section also loomed large in the African American imagination as an oasis for those on the wrong side of the law because of their opposition to US racism.[68]

Meanwhile, as leaders of the International Section, Eldridge and Kathleen were gaining a broader media profile. No African American racial justice organization had ever achieved this level of diasporic recognition and resources. Eldridge explained to the *New York Times* that the section showed "oppression is an international problem."[69] In another interview, Eldridge stated, "We feel that there's the mother country in America and that there's also the Black colony."[70]

From her home in Philadelphia, across the street from a church where she once addressed a Free Huey rally attended by hundreds of people, Barbara Easley-Cox explained that she was particularly impacted by the time she spent with women activists in African liberation movements while in the emancipated space of Algiers.[71] "It was a little community," she asserted. "'Cause I'd take my baby because they had babies, and I'd go to their house, and sit and eat, and we'd talk about things" (see figure 8.2). "That's where my knowledge of the world became more focused," she continued. "Listening to other people's historical battles . . . you realize that you're not the only group of little Black people . . . fighting for that freedom." In Algiers, Barbara also had a revelation similar to the one Malcolm X had in Mecca. "Once you travel abroad and you deal with other

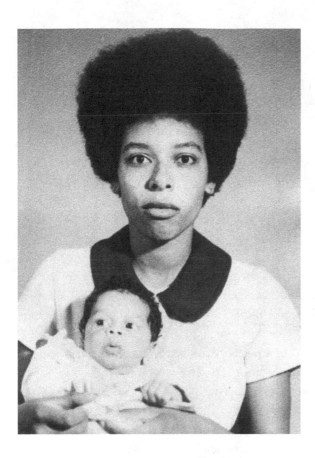

8.2. Barbara Easley-Cox and child during her time with the International Section of the Black Panther Party, 1970. Courtesy Barbara Easley-Cox.

peoples," she said, "you start realizing it is not a White-skinned person that is the enemy. It is a class distinction, and I think the class distinction is, you know, based on a few people having a whole lot and everybody else getting nothing."

Due in part to the effectiveness of the "Free Huey" campaign that Eldridge and Kathleen helped facilitate, on August 5, 1970, Newton was released from prison in Oakland. Over ten thousand people greeted him as he emerged, shirtless, from the same Alameda County Courthouse where so many Panthers had lined up in formation, marched, and chanted to liberate him.[72] Newton jumped on top of a vehicle so the multiracial multitude could fully see him.

Unsurprisingly, over two years of solitary confinement and the stress of facing fifteen years in prison changed Newton's demeanor and intentions for the party. He was, however, making important strides in addressing sexism and homophobia among men in the BPP. "We should try to unite with [women and Gay people] in a revolutionary fashion," he wrote.[73] "As we very well know, sometimes our first instinct . . . is to want to hit a homosexual in the mouth because we are afraid we might be homosexual; and we want to hit the woman or shut her up because we are afraid that she might castrate us." Newton continued, "We must gain security in ourselves and therefore have respect and feelings for all oppressed people."

HIJACKED

As the International Section enjoyed the relative safety of recognition and asylum in Algeria, Panthers and SNCC in the US were more and more besieged by the FBI's Counterintelligence Program (COINTELPRO). Black Panthers in New York City, Chicago, Kansas City, and other chapters became embroiled in psychological, legal, and physical confrontations with police departments that were executing the FBI's counterinsurgency strategy. The *Amsterdam News* printed extensive coverage of these conflicts. BPP activist Jorge Aponte was quoted stating, "White racist police know what power comes from the barrel of the gun. . . . We are a standing liberation army who intends to protect the life of Black people."[74] In "Panthers Backers Get Set," the *Amsterdam* described plans for "more than a thousand" Black Panther Party supporters to "march daily around the Criminal Courts building" at 100 Centre Street in protest of the increasing arrests of Panther activists. The paper also published photographs of rallies in which participants demanded, "Free the Slaves."[75]

Police hostility against the Black Panther Party escalated to the point that founders Huey P. Newton and Bobby Seale made an appeal to the United Nations—following in the footsteps of their idol Malcolm X. In a petition, Seale and Newton asserted that COINTELPRO—in combination with the broader US tradition of sanctioning violence against African Americans—violated the UN's Genocide Convention. Genocide is "killing members of the group and any intent to destroy in whole or in part a national racial or ethnic or religious group," Seale and Newton wrote.[76] "On the basis of simple justice . . . we further demand that the United

States government make reparations to those who have suffered the damages of racist and genocidal practices."

Increasingly, party members were assassinated and assaulted by local police, framed for crimes by paid informants, and targeted for misinformation campaigns that disrupted the interpersonal bonds necessary for collective action. In hindsight—with the benefit of a Senate investigation into the FBI's misdeeds, documents made available by the Freedom of Information Act, broadly cited scholarship, and testimony by witnesses and recalcitrant informants—we know that the Panthers were being subjected to a concerted attack.[77] At the time, the young activists leading this organization had only their experiences of aggression, studies of counterinsurgency methods that had been used against other liberation movements, and gut instinct to inform their suspicions. Sometimes members correctly attributed insults and attacks as originating from the FBI. Other times they believed slander that was created by agents and informants.

External pressures on the Black Panther Party eventually led to internal divisions between the West and East leadership factions. Threats from the BPP Central Committee, working under Newton's leadership, had already spurred New York chapter member Michael Cetewayo Tabor to flee to Algiers. Newton falsely accused well-respected Los Angeles chapter leader Geronimo Pratt of belonging to the CIA and expelled him from the party. After the Panther 21 were finally exonerated, the West Coast–based Central Committee ordered their expulsion as well. Alarmed by these actions, the International Section issued a statement calling for Pratt's and the New York chapter's reinstatement.

Newton and the West Coast branch responded with an issue of the Black Panther Party newspaper in March 1971. Its cover featured a photo of Kathleen in sunglasses with her fist raised in the Black Power salute. The headline exclaimed, "Free Kathleen and All Political Prisoners!" Inside, BPP leader Erica Huggins implored Kathleen to leave Eldridge and return to Oakland. Articles detailed Eldridge's alleged murder of Rahim and Eldridge's chronic years-long physical and emotional abuse of Kathleen. The newspaper also included a disturbing photograph that revealed that sometimes, behind Kathleen's trademark sunglasses, were black eyes from beatings by her husband. Kathleen and Eldridge appeared on a radio program and denied the charges. At the time, talk among the national membership asserted Newton's battles and expulsions had more to do with his growing addiction to cocaine and untreated emotional wounds from solitary confinement than with party ideology.

When Kathleen Cleaver returned to the US for a fundraising tour in 1971, she clarified how the organization's international presence and their interactions with men and women in different liberation movements had advanced the party's ideology. "Too many of the Black women are so brainwashed and anxious to help the men," she stated without irony. "The violence that Black men direct toward their own women . . . is something that Black women are subjected to as a result of the colonization of the man."[78]

The Cleavers and other members of the International Section joined with the New York chapter in an attempt to supplant Newton's leadership. Newton accused Eldridge of being an internationalist dilettante living off the largesse of a dictatorship. Although for a time the East Coast/International Section Panthers were able to function under the leadership of Bobby Seale, they ultimately disbanded.[79] Some members of the New York chapter, including Assata Shakur, organized into the Black Liberation Army (BLA). Newton directed the skeletal remains of the organization into a new direction, "survival pending revolution," which focused exclusively on the party's social service programs.[80]

As the BPP crumbled, the International Section was joined by Sekou Odinga and Larry Mack. Odinga, born Nathaniel Burns, first became involved in the Black Power movement through Malcolm X's Organization of Afro-American Unity. He helped build the BPP Bronx chapter in 1969. Once Odinga learned he was wanted for questioning in connection with a police shooting, he believed he was being targeted by COINTELPRO because of his political activism. He left the grid and joined the Black Liberation Army. Odinga and Mack arrived in Algiers after hijacking a plane from the US to Guinea.[81] Eventually, several other hijackers with connections of varying strength to the BPP—including George Wright, Pete and Charlotte O'Neal from Kansas City, and Melvin and Jean McNair—would make their way to Algiers and request political asylum. "Have you ever met a hijacker?" Kathleen Cleaver asked the author of this book during an interview in her Yale faculty office. "They are very special people."

The hijackers' arrival was not well received by the International Section's Algerian hosts. Before French colonialism, between the sixteenth and nineteenth centuries, the country's northern shore was part of what was known as the Barbary Coast—named for pirates who kidnapped people and stole property along the Mediterranean. The region's association with piracy developed into a racist Islamophobic stereotype of Algerians as brutish and criminal. The post-FLN government was displeased with the negative international attention that BPP hijackers were bringing back to their nation.

Tensions between the Cleavers and the Algerian Revolutionary Council grew over what to do with the BPP hijackers' sizable ransom. The Revolutionary Council was an authority formed by Boumédiène that supplanted the FLN's government and pushed for state-centered industrialization, financed by Algeria's oil reserves. The country had broken off diplomatic relations with the US several years earlier.[82] The council planned to keep the ransom, given they were funding the International Section's housing, international phone and telex bills, food allowances, and transportation—as well as enduring the global negative press around the criminal airplane stealing. Eldridge and the Panthers believed their social movement skills could pressure the Algerian government into changing their decision. They were wrong.

Eventually, it became clear that the Black Panther Party was no longer welcome in Algeria. Connie Matthews and Michael Cetewayo Tabor left for Zambia, another socialist African country that became the headquarters for the African National Congress in exile. The Cleavers were the final members of the International Section to leave Algiers, in 1973. Don Cox stayed in exile in the French Alps until his death in 2011. His partner, Barbara, returned to Philadelphia, where she remains politically active. After Algeria, Sekou Odinga continued taking part in clandestine activities with the Black Liberation Army, until he was convicted of assisting Assata Shakur's escape from the Clinton Correctional Facility in 1981. He remained in prison until 2014.

The New York chapter of the Black Panther Party disbanded. In Oakland, there were remnants of the original Black Panther Party for Self-Defense, which was founded just seven years earlier and continued to be under siege. From the same Alameda County Jail where Huey P. Newton was transformed by solitary confinement, David Hilliard reflected on the meaning of the Panthers' time in Algiers as he reread a dog-eared copy of *The Wretched of the Earth*. "I've gone through the cobblestoned streets of the Casbah . . . where Ali LaPointe . . . actually hid out," he mused. "We've come a long way . . . we've become a part of history."[83]

9

"Ready for the Revolution"
Prêt pour la Révolution
جاهزون للثورة
Tayari kwa Mapinduzi

SNCC HAD DETERIORATED in part for the same reasons the BPP waned—specifically, COINTELPRO attacks and an inability to sufficiently address sexism toward women in leadership. Like many SNCC activists, MFDP leader Fannie Lou Hamer continued her activism on the community level after the Student Nonviolent Coordinating Committee ceased to fully function on the national level. In Mississippi she founded the Freedom Farm Co-op, which grew to have 640 acres of land. In a talk to the NAACP Legal Defense Fund in New York—nearly seven years after her life-changing journey to the emancipated space of Conakry—Mrs. Hamer frankly detailed the challenges of forging alliances between Black women and White women. The White woman was finally "coming to the realization . . . her freedom is shackled in chains to mine, and she realizes for the first time that she is not free until I am free," Hamer stated.[1] She also detailed a perspective that challenged feminist organizing among Black women in the movement. "I got a Black husband, six feet three, two hundred and forty pounds, with a 14 shoe, that I don't want to be liberated from," Hamer humorously informed the crowd. "But we are here to work side by side with this Black man in trying to bring liberation to all people."

Kwame Ture (formerly Stokely Carmichael) had made a brief appearance at the Pan-African Cultural Festival and met with Eldridge and Kathleen. By that time, Ture decided to relocate permanently to Guinea—accepting the personal invitations of President Sékou Touré and Honorary Co-president Kwame Nkrumah. In the US, he endured daily surveillance and harassment from the FBI and began to fear for his life.

Ruby Doris Smith Robinson, his colleague from the Freedom Rides who gleefully embraced wearing cornrows during the SNCC delegation to Guinea, had died in 1967 from what some SNCC activists believed was stress-related illness. Ture's mentor, Rev. Dr. Martin Luther King Jr., was assassinated in 1968. (Having committed fully to addressing economic inequality and opposing US imperialism in Vietnam, King was more aligned with Ture's worldview in the last year of his life than perhaps either of them could have expected.) Ture was also maligned by false accusations (generated by COINTELPRO operatives) of being an informant, which caused him to be alienated from his SNCC and Black Panther Party colleagues. Just a few years after he'd arrived as a freshman on Howard University's campus, Ture was physically and psychologically exhausted from the costs of his total commitment to social justice.

Ture envisioned using Conakry as a base from which to circulate the progressive ideas of African independence to African Americans. In 1969, he'd renamed himself Kwame Ture in tribute to his mentors Kwame Nkrumah and Sékou Touré. (Changing names associated with a family's former slaveowners to names that were Arabic, Swahili, or at least more African sounding became part of the political expression of African American youths during this period.) Ture, and his influential book *Black Power: The Politics of Liberation*, written with political scientist Charles Hamilton, helped model a post–civil rights form of activism that combined cultural valorization and transnational coalition building. Like many in his generation of African Americans, by the early 1970s Ture had traded the sharp suit and clean fade associated with demonstrating a fitness for first-class citizenship, as well as the denim overalls that signified solidarity with

Mississippi sharecroppers, for traditional African dress. However, he retained his trademark sunglasses and overall concern with cool.

In 1972, he was invited to return to his HBCU alma mater to address students. "The one thing we know about life is that everything changes. Change is permanence," Ture asserted.[2] He may have also been alluding to the death of his mentor Kwame Nkrumah, who succumbed to prostate cancer that year after becoming increasingly paranoid about being assassinated or kidnapped during his exile in Conakry. With LaPointe, Lumumba, Malcolm, Fanon, King, and Nkrumah gone, at age thirty-one Ture was an elder statesperson of the movement.

FAMILYHOOD

Pete and Charlotte O'Neal headed to Tanzania after the BPP's International Section disbanded. Prior to joining up with the Cleavers in Algiers, the O'Neals were leaders of the Kansas City chapter of the Black Panther Party.[3] Like Ali LaPointe of the FLN, Pete O'Neal worked as a pimp before he became involved in activism. After reading about the BPP, he decided to visit the organization's headquarters in Oakland to see if their work could be helpful to his community. Impressed by the discipline and empowerment the party offered, he returned to Kansas City and immediately started a local chapter. "When people think about the Black Panther Party, mostly because of the media, they think about men with guns and leather jackets and berets—which was true!" Pete stated in the documentary *A Panther in Africa*.[4] "But we were much more than that." Charlotte clarified, "We fed more than 750 children every day" with their chapter's School Breakfast Program.[5] As Pete and the Kansas City chapter became more visible and impactful, like a number of Panthers, he was targeted by the police. According to Pete, he and Charlotte decided to go into exile once he was convicted of illegally transporting a gun across state lines because "the FBI had seriously indicated that I would die if I went to prison."[6]

SNCC alumni who were part of the Drum and Spear Collective in Washington, DC, also went to Tanzania in the early 1970s. This group was led by Charles Cobb, Geri Augusto, Jennifer Lawson, and Courtland Cox. Like Malcolm X and the BPP's International Section, these Black Power activists were pushed toward diasporic engagement by their frustrations with dominant elites in the US. Reflecting on his first trip to Tanzania, Cox remembered, "After being in Lowndes, looking back at Black Power . . . I just knew that what we had here [in the US] wasn't sufficient."[7] By the time Drum and Spear Collective members began traveling to Tanzania in 1970, remaining SNCC leaders had been targeted by COINTELPRO and many of the African American neighborhoods destroyed in the rebellions following King's assassination were left in disarray.

The draw of Tanzania was the ideology of President Julius Nyerere and the emancipated space of Dar es Salaam. Nyerere's Ujamaa, the term for familyhood in Swahili, interpreted socialism through the lens of what he described as traditional African values. Nyerere "opened up a space that allowed people to think differently," Cox said.[8] "He was open to talking about what it meant to really govern in a way that was beyond neo-colonialism." At the University of Dar es Salaam, the Drum and Spear Collective found a "boiling pot of radical ideas" similar to what Howard University had been during the days of the Nonviolent Action Group. In Dar es Salaam, African American activists became more familiar with Nyerere's particular blend of cultural reappropriation and economic justice, which was specifically appealing to Black Power movement activists who had seen the limits of an exclusively race-based or economics-based approach to social justice. "I realized it's not just race, it's also race and class," Jennifer Lawson remembered.[9] Tanzania appeared to offer the fulfillment of the deferred dreams of Nkrumah, Lumumba, Fanon, Malcolm, and King.

Since he met Malcolm X at the OAU's Cairo summit in 1964, Tanzanian president Julius Nyerere actively encouraged African Americans to go to Tanzania and participate in TANU's project of socialist African nation-building. By the early 1970s, the number of African Americans in Tanzania had grown to nearly a thousand. Consistent with his diasporic vision, Nyerere agreed Tanzania would host the sixth Pan-African Congress (6PAC). Among the congress organizers were Drum and Spear Collective members Augusto, Cobb, and Cox—as well as former SNCC activist Judy Claude. In spite of not officially representing any government, the collective negotiated with heads of state, including Guinea's Sékou Touré and Nyerere.[10] This effort illuminated how the difference in power between grassroots initiatives and national governments challenged solidarity in this diaspora underground. Geri Augusto remembered, "I subsequently became a diplomat for all intents and purposes." According to Ms. Augusto, I was "moving in that kind of supranational arena with experienced, seasoned—and in many cases vile—politicians."[11]

6PAC

The first Pan-African Congress (PAC) was organized by W. E. B. Du Bois in 1919 to petition the Versailles Peace Treaty Conference (which ended World War I) to support African independence. The fifth congress, in Manchester, England—following World War II—was characterized by a working-class perspective, which was a stark contrast to the tone set by elites who organized and dominated the first four PACs. By 1974, Cold War allegiances, political instability, and struggles with neocolonialism varied significantly from region to region in the diaspora and on the continent. This required organizers to set an agenda that recognized fulfilling the promise of Accra's 1957 independence celebrations was a continuing challenge within Africa and throughout the diaspora. According to historian La TaSha Levy, 6PAC reflected how the ideology of Pan-Africanism had evolved "into a third stage of development that emphasized anti-imperialism, stressed the necessity of class struggle, and foresaw the need for socialism based on mass participation."[12] Participants sought to deliberate how diasporic engagement and Black insurgency could overcome the stubborn obstacles of neocolonialism, White settler colonialist regimes (such as those in apartheid South Africa and Rhodesia), and the continued subjection of colonized and non-self-governing territories. The sixth Pan-African Congress was the first one to be held in Africa or any majority-Black nation.

6PAC opened June 20, 1974, at Nkrumah Hall on the University of Dar es Salaam campus. Like the Pan-African Cultural Festival in Algiers and the All-African People's Conference in Accra, this gathering promised to be another emancipated space that would advance diasporic antiracist activism. Sékou Touré sent a recorded greeting. Nyerere made opening statements that saluted the congress's forefathers, including Marcus Garvey and Nkrumah. He also articulated a long-term vision for Black liberation that would attack economic inequality with an awareness that the fates of Black communities are linked across borders. "We now have to recognize that an end to colonialism is not an end to the oppression of man. . . . Within nations, and in the world taken as a whole, it is an economic disadvantage to have a Black skin," Nyerere stated. "Our gains are not only grossly insufficient; they are also insecure until [racism] is overcome everywhere."[13]

There were over two hundred people in the US contingent. Prior to 6PAC, some delegates critiqued TANU's organization of the conference as merely offering the appearance of collaboration and democracy rather than truly sharing decision-making power.[14] Courtland Cox hoped the meeting would "generate a renewal of commitment to a united struggle on the part of Africa, and African people everywhere."[15] This renewal was sorely needed because many Black Power and African independence activists bore the bruises of arrests, beatings, exile, and incarceration.

Ultimately, 6PAC could not provide a pathway to resolve the contradictions that came to inhibit further exchanges and action within this iteration of a diaspora underground. Nyerere and his governing party conceived the gathering as a state-to-state diplomatic event. The Organization of African Unity (OAU) decided representatives from liberation movements headquartered in Dar es Salaam and elsewhere would be only "observers"—not delegates like the independence movements that had already won state power.[16] With the exception of African American activists and representatives from nationalist movements in the remaining African colonies, progressive groups were not particularly welcome.[17]

TANU's and the OAU's positions revealed how many of the social movement organizations that made African independence possible were no longer existent, as in Congo, or had adapted to the administrative and bureaucratic realities of governance, as in Tanzania and Guinea. The ascent of these organizations into firmly entrenched state authorities contrasted severely with the increasingly battered and fragmented nature of African American insurgency. By 1974, the OAAU, SNCC, and the Black Panther Party were largely defunct as national organizations. Transnational activist exchanges require all parties to be activists, and the grassroots element of African state politics was disappearing from view.

In addition, neither African independence nor Black Power was fully able to develop a plan of action that would address the intersections of race, class, gender, and sexual orientation. At 6PAC, Nyerere and other leaders suggested that the way forward was "disengagement from international capital" and "the construction of socialist society."[18] However, participants did not seem to have a clear articulation of how to address, in cultural theorist Stuart Hall's words, how "race is the modality in which class is lived." For Black social movements, dismantling policies and practices that economically undermine their communities remains as challenging today as it was in 1974 for two key reasons: First, people of African descent have a sense of "linked fate" across class lines because of the impact their racial identity has on their life outcomes, which, ironically, can heighten inter-class animosity.[19] Affluent Black elites can resent being associated with the lower-class members of their community. Blue- and no-collar community members can resent elites for failing to lift as they climb. After 6PAC, historian Walter Rodney pointed out that most African independence organizations (including Ghana's Convention People's Party) became platforms that advanced the leadership of the bourgeois *evolué* class but were unable to address issues such as scarcity of educational opportunity and health care.[20] Similarly, in the US, Black Power's legacy of cultural empowerment became in some ways a code for class mobility. Participating in Black studies programs, embracing natural hairstyles and African names, and engaging in heritage tourism throughout the continent is more complex for African Americans without access to higher education or surplus capital.

Second, as Fanon powerfully articulated in *The Wretched of the Earth*, and scholars such as Cathy Cohen echoed in later work, because of the linked fate phenomenon Black elites throughout the diaspora can disguise adherence to heteronormativity and patriarchy as "national" or "community" interests.[21] The term "intersectionality" was not to be coined and popularized by critical race theorist Kimberlé Crenshaw until the 1990s. However, feminist activists in African independence and Black Power attempted to address the impact of gender inequality in their organizations and among their constituencies. In addition, LGBTQ activists had made significant contributions. The US delegation to 6PAC included veteran activists such as Queen Mother Moore and Mae Mallory. Congress workshops, such as "Women's Contribution to the Pan-African Struggle," further illuminated the crucial role women made building the movement. 6PAC's "Resolution on Black Women" declared "total support to the political struggles for equality undertaken by Black women" and called on "all the states and organizations participating in this Congress to tackle the problems of the oppression of women thoroughly and profoundly."[22]

In spite of these positive actions, both 6PAC and this diaspora underground remained plagued by society's patriarchal and homophobic ideologies. Feminist activist Sylvia Hill—who attended the congress and would later be a leader of the African Liberation Support Committee, based in Washington, DC—observed that while platitudes toward women's significance were being made during congress proceedings, she experienced microaggressions from men in the US delegation.[23] Although 6PAC took place five years after the Stonewall Rebellion, led by African American trans woman Marsha P. Johnson, no congress resolutions explicitly supported LGBTQ people in the diaspora. This diaspora underground's inability to develop platforms and organizational structures that rigorously included and advanced the human rights of Black women and the LGBTQ community would also contribute to its decline.

BUILDING BRIDGES

While in Conakry, Kwame Ture founded the All-African People's Revolutionary Party (AAPRP) to manifest his vision of a diasporic progressive political force. The title was influenced by the All-African People's Party that Nkrumah advanced in the late 1950s. The AAPRP aimed to unite people of African descent in a struggle for antiracist socialism. Ture argued that grassroots organization and armed struggle would be necessary to achieve complete racial, political, and economic equality. "We must organize!" he exclaimed in a speech at Howard, one of several HBCUs he would lecture at through the '70s and '80s. "It is when we are organized that we are invincible."

After 6PAC, African American political engagement with Africa continued with the African Liberation Support Committee (ALSC), which raised awareness about the second wave of African independence struggle in Angola, Mozambique, Namibia, Zimbabwe, and South Africa. Support from the ALSC evolved out of this diaspora underground. Progressive African political and cultural movements continue to engage with African American communities around issues including LGBTQ equality and environmental justice. Although Ujamaa was not a political and economic success, transnational unity continues to be promoted by indigenous institutions—including HBCUs and Black media—throughout the African diaspora.

Fellow SNCC activists James Forman, Cleveland Sellers, and others also continued their advocacy for transnational connections between independent African nations and the African American community once SNCC was no longer viable as an organization. "I am committed to doing whatever I can to build bridges between Blacks in this country and revolutionary groups in Africa," Sellers wrote in his memoir.[24] "When Africa is free, her sons and daughters . . . will have a solid base for their struggles." The SNCC insurgency that began with sit-ins in 1960 evolved into and influenced the African Liberation Support Committee as well as the struggle to impose US sanctions against the apartheid government in South Africa.

Although the CIA continued to have Ture under surveillance until the 1980s, and Sékou Touré's regime in Guinea became less and less democratic, he persisted in his political activism. The young firebrand who demanded Black Power now seemed to evolve into someone who accepted that profound political change requires decades of persistence. Each day he greeted people on the phone from his home in Conakry with "Ready for the Revolution!"—until his death from prostate cancer in 1998. The All-African People's Revolutionary Party's work continues as of this book's initial publication with chapters in Washington, DC; Guinea-Bissau; Oakland; Côte d'Ivoire; and other places in this diaspora underground.

Former BPP International Section members Pete O'Neal and Charlotte O'Neal stayed in Tanzania and founded the United African Alliance Community Center (UAACC) in a village outside of Arusha. Their organization utilizes the organizing techniques they learned in the Black Panther Party to provide empowerment and educational resources—including STEM and arts training for youths—to their adopted Maasai and Wameru communities in Tanzania.[25] The O'Neals also facilitate links between the diaspora and Tanzanians through their programs, which include eco-socialism and art tours. "It's difficult to distinguish the community work we were doing then and what we are doing now," Pete O'Neal stated.[26] Their goal continues to be to "create a microcosm of what we think the world should be." The African Liberation Support Committee movement, the antiapartheid struggle, and the O'Neals' nongovernmental organization exemplify how sustained transnational exchanges between Black communities are the final stage of a diaspora underground.

In the US, demands for Black Power developed into the practice of what scholar Cynthia Young describes as Soul Power.[27] The penetration of Soul Power into mainstream global consciousness was initially seen in the 1970s: in Afros and other natural hair care trends, *Soul Train* lines, and Blaxploitation films. The innovative cultural forms of house and hip hop, the adoption of school breakfast programs by public schools throughout the country, and social movements for environmental justice and against gentrification also embraced Black Power's emphasis on the significance of self-determination and self-acceptance to racial justice.

The circulation of Soul Power has continued throughout this diaspora underground among new generations. This is evidenced in the early twenty-first century by the transnational impact of Congolese *sapeurs*, singer/songwriter Beyoncé's visual album *Black Is King*, the blockbuster film *Black Panther* (directed by Oakland native Ryan Coogler), and the natural hair movement's resurgence among Black women. Ideational travel throughout this diaspora underground is now expedited by social media outlets such as Facebook, Twitter, YouTube, and Instagram—which, for example, enabled antiracist activists to connect across borders with hashtags such as #BlackLivesMatter and #ArabSpring. Although more and more Black students are attending predominately White institutions (PWIs), HBCUs and Black studies programs continue to play an important role in facilitating transnational connections between African and African American communities. Similarly, as media influence has migrated from print publications to digital platforms, Black-controlled outlets on both sides of the Atlantic continue to shape perceptions of the relevance of international Black struggles to domestic concerns. While all of the hopes of African independence and Black Power have not yet been realized, the diaspora underground its activists and constituents built is still here. For the generations that followed, their work and blood sacrifice sowed the seeds of a love for liberation.

EPILOGUE

Black Lives Matter
Black Lives Matter

حياة السود مهمة
Maisha ya Weusi ni Muhimu

THIS BOOK PRESENTED a crucial case study of exchanges between African independence movements in Algeria, Democratic Republic of Congo, Ghana, Guinea, and Tanzania and the Black Power organizations the Black Panther Party, Organization of Afro-American Unity, and Student Nonviolent Coordinating Committee. The study began with the celebration of Ghana's independence in 1957 and concluded with the sixth Pan-African Congress (6PAC) in 1974. It explored my original theory of a diaspora underground (see figure 1.1, in chapter 1) about how and why social movements in the African diaspora forge connections across national borders.

Evidence presented in *Love for Liberation* corroborates the following assertions of the theory of a diaspora underground:

- Black social movements seek transnational connections during cycles of contention after they become frustrated with domestic elites.

- Institutions indigenous to Black communities facilitate these connections by channeling information about antiracist social movements across borders.
- Innovations and attributions of similarity follow these information exchanges.
- Black social movement activists engage face-to-face in emancipated spaces, which are physical environments created and regulated within the African diaspora that are autonomous from the gaze and authority of dominant elites.
- Engagement within a diaspora underground perpetuates a transnational perspective on racial inequality. This engagement also promotes relationship building between diasporic communities that continues after cycles of contention have ended.

The theory of a diaspora underground reveals how antiracist activists utilize transnational engagement to overcome the inevitable obstacles that arise during cycles of contention. It also illuminates the robust spirit of resistance engendered by understanding racial inequality as a human rights issue and Black identity as international in scope.

For example, SNCC activists became frustrated with dominant elites in the US when their sit-ins, voter registration drives, and mass demonstrations failed to fully recalibrate racial dynamics of power in the US. As they participated in the movement, indigenous institutions—such as the Black press outlet the *Afro-American* and the historically Black college (HBCU) Howard University—shared information with the African American community about the successes of African independence movements in countries such as Algeria, Ghana, and the Democratic Republic of Congo. As these organizers learned of these successes, their understanding of racial inequality as an international issue and the urgency of making headway against White supremacy in the United States evolved. These new ideas also helped shape new tactics, including Freedom Summer and Freedom Schools. As their frustrations over the lack of responsiveness by dominant elites deepened, SNCC activists engaged with Sékou Touré and other participants in the Guinean independence movement during a journey to the emancipated space of Conakry. They also participated in the Pan-African Cultural Festival in Algiers and 6PAC. After SNCC's viability as an antiracist organization waned, its activists and constituencies continued with their transnational approach to addressing racial inequality and working in solidarity with African independence–related issues.

THE STRUGGLE CONTINUES

Unfortunately, as of the publication of this book and over 125 years after the Berlin Conference, the African region of Western Sahara, as well as Saint Helena, Ascension, and Tristan da Cunha remain on the United Nations' list of non-self-governing territories.[1] The rest of the continent is still searching for economic and governing practices that fully reflect the democratic social movement ideals that liberated so many nations from the colonizing yoke. As Nkrumah warned during his optimistic speech on that exuberant night in 1957, healing the wounds caused by colonialism and forging true self-determination would require intertribal cooperation, the respect of foreign political and economic authorities, and sustained solidarity throughout the diaspora. While some African countries made tremendous strides toward cultural, economic, and political development, the prize of a truly egalitarian and democratic society remains mostly out of reach. After independence, some liberation movements morphed into oligarchies that, according to African theorist Achille Mbembe, imitated former colonizers by appropriating public goods for private gain.[2]

For example, ruling elites in Ghana have often actualized the Convention People's Party's independence slogan, "Forward Ever, Backwards Never," into public policy.[3] Since Nkrumah was ousted, the nation's government has become a viable democracy. Its economy has survived serious challenges and currently subsists on a diversified portfolio of industrial minerals, petroleum, and manufacturing. It has one of the most comprehensive social safety nets on the continent, including universal health care and a public education system without significant gender disparities in access. Nkrumah's cultural program of honoring Ghana's Pan-African ties and multiethnic heritage has also continued. The country's Cape Coast and El Mina slave trading forts have been designated as UNESCO World Heritage Sites. In addition, African Americans are eligible for Ghanaian citizenship.

However, many Ghanaians do not enjoy the freedoms of speech, expression, and assembly their constitution guarantees. Homosexuality is prohibited by law and homophobic violence is common. Different regimes, including Nkrumah's, have arrested dissenters and journalists.

Guinea has struggled with peaceful democratic transitions since Sékou Touré died in 1984 and the PDG was removed from power in a bloodless coup. Violence, demonstrations, allegations of electoral fraud, and interethnic conflict between the Fula and Malinke continue to inhibit democratic stability. Although socialist reforms were introduced in the 1980s, Guineans do not generally benefit from the nation's extraordinary mineral reserves (including bauxite, iron ore, gold, and uranium). The nation's struggles to produce sufficient food for subsistence are due in part to widespread corruption. The state also fails to provide basic human services, such as public education after the sixth grade and health care. Homosexuality is illegal in Guinea, which also has one of the highest rates of female genital mutilation in the world.

In some ways the People's Democratic Republic of Algeria has fulfilled the promise of the FLN. The nationalization of the country's oil reserves helped Algeria achieve the highest human development index of any country on the African mainland. By highlighting the diversity and achievements of Algerian as well as Arabic culture and history, educational and cultural institutions have put an end to the soul-crushing cultural imperialism of the colonial era—which Fanon detailed in *The Wretched of the Earth*.

However, since Boumédiène's coup against Ahmed Ben Bella, Algerian authorities have failed to support the full human rights enjoyment of the country's citizens. As of 2020, homosexuality remains illegal. Women face systemic exclusion. Bloggers, journalists, and protesters who criticize the government are routinely jailed. The religious freedoms of non-Muslims are limited. It seems Algeria's political, cultural, and economic autonomy has survived at the expense of its most vulnerable community members.

In contrast, the independence movement in the Democratic Republic of Congo never recovered from the international community's complicity with the assassination of Patrice Lumumba. Colonel-turned-president Joseph Mobutu thrived for three decades as a US ally who allegedly embezzled billions of dollars in international aid from the Congolese people and brutally suppressed political opposition. The outcomes of elections that installed Joseph Kabila and later Raymond Tshibanda after Mobutu fled the country in 1996 were questioned by the international human rights community and protested by Congolese activists. Civil wars reflecting opposition to governing authorities, tribal and ethnic conflicts, and struggles for control over Congo's ample natural resources—including oil, diamonds, cobalt, and gold—continue to rage. As of 2021, the Democratic Republic of Congo remains, in political science terms, a weak state. The government cannot provide the basic level of physical security, access to resources, or physical infrastructure that its citizens need to survive. The impact of the government's failure is particularly deadly to women and children. Mass rape is consistently used as a weapon of civil war factions. Millions of children are at risk for starvation.

Similar to Algeria, Tanzania has successfully advanced its liberation movement's aims of political, economic, and cultural autonomy but is falling short in its support of full human rights enjoyment. The nation's economy thrives due to gold reserves, tourism, and banking. Poverty has substantially reduced since independence, but financial gains are mainly concentrated among urban elites. However, as of 2020, an incarnation of TANU named Chama Cha Mapinduzi (CCM, Party of the Revolution) continues to dominate under the presidency of John Magafuli. Discouragement of dissent and arrests of journalists appear to be on the rise. Although 30 percent of the National Assembly's seats are reserved for women, according to Human Rights Watch, systemic discrimination against women continues. Sex between men remains illegal in this nation and can be penalized with life imprisonment.

While pointing out the continued struggles of these African governments to provide full human rights enjoyment, economic stability, and free political participation for their citizens, it is important to note how their colonizers—Great Britain, France, and Belgium—as well as their Cold War interveners, the US and Russia, have failed spectacularly in similar ways. For example, as of 2020, the US government has banned openly trans people from serving in the military and failed to provide federal protections against workplace and educational discrimination for members of the LGBTQ community. Unlike Tanzania, the US and Great Britain have no minimum guarantee of representation for women in the national legislature. Women compose only 23.2 percent of US Congress representatives and 26 percent of US senators. America does not provide universal health care. In 2020, video reports of antiracist protesters in Seattle and New York City being kidnapped and thrown into unmarked vans by what appeared to be federal authorities were widely disseminated on social media. Euphemistically named "crowd control" techniques— including tear gas, noise cannons, and rubber bullets—are widely used by American police officers to suppress nonviolent demonstrations.

FOOTSTEPS

Although African independence and Black Power weren't able to fully actualize their goal of complete self-determination, today's generation of social justice activists appear to be taking cues from their limitations and the best of their examples. The Black Lives Matter movement (BLM) was founded in 2013 by three openly Queer Black women activists: Opal Tometi, Alicia Garza, and Patrisse Khan-Cullors.[4] It began with a hashtag, which is used on social media outlets such as Twitter and Instagram as a digital file folder to label posts and unite them under a specific theme or topic. #BlackLivesMatter helped coalesce online discussions about the acquittal of White Latino George Zimmerman in the killing of unarmed teenager Trayvon Martin in Sanford, Florida.

The still controversial assertion (for some) that Black Lives Matter, and the millions of social media impressions the term and hashtag have made, articulate the frustrations of an entire generation about the continued but often denied reality of racial injustice. A misleading discourse about America being "postracial" had enabled liberal indifference to anti-Black police misconduct. School-to-prison pipelines have been enacted and well funded in segregated public schools while teachers struggle to acquire basic supplies for their classrooms from their meager wages. Microaggressions in workplaces, the health-care system, and public space remain facts of Black life in spite of the concessions won by the social movements for civil rights, Black Power, and African independence.[5] BLM has helped the US and other nations understand that in spite of elites supporting a Black president (Barack Obama, whose father was an African independence activist) or welcoming a Black duchess (Meghan Markle) or declaring a society "color-blind" (France), White supremacist policies and practices continue to restrict the life chances and choices of Black people throughout the world.

In this Black Lives Matter cycle of contention, there is already evidence that the movement has sought transnational connections due to their frustrations with domestic elites. These frustrations exploded in 2014 during the supportive international response to the rebellion that followed the police killing of unarmed teenager Mike Brown, known as the Ferguson Uprising. Out of this uprising came a number of national demands, including "the de-militarization of local law enforcement across the country, repurposing of law enforcement funds to support community based alternatives to incarceration" and the development, legislation and enactment of a national plan of action for racial justice by the current presidential administration.[6] In spite of the cascade of support enjoyed by the movement and expressed vigorously via social media, federal, state, and local authorities made little or no progress toward these demands.

Following the examples of the OAAU, SNCC, BPP, and African independence movements, BLM participants appealed to the United Nations for international intervention in 2016. Testifying before the UN, cofounder Opal Tometi asserted, "In the footsteps of many courageous civil and human rights defenders that came before, I look to this meeting to be a forum for meaningful dialogue and action."[7] Indigenous press institutions and the Black Lives Matter hashtag also enabled activists to engage across national borders. Chapters have emerged in Marseilles, Brussels, Johannesburg, London, Birmingham, Berlin, Amsterdam, and other international cities in response to racially motivated violence and police shootings.[8]

It appears this new cycle of contention reflects the patterns of migration from Africa, Latin America, and the Caribbean to Europe, Canada, and the US that occurred in the late twentieth century. Black Power and African independence developed connections based on an understanding of the impact of the transatlantic slave trade on people of African descent born in the US. However, Black Lives Matter activists are frequently first- or second-generation descendants of Black immigrants who have homeland relationships to Europe, the Caribbean, and/or Africa.[9]

BLM also embraces the diasporic, intersectional approach to achieving racial justice that Black Power and African independence began to develop but did not quite embody. Protest chants and social media posts in support of BLM have also exclaimed, "Black Trans Lives Matter!" "Black Women's Lives Matter!" "Black Immigrant Lives Matter!" and "Black Queer Lives Matter!" to indicate how the movement's understanding of Blackness embraces its more vulnerable members. Khan-Cullors explained, "We aren't going to give up parts of our community in an effort to save some of our community. It's either all of us, or its none of us."[10]

SALUTE

The emergence of Black Lives Matter as a transnational, intersectional movement suggests that another diaspora underground is in the making. In 2020, another wave of protests erupted throughout the US and internationally in response to the police murders of unarmed George Floyd in Minneapolis; unarmed Elijah McClain in Aurora, Colorado; and unarmed, sleeping Breonna Taylor in Louisville, Kentucky. The gruesome reality of White supremacist violence against protesters from all backgrounds as well as victims of police misconduct—often captured on digital video and disseminated instantly via the internet—also spurred more difficult and productive dialogues about the continued realities of anti-Black racism at school, at work, in interpersonal relationships, and in the health-care system. More than ever, dominant institutions ranging from Netflix to Ben and Jerry's have directly proclaimed, "Black Lives Matter." Among White communities, candid conversations and trainings about White privilege, White fragility, and the best practices of allyship are increasingly popular online and in person.[11]

However, BLM activists continue to experience the discrediting, violence, false arrests, and efforts at co-optation experienced by African independence and Black Power. Some community members question whether protesting or voting are worth it. Understanding that this new diaspora underground is one of many—which were created by the total commitment and profound sacrifice of people who came before us— daunts some into believing change is not possible. It's fair for young people who are newly "woke" and those of us who have long been aware of the disappointments, incarceration, exile, and assassinations that often greet racial justice activists to be skeptical. How do we know that a diaspora underground is anything more than an adventurous loop that traps Black people in the vain hope that White supremacy can end?

Along with sit-ins (now referred to as "occupations") and mass demonstrations, a popular action during the era of African independence and Black Power that has made a comeback during the BLM cycle of contention is the raised fist. While this act of solidarity by racial justice activists was—and continues to be—distorted by the mainstream media as aggressive or defiant, in fact, the raised fist (sometimes covered in a black glove) is and always has been a form of salute. A salute to everyday Black people throughout the African diaspora who must use their resourcefulness, wit, and grace to survive against the overwhelming odds created by White supremacist policies and practices. A salute to ancestors—like Ali LaPointe, Patrice Lumumba, the four little girls in Birmingham, Alabama, and Malcolm X—who gave their lives in the past so that today's struggle is possible. A salute to those who remain in exile, in prison, or on the ground as indigenous leaders—the folks who, according to SNCC facilitator Ella Baker, work on a regular basis outside of the limelight to cohere and uplift their communities. A salute to the miraculous, diasporic splendor of Black culture and the ways in which it helps us find joy, community, and self-love in spite of White supremacist violence. The salute remains a powerful and unifying act because Black suffering and excellence are so often made invisible by the negligence and hostility of dominant institutions.

In researching this book, I have been fortunate enough to walk in the footsteps of African independence and Black Power activists. I've visited archival collections and had the opportunity to interview dozens of survivors throughout the US, Ghana, South Africa, and Zambia (see "Interviews, Archival Materials, and Periodicals"). Immersing myself in their legacy, and witnessing its direct impact on antiracist activism today, has cured me of my skepticism and alerted me to my responsibility.

A diaspora underground's ability to facilitate innovations in social movement ideas and tactics, exchanges between activists in emancipated spaces, and sustained transnational engagement from which new cycles of contention can emerge is not solely reliant on the work of social movement activists. It also requires support from committed indigenous institutions and constituencies. The force of antiracist activism is not a mystical giant in the hillside over which we—everyday community members and allies—have no control. On the contrary, the foundation for observable social change that a diaspora underground creates demands our cognitive liberation—faith that a better world is what we deserve, possible, and on her way. It also requires our willingness to use concrete action as an indicator of that faith. Kwame Ture's call for Black Power was so powerful because of the crowd's response on that warm night in Mississippi and the responses of so many crowds afterward. It was also amplified by the willingness of the Black press and HBCUs to help clarify the meaning of his message although it was distorted by dominant institutions.

Similarly, today, the success of Black Lives Matter in making our dominant institutions more inclusive and less violent—a change that positively impacts everyone—will depend on all of us. So, dear reader, I conclude by asking you to consider how you can salute the Black Radical Tradition and help construct this new diaspora underground. In addition to raising your fist to see and be seen, are you willing to show up at mass demonstrations and help register voters? To fill out yet another digital petition and email a representative or police chief? Are you willing to support Black studies curricula in schools, the scholarship funds of HBCUs, and Black-owned media? To participate in and help construct emancipated spaces? To become an indigenous leader against racism for your block, house of worship, or social circle? Only concrete action can buoy our faith in the possibility of change. The freedom, connections, and visibility that the African diaspora enjoys today is proof that organizing works—if we work it.

ACKNOWLEDGMENTS

I AM FIRST AND foremost grateful to the activists who lived the history described in this book. We will never know the names of every person who contributed to African independence and Black Power. I extend my ceaseless appreciation to those famous and lesser known, as well as their families, who made tremendous sacrifices so we can all enjoy more freedom and autonomy today. In addition, I am compelled to thank the scholars of diaspora, Pan-Africanism, and Black social movements whose work inspired me to persist with this project and persevere in my academic and artistic careers.

I'm also indebted to the activists who agreed to be interviewed for this book and the many archivists who tolerated my questions and anxiety as I delved into this history. I am especially thankful to the librarians at the New York Public Library's Schomburg Center for Research in Black Cultures, where I was a scholar-in-residence funded by the National Endowment for the Humanities (NEH). Without the time and access to Schomburg resources this funding provided, the completion of this book would not have been possible. At the Schomburg, I also benefited from the feedback, examples, and mentorship of my fellow scholars, as well as our leader, Dr. Colin Palmer, and the head of the Schomburg at that time, Dr. Khalil Muhammad.

The journey of writing this book began while I was a postdoctoral fellow at Northwestern University's Department of African American Studies. The guidance and encouragement of Dr. Dwight McBride, Dr. Martha Biondi, Dr. Barnor Hesse, Dr. Celeste Watkins-Hayes, Dr. Nitasha Sharma, Dr. Alexander Welheliye, Dr. Richard Iton, and the legendary Dr. Darlene Hines helped me overcome some of my impostor syndrome. My research collaborations with students during this time were also vital to the development of the aims of this book.

I continued researching *Love for Liberation* while I taught at Santa Clara University and enjoyed the mentorship of Dr. Juliana Chang and Dr. Linda Garber. Although my progress was not continuous, all advancements were assisted by my participation in the Surplussers Writing Group, which included Dr. Leigh Raiford, Dr. Michael Cohen, Dr. Grace Wang, Dr. Victoria Langland, Dr. Nadia Ellis, and Dr. Susette Min. Communing regularly with such brilliant scholars—who shared my passion for engaged research about race, politics, and culture—buoyed my spirit and strengthened my resolve to write the best book I could. I also consider myself fortunate to count the committed, prolific, and wickedly insightful scholars Dr. Janet Chang, Dr. Naomi Murakawa, and Dr. Ruth Nicole Brown among my allies, close friends, and peer mentors.

As I continued writing back on the East Coast, my infallible and resourceful research assistant, April Grigsby, provided crucial support. I am also grateful to Vedan Anthony-North, Dr. Brittany Meché, and Shannon Shird—the trio of brilliant superstars who helped me elevate the work of my production entity, Progressive Pupil, which makes Black studies for everybody. These women's sterling contributions, along with the work of the innovative participants in the New Leaders for Social Change program, allowed me to balance my filmmaking and community engagement with the demands of this book. I continue to be impressed and inspired by the creativity and verve they bring to their own work.

I am thankful to have a diverse chosen family, whose members played a critical role in helping me maintain balance and optimism throughout the process of writing *Love for Liberation*. David Murphy, Brian A. Kates, and Svenja Heinrich have encouraged my tiny triumphs since I completed the dissertation on which this book is based at Yale University many moons ago. Dinner Club rendezvous with Dr. Aisha Mays, Danielle Cherry, and Sarah Kornhauser forced me to leave the house, stay grounded, and celebrate life. The Inkwell chat's Dr. Azure Thompson, Courtney Liddell, Dr. Karinn Glover, Tiffany Washington, and Latressa Fulton, MPH, always illuminate the myriad of ways Black studies affirms, empowers, and enlightens in everyday life. Cecily Fox encourages me to take care of my body as well as I care for my mind.

In the final stretch of completing this work, I faced considerable professional and financial challenges that led me to doubt if my life and this book would continue. I would not have survived without the encouragement, empathy, and shelter of the Perry family—Alison, Jeanne, and Oliver. I am exceptionally grateful to the brilliant Dr. Courtney Baker, author of *Humane Insight: Looking at Images of African American Suffering and Death*. In addition to sharing her home, library, and previous publishing experiences with me, Dr. Baker literally provided a lifesaving net for me and this project. Hopefully, this work will pay her generosity forward and support the work of other students, scholars, and activists with a love for liberation.

REMAINING NON-SELF-GOVERNING TERRITORIES

(According to the United Nations)

American Samoa
Anguilla
Bermuda
British Virgin Islands
Cayman Islands
Falkland Islands
French Polynesia (including Tahiti and Bora-Bora)
Gibraltar
Guam
Montserrat
New Caledonia
Pitcairn, Henderson, Ducie, and Oeno Islands
Saint Helena, Ascension, and Tristan da Cunha
Tokelau
Turks and Caicos Islands
United States Virgin Islands
Western Sahara

NOTES

INTRODUCTION

1 Robin J. Hayes, *Black and Cuba*, documentary film (Progressive Pupil, 2014).

2 An excellent overview of diaspora studies can be found in Kim D. Butler, "Defining Diaspora, Refining a Discourse," *Diaspora: A Journal of Transnational Studies* 10, no. 2 (2001): 189–219.

3 Benedict Anderson, *Imagined Communities: Reflections on the Origin and Spread of Nationalism* (London: Verso Books, 1983), 4–7.

4 For an explanation of how elites create and perpetuate dominant ideologies that the majority in a society come to accept as "commonsense" and how they adapt these ideologies to dissent by the subaltern over time, see a discussion of hegemony in Antonio Gramsci, *Selections from the Prison Notebooks of Antonio Gramsci*, trans. Quintin Hoare and Geoffrey Nowell Smith (New York: International Publishers, 2005), 215–17.

5 Brent Hayes Edwards, *The Practice of Diaspora: Literature, Translation, and the Rise of Black Internationalism* (Cambridge: Harvard University Press, 2009), 15.

6 Edwards, *Practice of Diaspora*, 15.

7 Butler, "Defining Diaspora"; Saidiya Hartman, *Lose Your Mother: A Journey along the Atlantic Slave Route* (New York: Macmillan, 2008); Tiffany Ruby Patterson and Robin D. G. Kelley, "Unfinished Migrations: Reflections on the African Diaspora and the Making of the Modern World," *African Studies Review* 43, no. 1 (2000): 11–45.

8 Edwards, *Practice of Diaspora*.

9 Jean-François Bayart and Stephen Ellis, "Africa in the World: A History of Extraversion," *African Affairs* 99, no. 395 (2000): 256.

10 Basil Davidson, *Africa in History* (New York: Touchstone, 1995).

11 Anderson, *Imagined Communities*; William L. Van DeBurg, ed., *Modern Black Nationalism: From Marcus Garvey to Louis Farrakhan* (New York: New York University Press, 1997).

12 Alexander George and Andrew Bennett, *Case Studies and Theory Development in the Social Sciences* (Cambridge, MA: MIT Press, 2005); Henry E. Brady and David Collier, eds., *Rethinking Social Inquiry: Diverse Tools, Shared Standards* (Lanham: Rowman & Littlefield, 2010).

13 Katharine Q. Seelye, "John Lewis, Towering Figure of the Civil Rights Era, Dies at 80," *New York Times*, July 17, 2020.

14 William Sales, *From Civil Rights to Black Liberation: Malcolm X and the Organization of Afro-American Unity* (Boston: South End, 1994); David Hilliard and Lewis Cole, *This Side of Glory: The Autobiography of David Hilliard and the Story of the Black Panther Party* (Boston: Little, Brown, 1993); Clayborne Carson, *In Struggle: SNCC and the Black Awakening of the 1960s* (Cambridge, MA: Harvard University Press, 1995).

15 Michael Hanchard, *Party/Politics: Horizons in Black Poltical Thought* (Oxford: Oxford University Press, 2006); Minkah Makalani, *In the Cause of Freedom: Radical Black Internationalism from Harlem to London, 1917–1939* (Chapel Hill: University of North Carolina Press, 2011).

CHAPTER 1: DIASPORA UNDERGROUND

1 Robin J. Hayes and Christina M. Greer, "The International Dimensions of Everyday Black Political Participation," *Journal of African American Studies* 18, no. 3 (2014): 353–71.

2 The concept of space-time originated in mathematics theory by Minkowski and is most commonly applied in physics. See Hermann Minkowski, *Space and Time: Minkowski's Papers on Relativity* (Montreal: Minkowski Institute Press, 2012 [1909]), 39–54.

3 Robin D. G. Kelley, *Freedom Dreams: The Black Radical Imagination* (Boston: Beacon, 2002); Cedric J. Robinson, *Black Marxism: The Making of a Black Radical Tradition* (Chapel Hill: University of North Carolina Press, 2005).

4 Examples of which are described in Simon Anekwe, "Tells Why Ghana Ousted Nkrumah," *Amsterdam News*, October 15, 1966, 1 and 50; Ward Churchill and Jim Vander Wall, *The COINTELPRO Papers: Documents from the FBI's Secret Wars against Dissent* (Boston: South End, 2002); James Forman, *The Making of Black Revolutionaries: A Personal Account* (New York: Macmillan, 1972); and Robert Legvold, "The Super Rivals: Conflict in the Third World," *Foreign Affairs* 57, no. 4 (Spring 1979): 755–78.

5 Lin-Manuel Miranda, "The Room Where It Happens," *Hamilton: An American Musical*, Public Theater, New York, debuted January 15, 2015.

6 Cathy Cohen, *The Boundaries of Blackness: AIDS and the Breakdown of Black Politics* (Chicago: University of Chicago Press, 1999).

7 "For Us, By Us" was a slogan promoting Black solidarity and economic cooperation popularized by the African American–owned fashion label FUBU.

8 Robert Farris Thompson, *Flash of the Spirit: African and Afro-American Art and Philosophy* (New York: Random House, 1983).

9 Sidney G. Tarrow, *Power in Movement: Social Movements and Contentious Politics* (Cambridge: Cambridge University Press, 1998), 145.

10 Robert Alan Dahl, *Dilemmas of Pluralist Democracy: Autonomy vs. Control* (New Haven, CT: Yale University Press, 1982); James Madison, "Federalist no. 51," November 22, 1787; Iris Marion Young, *Justice and the Politics of Difference* (Princeton, NJ: Princeton University Press, 2011).

11 Tarrow, *Power in Movement*, 144–45.

12 Hasan Jeffries, *Bloody Lowndes: Civil Rights and Black Power in Alabama's Black Belt* (New York: New York University Press, 2010), 187.

13 Margaret E. Keck and Kathryn Sikkink, *Activists beyond Borders: Advocacy Networks in International Politics* (Ithaca, NY: Cornell University Press, 2014), 10–12.

14 Hanspeter Kriesi, "Cross-national Diffusion of Protest," in *New Social Movements in Western Europe*, ed. Hanspeter Kriesi et al. (Minneapolis: University of Minnesota Press, 1993), 182.

15 Michael Omi and Howard Winant, *Racial Formation in the United States: 1960s–1990s* (New York: Routledge, 1994), 19.

16 Ruth Wilson Gilmore, *Golden Gulag: Prisons, Surplus, Crisis, and Opposition in Globalizing California* (Berkeley: University of California Press, 2007), 28.

17 Robinson, *Black Marxism*, 185–240.

18 Doug McAdam and Dieter Rucht, "The Cross-national Diffusion of Social Movement Ideas," *Annals of the American Academy of Political and Social Science* 528, no. 1 (July 1993): 56–74; Kriesi, "Cross-national Diffusion of Protest"; David A. Snow and Robert D. Benford, "Alternative Types of Cross-national Diffusion in the Social Movement Arena," in *Social Movements in a Globalizing World*, ed. Donatella della Porta, Hanspeter Kriesi, and Dieter Rucht (New York: St. Martin's, 1999), 23–39.

19 Jean L. Cohen, "Strategy or Identity: New Theoretical Paradigms and Contemporary Social Movements," *Social Research* 52, no. 4 (Winter 1985): 684; Dara Z. Strolovitch, *Affirmative Advocacy: Race, Class, and Gender in Interest Group Politics* (Chicago: University of Chicago Press, 2008); Kriesi, "Cross-national Diffusion of Protest," 188–90; McAdam and Rucht, "Social Movement Ideas," 60–63.

20 Kriesi, "Cross-national Diffusion of Protest," 184–85.

21 Hayes and Greer, "Everyday Black Political Participation," 356–58; Robin J. Hayes, "'A Free Black Mind Is a Concealed Weapon': Institutions and Social Movements in the African Diaspora," in *Transnational Blackness: Navigating the Global Color Line*, ed. Vanesa Agard-Jones and Manning Marable (New York: Palgrave-Macmillan, 2008), 175–85.

22 Aldon Morris and Naomi Braine, "Social Movements and Oppositional Consciousness," in *Oppositional Consciousness: The Subjective Roots of Social Protest*, ed. Jane Mansbridge and Aldon Morris (Chicago: University of Chicago Press, 2001), 25.

23 Doug McAdam, Sidney Tarrow, and Charles Tilly, *Dynamics of Contention* (Cambridge: Cambridge University Press, 2001), 28.

24 McAdam, Tarrow, and Tilly, *Dynamics of Contention*, 157–58.

25 Paul Gilroy, *Against Race: Imagining Political Culture beyond the Color Line* (Cambridge, MA: Harvard University Press, 2000), 106.

26 Kamari Maxine Clarke, *Mapping Yorùbá Networks: Power and Agency in the Making of Transnational Communities* (Durham, NC: Duke University Press, 2004), 31, 32.

27 Cohen, *Boundaries of Blackness*, 187.

28 Frances Fox Piven and Richard A. Cloward, *Poor People's Movements: Why They Succeed, How They Fail* (New York: Vintage, 1978), 14–21.

29 Gunnar Myrdal, *An American Dilemma: The Negro Problem and Modern Democracy* (New York: Harper, 1944), 911.

30 Verta Taylor and Nancy E. Whittier, "Collective Identity in Social Movement Communities," in *Frontiers in Social Movement Theory*, ed. Aldon Morris and Carol McClurg Mueller (New Haven, CT: Yale University Press, 1992), 110–11.

31 Cohen, *Boundaries of Blackness*, 187.

32 Evelyn Brooks Higginbotham, *Righteous Discontent: The Women's Movement in the Black Baptist Church* (Cambridge, MA: Harvard University Press, 1993), 198.

33 Cohen, *Boundaries of Blackness*, 74.

34 Clarke, *Mapping Yorùbá Networks*, 40.

35 Kimberlé Crenshaw, "Mapping the Margins: Intersectionality, Identity Politics, and Violence against Women of Color," *Stanford Law Review* 43 (1990): 1241–99.

36 Mayer N. Zald, "Culture, Ideology and Strategic Framing," in *Comparative Perspectives on Social Movements: Political Opportunities, Mobilizing Structures, and Cultural Framings*, ed. Doug McAdam, John D. McCarthy, and Mayer N. Zald (Cambridge: Cambridge University Press, 1996), 266–67; Doug McAdam, *Political Process and the Development of Black Insurgency, 1930–1970* (Chicago: University of Chicago Press, 1982), 46.

37 Melissa Harris-Lacewell, *Barbershops, Bibles and Bet: Everyday Talk and Black Political Thought* (Princeton, NJ: Princeton University Press, 2004), 12–15; Michael Hanchard, *Party/Politics: Horizons in Black Political Thought* (Oxford: Oxford University Press, 2006), 27–33.

38 Antonio Gramsci, *Selections from the Prison Notebooks of Antonio Gramsci*, trans. Quintin Hoare and Geoffrey Nowell Smith (New York: International Publishers, 2005), 471.

39 Cohen, *Boundaries of Blackness*, 151.

40 McAdam and Rucht, "Social Movement Ideas," 60.

41 Peter L. Berger and Thomas Luckmann, *The Social Construction of Reality: A Treatise in the Sociology of Knowledge* (Garden City, NJ: Doubleday, 1966), 2–3, 159.

42 Bernard Magubane, *The Ties That Bind: African-American Consciousness of Africa* (Trenton, NJ: Africa World, 1987), 106.

43 See analysis of these tropes in Jan Nederveen Pieterse, *White on Black: Images of Africa and Blacks in Western Popular Culture* (New Haven, CT: Yale University Press, 1995); and Lola Young, "Imperial Culture: The Primitive, the Savage and White Civilization," in *Fear of the Dark: "Race," Gender and Sexuality in the Cinema* (New York: Routledge, 2000).

44 Sidney LeMelle and Robin D. G. Kelley, "Imagining Home: Pan-Africanism Revisited," in *Imagining Home: Class, Culture and Nationalism in the African Diaspora*, ed. Sidney LeMelle and Robin D. G. Kelley (London: Verso Books, 1994), 7–9.

45 Arjun Appadurai, *Modernity at Large* (Minneapolis: University of Minnesota Press, 1996), 33.

46 Penny M. Von Eschen, *Race against Empire: Black Americans and Anti-colonialism, 1937–1957* (Ithaca, NY: Cornell University Press, 1997), 9.

47 Paul Gilroy, *The Black Atlantic: Modernity and Double-Consciousness* (Cambridge, MA: Harvard University Press, 1993); Brenda Gayle Plummer, *In Search of Power: African Americans in the Era of Decolonization, 1956–1974* (Cambridge: Cambridge University Press, 2013).

48 Clayborne Carson, *In Struggle: SNCC and the Black Awakening of the 1960s* (Cambridge, MA: Harvard University Press, 1995), 134–36.

49 Raymond Williams, *Marxism and Literature* (Oxford: Oxford University Press, 1977), 132.

50 Charles Taylor, *The Ethics of Authenticity* (Cambridge, MA: Harvard University Press, 1991), 25–29.

51 Taylor, *Ethics of Authenticity*, 25; Jean-Jacques Rousseau, *A Discourse on Inequality* (New York: Penguin, 1984).

52 Taylor, *Ethics of Authenticity*, 29.

53 Michael Dawson, *Behind the Mule: Race and Class in African-American Politics* (Princeton, NJ: Princeton University Press, 1994), 64–68. For more on cultural imperialism as a face of oppression, see Young, *Politics of Difference*, 39–65.

54 Simone Browne, *Dark Matters: On the Surveillance of Blackness* (Durham, NC: Duke University Press, 2015).

55 James C. Scott, *Domination and the Arts of Resistance: Hidden Transcripts* (New Haven, CT: Yale University Press, 1990), 18–20.

56 Kathleen Neal Cleaver, "Back to Africa: The Evolution of the International Section of the Black Panther Party (1969–1972)," in *The Black Panther Party (Reconsidered)*, ed. Charles E. Jones (Baltimore: Black Classic, 1998), 223.

57 Joseph Raz, *The Morality of Freedom* (Cambridge: Oxford University Press, 1986).

58 Clarke, *Mapping Yorùbá Networks*, 34.

59 Stuart Hall, "Race, Articulation, and Societies Structured in Dominance," in *Black British Cultural Studies: A Reader*, ed. Houston A. Baker and Manthia Diawara (Chicago: University of Chicago Press, 1996), 16–60; Stuart Hall, "Cultural Identity and Diaspora," in *Identity: Community, Culture, Difference*, ed. Jonathan Rutherford (London: Lawrence & Wishart, 1990).

60 Robin D. G. Kelley, *Hammer and Hoe: Alabama Communists during the Great Depression* (Chapel Hill: University of North Carolina Press, 1990), 10.

61 Brent Hayes Edwards, *The Practice of Diaspora: Literature, Translation, and the Rise of Black Internationalism* (Cambridge, MA: Harvard University Press, 2009).

62 Von Eschen, *Race against Empire*.

63 Nancy Fraser, "Rethinking the Public Sphere: A Contribution to the Critique of Actually Existing Democracy," *Social Text* 25/26 (1990): 67.

64 Robert J. C. Young, *Postcolonialism: An Historical Introduction* (Oxford: Blackwell, 2001).

65 Malcolm X, "Appeal to African Heads of State," in *Malcolm X Speaks: Selected Speeches and Statements*, ed. George Breitman (New York: Grove, 1965), 77.

CHAPTER 2: "NEW AFRICAN IN THE WORLD"

1 "To be sure, slavery and slave trading were already firmly entrenched in many African societies before their contact with Europe. In most situations, men as well as women captured in local warfare became slaves. In general, however, slaves in African communities were often treated as junior members of the society with specific rights, and many were ultimately absorbed into their masters' families as full members. Given traditional methods of agricultural production in Africa, slavery in Africa was quite different from that which existed in the commercial plantation environments of the New World." *Early European Contact and the Slave Trade*, accessed February 10, 2016, www.ghanaweb.com/GhanaHomePage/history /slave-trade.php.

2 Author's tour of Cape Coast Castle, Cape Coast Ghana, August 12, 2009.

3 C. B. Powell and Lester Granger, "Can Ghana Make It?," *Amsterdam News*, April 6, 1957, 26; Martin Luther King Jr., "The Birth of a New Nation," sermon delivered at Dexter Avenue Baptist Church, April 7, 1957, Martin Luther King, Jr. Papers Project, Stanford University, https://kinginstitute.stanford.edu/king-papers/doc uments/birth-new-nation-sermon-delivered-dexter-avenue-baptist-church.

4 "God Bless Our Homeland Ghana," written and composed by Philip Gbeho, 1957; Lester Granger, "Manhattan and Beyond," *Amsterdam News*, March 23, 1957, 6.

5 Kwame Nkrumah, "Prime Minister's Midnight Speech on the Eve of Independence," 1957, p. 1, Kwame Nkrumah Papers, Manuscript Division, Moorland-Spingarn Research Center, Howard University, Washington, DC.

6 "Proudly We Can Be Africans," *Baltimore Afro-American*, April 6, 1957, 4.

7 Powell and Granger, "Can Ghana Make It?"

8 "On the Day: March 6, 1957," *BBC News*, accessed June 1, 2016, http://news.bbc.co .uk/onthisday/hi/dates/stories/march/6/newsid_2515000/2515459.stm.

9 Ethel L. Payne, "Ghana—Its Independence Has Great Impact in Africa," *Chicago Defender*, March 16, 1957, 11.

10 "Nixon, Powell, Diggs to Ghana Celebration," *Amsterdam News*, February 16, 1957, 1.

11 Stephen J. Whitfield, *A Death in the Delta: The Story of Emmett Till* (Baltimore: Johns Hopkins University Press, 1991), 33–70.

12 Charles V. Hamilton, *Adam Clayton Powell, Jr.: The Political Biography of an American Dilemma* (New York: Atheneum, 1991).

13 "Dr. King Gets Invites from India, Ghana," *Amsterdam News*, February 16, 1957, 2; "M. L. King Meets Nixon in Ghana," *Pittsburgh Courier*, March 16, 1957.

14 "King Gets Invites," 2.

15 "King Meets Nixon."

16 Martin Luther King Jr., interview by Etta Moten Barnett, March 6, 1957, Martin Luther King, Jr. Papers Project, Stanford University, https://kinginstitute.stanford.edu/king-papers/documents/interview-etta-moten-barnett.

17 King, "Birth of a New Nation."

18 "New Gold Coast Flag to Be Unveiled Here," *Amsterdam News*, February 9, 1957, 2.

19 For more on the origins of Pan-Africanism, see Minkah Makalani, *In the Cause of Freedom: Radical Black Internationalism from Harlem to London, 1917–1939* (Chapel Hill: University of North Carolina Press, 2011); Michael C. Dawson, *Black Visions: The Roots of Contemporary African-American Political Ideologies* (Chicago: University of Chicago Press, 2001); and Ronald W. Walters, *Pan Africanism in the African Diaspora: An Analysis of Modern Afrocentric Political Movements* (Detroit: Wayne State University Press, 1997).

20 "Ghana's Crusade," *Baltimore Afro-American*, October 19, 1957, 4.

21 George Shepperson, "'Pan-Africanism' and 'pan-Africanism'": Some Historical Notes." *Phylon* 23, no. 4 (1962): 348.

22 For more on the Garveys and the Universal Negro Improvement Association, see Amy Jacques Garvey, *More Philosophy and Opinions of Marcus Garvey* (New York: Routledge, 2012); Marcus Garvey, *The Marcus Garvey and Universal Negro Improvement Association Papers* (Berkeley: University of California Press, 1991); and Ronald J. Stephens and Adam Ewing, eds., *Global Garveyism* (Gainesville: University Press of Florida, 2019).

23 Garvey, *Universal Negro Improvement Association*.

24 Shepperson, "Pan-Africanism," 348.

25 John Henrik Clarke, "Kwame Nkrumah: His Years in America," *Black Scholar* 6, no. 2 (1974): 9–16.

26 "Ghana: A New Nation Is Born in Africa," *Chicago Defender*, March 2, 1957, 4.

27 Louis Lautier, "Stormy Road Marked Career of Nkrumah," *Baltimore Afro-American*, March 23, 1957, 11; David Rooney, *Kwame Nkrumah: The Political Kingdom in the Third World* (London: IB Tauris, 1988), 16.

28 Marika Sherwood, *Kwame Nkrumah: The Years Abroad, 1935–1947* (Oxford: African Books Collective, 1996), 117.

29 Nkrumah, "Prime Minister's Midnight Speech," 1–2.

30 David Killingray, "Military and Labour Recruitment in the Gold Coast during the Second World War," *Journal of African History* 23, no. 1 (1982): 83–95.

31 "Ghana Veterans and the 1948 Accra Riots," *BBC World Service*, accessed June 1, 2016, www.bbc.co.uk/programmes/p01t1os9.

32 Kwame Nkrumah, "Gold Coast's Claim to Immediate Independence: Speech Made in National Assembly," 1955, p. 8, Kwame Nkrumah Papers, Manuscript Division, Moorland-Spingarn Research Center, Howard University, Washington, DC.

33 Charles Arden-Clarke, "Eight Years of Transition in Ghana," *African Affairs* 57, no. 226 (1958): 31.

34 Minion K. C. Morrison, "Political Parties in Ghana through Four Republics: A Path to Democratic Consolidation," *Comparative Politics* (2004): 423.

35 Arden-Clarke, "Eight Years of Transition," 31.

36 Stokely Carmichael, "What We Want," in *Let Nobody Turn Us Around: Voices of Resistance, Reform and Renewal*, ed. Manning Marable and Leith Mullings (Lanham, MD: Rowman & Littlefield, 2000), 442–48.

37 Arden-Clarke, "Eight Years of Transition," 31.

38 Nkrumah, "Gold Coast's Claim," 8.

39 Arden-Clarke, "Eight Years of Transition," 37; Morrison, "Political Parties in Ghana," 423.

40 Lautier, "Stormy Road Marked Career," 11; Nkrumah, "Gold Coast's Claim."

41 James L. Hicks, "Ghana Celebrates Freedom on March 6th," *Amsterdam News*, March 2, 1957, 6.

42 "Proudly We Can Be Africans."

43 "Ghana Celebrates World Bank Entry," *Chicago Defender*, October 5, 1957, 3.

44 Payne, "Ghana—Its Independence."

45 Nkrumah, "Prime Minister's Midnight Speech."

CHAPTER 3: "A FREE BLACK MIND"

1 Alistair Horne, *A Savage War of Peace: Algeria, 1954–1962* (New York: New York Review of Books Classics, 2011), locs. 449–1660 of 15340, Kindle.

2 Colonial schools and governments serve as what French theorist Michel Foucault termed "disciplinary institutions." Michel Foucault, *Discipline and Punish: The Birth of the Prison* (New York: Vintage, 1977), 300; Frantz Fanon, *The Wretched of the Earth* (New York: Grove, 1963 [1961]), 148–248.

3 Gregory Mann, "What Was the *Indigénat*? The 'Empire of Law' in French West Africa," *The Journal of African History* 50, no. 3 (2009): 331–33.

4 Celebrated *pieds-noirs* include author Albert Camus and fashion designer Yves Saint-Laurent.

5 Horne, *Savage War of Peace*, loc. 1284 of 15340.

6 Horne, *Savage War of Peace*, loc. 1300 of 15340.

7 Mahmood Mamdani, *Citizen and Subject: Contemporary Africa and the Legacy of Late Colonialism* (Princeton, NJ: Princeton University Press, 1996), 126–27; Mann, "What Was the *Indigénat*?"

8 Horne, *Savage War of Peace*, locs. 1139–40 of 15340.

9 Horne, *Savage War of Peace*, loc. 1117 of 15340. For more on stereotypes of African Americans in US popular culture, see the documentary film by Marlon T. Riggs and Esther Rolle, *Ethnic Notions: Black People in White Minds* (California Newsreel, 1987).

10 Horne, *Savage War of Peace*, loc. 1117 of 15340.

11 Brent Hayes Edwards, "Uses of Diaspora," *Social Text* 19, no. 1 (2001): 48.

12 Aimé Césaire, *Discourse on Colonialism*, trans. Joan Pinkham (New York: Monthly Review Press, 1955), 37.

13 See, for example, Jean-Paul Sartre, "Colonialism Is a System," *Interventions* 3, no. 1 (2001 [1956]): 127–40; Frantz Fanon, *Black Skin, White Masks* (New York: Grove, 2008 [1952]).

14 This paragraph's description of the origins of the FLN is indebted to Horne, *Savage War of Peace*, locs. 1501–1614 of 15340.

15 This paragraph's description of the first incident of the Algerian Revolution is indebted to Horne, *Savage War of Peace*, locs. 1673–1916 of 15340.

16 Horne, *Savage War of Peace*, loc. 1916 of 15340.

17 Horne, *Savage War of Peace*, locs. 3599–602 of 15340.

18 Horne, *Savage War of Peace*, loc. 3379 of 15340.

19 Horne, *Savage War of Peace*, loc. 1117 of 15340.

20 Horne, *Savage War of Peace*, locs. 3775, 4297 of 15340.

21 Horne, *Savage War of Peace*, loc. 3807 of 15340. The incident is grippingly portrayed in the narrative Third Cinema classic *The Battle of Algiers* (Criterion Collection, 2004), directed by Gillo Pontecorvo.

22 Horne, *Savage War of Peace*, loc. 3808 of 15340.

23 Horne, *Savage War of Peace*, loc. 3725 of 15340.

24 Horne, *Savage War of Peace*, loc. 3807 of 15340.

25 The following description of Yacet's interaction with Tillion is indebted to Horne, *Savage War of Peace*, locs. 4424–25 of 15340.

26 Raymund T. Yingling and Robert W. Ginnane, "The Geneva Conventions of 1949," *American Journal of International Law* 46, no. 3 (1952): 395.

27 Yingling and Ginnane, "Geneva Conventions of 1949," 396.

28 Yingling and Ginnane, "Geneva Conventions of 1949," 395.

29 Horne, *Savage War of Peace*, loc. 4026 of 15340.

30 Walter A. Schrepel, "Paras and Centurions: Lessons Learned from the Battle of Algiers," *Peace and Conflict: Journal of Peace Psychology* 11, no. 1 (2005): 76, ProQuest.

31 Schrepel, "Paras and Centurions," 76.

32 Horne, *Savage War of Peace*, loc. 4070 of 15340.

33 Horne, *Savage War of Peace*, loc. 4127 of 15340.

34 Paul Aussaresses, *The Battle of the Casbah: Terrorism and Counterterrorism in Algeria 1955–1957* (New York: Enigma Books, 2013); Horne, *Savage War of Peace*, loc. 4167 of 15340.

35 Horne, *Savage War of Peace*, loc. 4026 of 15340.

36 Schrepel, "Paras and Centurions," 77.

37 Horne, *Savage War of Peace*, loc. 4520 of 15340.

38 Horne, *Savage War of Peace*, loc. 4521 of 15340.

39 The above description of LaPointe's death is indebted to Horne, *Savage War of Peace*, loc. 4520 of 15340.

40 Horne, *Savage War of Peace*, loc. 4522 of 15340.

41 Leigh Raiford, *Imprisoned in a Luminous Glare: Photography and the African American Freedom Struggle* (Chapel Hill: University of North Carolina Press, 2011).

42 Jean-François Sirinelli, "Algerie, manifeste des 121: Déclaration sur le droit à l'insoumission dans la Guerre d'Algérie," *Libération*, republished January 12, 1998, www.liberation.fr/cahier-special/1998/01/12/algerie-manifeste-des-121-declaration -sur-le-droit-a-l-insoumission-dans-la-guerre-d-algerie_544819.

43 "Independence for Algeria," *Chicago Defender*, October 12, 1957, 10.

44 Horne, *Savage War of Peace*, loc. 4524 of 15340.

45 Horne, *Savage War of Peace*, loc. 2944 of 15340.

46 Fanon, *Black Skin, White Masks*, 143.

47 David Macey, *Frantz Fanon: A Biography* (New York: Verso Books, 2012).

48 Isaac Julien, *Frantz Fanon: Black Skin, White Mask*, documentary film (Film Movement Classics, 1996).

49 Frantz Fanon, "Letter to the Resident Minister," in *Toward the African Revolution, Political Essays* (New York: Grove, 1988 [1969]), 53.

50 Fanon, "Letter to the Resident Minister," ix.

51 Frantz Fanon, "Racism and Culture," in *Toward the African Revolution, Political Essays* (New York: Grove, 1988 [1969]), 31.

52 Phineas Malinga, "Ahmed Sékou Touré: An African Tragedy," *African Communist* 100 (1985): 58–64, *ebGuinee*.

53 R. W. Johnson, "Sekou Touré and the Guinean Revolution," *African Affairs* 69, no. 277 (1970): 350, www.jstor.org/stable/720210.

54 Fanon, *Wretched of the Earth*.

55 Johnson, "Sekou Touré and the Guinean Revolution," 352.

56 Malinga, "Ahmed Sékou Touré," 58–64.

57 "A New Nation Is Born," *Baltimore Afro-American*, October 11, 1958, 4; "Elections in Guinea," African Elections Database, accessed July 29, 2016, http://african elections.tripod.com/gn.html#1958_Constitutional_Referendum.

58 "New Nation Is Born," 4.

59 "French Guinea Gains Independence," *Chicago Defender*, October 11, 1958, 10.

60 Doug McAdam, *Political Process and the Development of Black Insurgency, 1930–1970* (Chicago: University of Chicago Press, 1982).

61 Charles M. Payne, *I've Got the Light of Freedom: The Organizing Tradition and the Mississippi Freedom Struggle* (Berkeley: University of California Press, 1995).

62 McAdam, *Political Process*, 51.

63 "Nation Horrified by Murder of Chicago Youth," *Jet*, September 15, 1955, 6–9; James Forman, *The Making of Black Revolutionaries: A Personal Account* (New York: Macmillan, 1972), 30–35.

64 Timothy B. Tyson, "Robert F. Williams, 'Black Power,' and the Roots of the African American Freedom Struggle," *Journal of American History* 85, no. 2 (1998): 550.

65 Tyson, "Robert F. Williams," 550.

66 Tyson, "Robert F. Williams," 548.

67 Robert Franklin Williams, *Negroes with Guns* (Detroit: Wayne State University Press, 1962).

68 Tyson, "Robert F. Williams," 544.

69 "Ghana Envoy Jim Crowed in Maryland," *Amsterdam News*, October 12, 1957, 1, 29.

70 "'Dear Head Nigger': Hate Letter Shocks U.N.," *Amsterdam News*, April 22, 1961, 39.

71 "'Freedom Not Free,' Ghanaian Asserts," *Baltimore Afro-American*, June 14, 1958, 19.

72 "Dynamic African Leader Invades US," *Chicago Defender*, November 7, 1959, 21.

73 "Dynamic African Leader Invades US."

74 "A Day with the First Lady of Guinea During Blair House Visit in D.C.," *Chicago Defender*, November 14, 1959, 21.

75 "Day with the First Lady"; "Tells Role of Women in Guinea," *Baltimore Afro-American*, November 7, 1959, 5; Evelyn Brooks Higginbotham, *Righteous Discontent: The Women's Movement in the Black Baptist Church, 1880–1920* (Cambridge, MA: Harvard University Press, 1993).

76 John Lewis and Michael D'Orso, *Walking with the Wind: A Memoir of the Movement* (New York: Simon and Schuster, 1998), 81; William Edward Burghardt Du Bois, *The Souls of Black Folk: Essays and Sketches* (Chicago: A. C. McClurg, 1903).

77 James Forman, "Letter to George Houser" (July 18, 1962), in *Student Nonviolent Coordinating Committee Papers, 1959–1972* (Sanford, NC: Microfilming Corporation of America, [1982]); Forman, *Making of Black Revolutionaries*, 105.

78 Stokely Carmichael and Michael Ekwueme Thelwell, *Ready for Revolution: The Life and Struggles of Stokely Carmichael (Kwame Ture)* (New York: Scribner, 2003), 163–64.

79 Carmichael and Thelwell, *Ready for Revolution*, 165.

80 James Baldwin, "A Negro Assays on the Negro Mood," *New York Times*, March 12, 1961, 25.

81 Howard Zinn, *SNCC: The New Abolitionists* (Boston: Beacon, 1964), 6, 18.

82 John Lewis, Freedom Riders 50th Anniversary Conference, Chicago, May 22, 2011.

83 Zinn, *New Abolitionists*, 16, 29; Clayborne Carson, *In Struggle: SNCC and the Black Awakening of the 1960s* (Cambridge, MA: Harvard University Press, 1995), 12.

84 "The Sit-Ins—Off Campus and Into Movement," Civil Rights Movement Archive, Civil Rights Movement Veterans, accessed August 2, 2016, www.crmvet.org /images/imgcoll.htm.

85 Sociologists including Charles Tilly, Andrew Jamison, and Ron Eyerman observe that social movements shape public space and create new meanings through their performance of dissent. Describing nonviolent civil disobedience as "performance" does not subvert its sincerity or significance. It accurately reflects the considerable deliberation and agency involved in protests such as boycotts and occupations. Charles Tilly, "Social Movements as Historically Specific Clusters of Political Performances," *Berkeley Journal of Sociology* 38 (1993): 1–30; Andrew Jamison and Ron Eyerman, *Social Movements: A Cognitive Approach* (University Park: Penn State Press, 1991).

86 Zinn, *New Abolitionists*, 24.

87 Zinn, *New Abolitionists*, 21.

88 Barbara Ransby, *Ella Baker and the Black Freedom Movement: A Radical Democratic Vision* (Chapel Hill: University of North Carolina Press, 2003).

89 Ransby, *Black Freedom Movement*.

90 Zinn, *New Abolitionists*, 33.

91 Carson, *In Struggle*, 23.

92 Ella Baker, "Bigger Than a Hamburger," *Southern Patriot*, May 1960, www.crmvet .org/docs/sncc2.htm.

93 SNCC Legacy Project, *One Person, One Vote: The Story of SNCC and the Legacy of the Civil Rights Struggle*, Duke University Library, 2016, www.sncclegacyproject.org /projects/one-person-one-vote.

94 In her oft-cited classic, *The Boundaries of Blackness*, political scientist Cathy Cohen shows how African American elites further marginalize the least advantaged members of their group by enforcing mainstream values and excluding them from resources available within indigenous institutions such as churches, the Black press, etc.

95 Franklin E. Frazier, *The Black Bourgeoisie* (Glencoe: Free Press, 1957).

96 Cleveland Sellers, *The River of No Return: The Autobiography of a Black Militant and the Life and Death of SNCC* (New York: William Morrow, 1973).

97 A. Peter Bailey, interview by Robin J. Hayes, Silver Spring, MD, 2005.

98 Carmichael and Thelwell, *Ready for Revolution*.

99 Aldon Morris, *Origins of the Civil Rights Movement: Black Communities Organizing for Change* (New York: Free Press, 1984).

100 Sellers, *River of No Return*.

101 Harry G. Lefever, *Undaunted by the Fight: Spelman College and the Civil Rights Movement, 1957–1967* (Macon, GA: Mercer University Press, 2005); Howard Zinn, *You Can't Be Neutral on a Moving Train: A Personal History of Our Times* (Boston: Beacon, 2010).

102 Lefever, *Undaunted by the Fight*.

103 "Ruby Doris Smith Robinson," SNCC Digital Gateway, SNCC Legacy Project and Duke University, https://snccdigital.org/people/ruby-doris-smith-robinson.

104 Carmichael and Thelwell, *Ready for Revolution*.

105 Lefever, *Undaunted by the Fight*.

106 Zinn, *New Abolitionists*, 21.

107 Lefever, *Undaunted by the Fight*.

108 Carmichael and Thelwell, *Ready for Revolution*.

109 Carmichael and Thelwell, *Ready for Revolution*.

110 Carmichael and Thelwell, *Ready for Revolution*.

111 Carmichael and Thelwell, *Ready for Revolution*.

112 Raymond Arsenault, *Freedom Riders: 1961 and the Struggle for Racial Justice* (Oxford: Oxford University Press, 2006).

113 Robert (Bob) Moses, interview by Robin J. Hayes, Jackson, MS, 2005.

114 Carmichael and Thelwell, *Ready for Revolution*, 194.

115 "Civil Rights Movement History 1961," Civil Rights Movement Archive, Civil Rights Movement Veterans, www.crmvet.org/tim/timhis61.htm#1961frides.

116 David M. Oshinsky, *Worse Than Slavery: Parchman Farm and the Ordeal of Jim Crow Justice* (New York: Simon and Schuster, 1997), 235.

117 Carson, *In Struggle*, 38; Oshinsky, *Worse Than Slavery*, 235.

118 Oshinsky, *Worse Than Slavery*, 235.

119 Carmichael and Thelwell, *Ready for Revolution*, 194.

120 Carmichael and Thelwell, *Ready for Revolution*, 194.

121 Payne, *Light of Freedom*, 98.

122 "Civil Rights Movement History."

123 Doug McAdam, "Tactical Innovation and the Pace of Insurgency," *American Sociological Review* 48, no. 6 (December 1983): 745–46.

124 Robert D. Benford and Scott A. Hunt, "Dramaturgy and Social Movements: The Social Construction and Communication of Power," *Sociological Inquiry* 62, no. 1 (1992): 43–46.

125 Carson, *In Struggle*, 34.

126 For more on the impact of this compromise, see William Edward Burghardt Du Bois, *Black Reconstruction in America: Toward a History of the Part Which Black Folk Played in the Attempt to Reconstruct Democracy in America, 1860–1880* (Oxford: Oxford University Press, 2014). For an example of how this compromise was legitimated using racist stereotypes about African Americans, see D. W. Griffith's narrative film *The Birth of a Nation* (David W. Griffith Corporation and Epoch Producing Corporation, 1915).

CHAPTER 4: "INDEPENDENCE WITH DANGER"

1 James Hunter Meriwether, *Proudly We Can Be Africans: Black Americans and Africa, 1935–1961* (Chapel Hill: University of North Carolina Press, 2002), 181.

2 The following description of the Berlin Conference is indebted to Adam Hochschild, *King Leopold's Ghost: A Story of Greed, Terror, and Heroism in Colonial Africa* (Boston: Houghton Mifflin Harcourt, 1999), 228–30.

3 Meriwether, *Proudly We Can Be*, 210. For graphic evidence of the abuses endured by the Congolese during Leopold's rule, see Mark Twain, *King Leopold's Soliloquy: A Defense of His Congo Rule* (Boston: P. R. Warren, 1905); Eddie Pimental, "Civilization and the Congo Free State," December 12, 2019, https://arcg.is/joi1z.

4 Herbert M. Howe, *Ambiguous Order: Military Forces in African States* (Boulder: Lynne Rienner, 2001), 231.

5 Meriwether, *Proudly We Can Be*, 211; Hochschild, *King Leopold's Ghost*, 226–32.

6 Ruth M. Slade, *King Leopold's Congo: Aspects of the Development of Race Relations in the Congo Independent State* (Oxford: Oxford University Press, 1962), 179.

7 Joseph Conrad, *Heart of Darkness* [1902], in Joseph Conrad, Heart of Darkness *and Selections from* The Congo Diary (New York: Modern Library, 1999), 1–96.

8 Francis Ford Coppola, *Apocalypse Now*, narrative film (United Artists, 1979); *Spec Ops: The Line*, video game (Yager Development, 2012); Matthew Thomas Payne, "War Bytes: The Critique of Militainment in *Spec Ops: The Line*," *Critical Studies in Media Communication* 31, no. 4 (2014): 265–82.

9 Eduardo Bonilla-Silva, *Racism without Racists: Color-Blind Racism and the Persistence of Racial Inequality in the United States* (Lanham, MD: Rowman and Littlefield, 2006); Charles W. Mills, *The Racial Contract* (Ithaca, NY: Cornell University Press, 1997), 68; Jane Anna Gordon and Neil Roberts, "Introduction: The Project of Creolizing Rousseau," *C. L. R. James Journal: A Review of Caribbean Ideas* 15, no. 1 (Spring 2009): 78.

10 Chinua Achebe, "An Image of Africa," *Massachusetts Review* 18, no. 4 (1977): 787.

11 Achille Mbembe, *On the Postcolony* (Berkeley: University of California Press, 2001).

12 Achebe, "Image of Africa," 787.

13 Hochschild, *King Leopold's Ghost*, 238.

14 Georg Wilhelm Friedrich Hegel and John Sibree, *The Philosophy of History* (Chelmsford: Courier, 2004); Olufemi Taiwo, "Exorcising Hegel's Ghost: Africa's Challenge to Philosophy," *African Studies Quarterly* 1, no. 4 (1998): 3–16.

15 Achebe, "Image of Africa," 790.

16 Meriwether, *Proudly We Can Be*, 211; Robert Craig Johnson, "Heart of Darkness: The Tragedy of the Congo, 1960–1970," *Chandelle: A Journal of Aviation History* 2, no. 3, http://worldatwar.net/chandelle/v2/v2n3/congo.html.

17 "Heart of Darkness."

18 Meriwether, *Proudly We Can Be*, 212.

19 Georges Nzongola-Ntalaja, *The Congo: From Leopold to Kabila: A People's History* (London: Zed Books, 2002).

20 Nzongola-Ntalaja, *Congo*.

21 Nzongola-Ntalaja, *Congo*, 267.

22 Nzongola-Ntalaja, *Congo*, 32.

23 Meriwether, *Proudly We Can Be*, 211.

24 Leo Zeilig, *Lumumba: Africa's Lost Leader* (London: Haus, 2008), 18; "Patrice Lumumba," People's Friendship University of Russia, http://people.sci.pfu.edu.ru/asemenov/LUMUMBA/Lumumba.htm; "Patrice Émery Lumumba," South African History Online, accessed February 26, 2017, www.sahistory.org.za/people/patrice-lumumba.

25 Zeilig, *Lumumba*, 18.

26 Oliver Klein and Lauren Licata, "When Group Representations Serve Social Change: The Speeches of Patrice Lumumba During the Congolese Decolonization," *British Journal of Social Psychology* (2003): 42, 586, 588.

27 Meriwether, *Proudly We Can Be*, 211–12.

28 Nzongola-Ntalaja, *Congo*, 68.

29 David Rooney, *Kwame Nkrumah: The Political Kingdom in the Third World* (New York: St. Martin's Press, 1988).

30 Ali Mazrui, *Nkrumah's Legacy and Africa's Triple Heritage between Globalization and Counter Terrorism* (Accra: Ghana Universities Press, 2004).

31 The additional nations who organized the first conference were Ethiopia, Liberia, Libya, Morocco, Tunisia, and the United Arab Republic (later Egypt and Syria). Apartheid South Africa was not included.

32 Georges Nzongola-Ntalaja, *Patrice Lumumba* (Athens: Ohio University Press, 2014), 71.

33 Kwame Nkrumah and Jomo Kenyatta Ochwada, "Africans Demand Liberation," digitized newsreel footage (Pathé News, 1958), British Pathé.

34 Nkrumah and Kenyatta Ochwada, "Africans Demand Liberation."

35 Nkrumah and Kenyatta Ochwada, "Africans Demand Liberation."

36 Nzongola-Ntalaja, *Patrice*, 71.

37 Zeilig, *Lumumba*, 67.

38 "Heart of Darkness."

39 "Nationalist Congo Riots Stun Belgians in Africa," *Chicago Defender*, January 17, 1959, 1, 5.

40 Nzongola-Ntalaja, *Patrice*, 75–76.

41 Nzongola-Ntalaja, *Patrice*, 75–76.

42 Nzongola-Ntalaja, *Patrice*, 79.

43 "Congolese Jeer King of Belgium," *Chicago Defender*, January 9, 1960, 3.

44 "Heart of Darkness."

45 Meriwether, *Proudly We Can Be*, 213.

46 "King Baudouin Declares Congo Independent," digitized newsreel footage (Pathé News, July 1960), British Pathé.

47 Bonilla-Silva, *Racism without Racists*.

48 Mills, *Racial Contract*.

49 "Patrice Lumumba's Independence Day Speech, June 30, 1960," *San Francisco Bay View*, June 30, 2009.

50 George M. Fredrickson, *Racism: A Short History* (Princeton University Press, 2015), 100–101.

51 Meriwether, *Proudly We Can Be*, 213.

52 "Marred: M. Lumumba's Offensive Speech in King's Presence," *Guardian*, July 1, 1960, www.theguardian.com/world/1960/jul/01/congo.

53 "Bishop in Congo Condemns Propaganda," *Amsterdam News*, August 13, 1960, 23.

54 "Report from Africa: Dr. Pierce Tells of Whites Fear," *Amsterdam News*, July 30, 1960, 1, 35.

55 Meriwether, *Proudly We Can Be*, 215.

56 "Nkrumah Leads States Supporting Lumumba," *Amsterdam News*, October 1, 1960, 8.

57 "Ghana's Stand on the Congo," *Amsterdam News*, September 17, 1960, 11.

58 The following paragraph is indebted to Meriwether, *Proudly We Can Be*, 215–17.

59 "Congo Senator Is Harlem Street Speaker," *Amsterdam News*, July 30, 1960, 1.

60 Stokely Carmichael and Michael Ekwueme Thelwell, *Ready for Revolution: The Life and Struggles of Stokely Carmichael (Kwame Ture)* (New York: Scribner, 2003).

61 Carmichael recalled that in the late 1950s and early 1960s, former members of Marcus Garvey's Universal Negro Improvement Association, including Queen Mother Moore, would routinely speak from stepladders adorned with red, black, and green flags (a symbol of Pan-Africanism). Carmichael and Thelwell, *Ready for Revolution.*

62 "Harlem Street Speaker."

63 "The Way It Is," *Amsterdam News,* July 30, 1960, 10.

64 Roy Wilkins, "Along This Way: Freedom Fighters," *Amsterdam News,* January 27, 1962, 11.

65 Meriwether, *Proudly We Can Be,* 222.

66 David F. Schmitz, "Senator Frank Church, the Ford Administration, and the Challenges of Post-Vietnam Foreign Policy," *Peace & Change* 21, no. 4 (1996): 438–63.

67 George Barner, "'Richest Country in the World?': Katanga Leader Bars Reunion with Congo," *Amsterdam News,* October 22, 1960, 35.

68 Meriwether, *Proudly We Can Be,* 219.

69 The following description of events is indebted to Nzongola-Ntalaja, *Congo,* 98, 110–13.

70 Ludo De Witte, *The Assassination of Lumumba* (New York: Verso Books, 2002).

71 Meriwether, *Proudly We Can Be,* 232.

72 Meriwether, *Proudly We Can Be,* 239.

73 Meriwether, *Proudly We Can Be,* 234.

74 "Demonstrations Organized in Europe and at the United Nations after the Death of Patrice Lumumba," digitized newsreel footage (Universal International News, 1961), Critical Past.

75 Ronald W. Walters, *Pan Africanism in the African Diaspora: An Analysis of Modern Afrocentric Politics* (Detroit: Wayne State University Press, 1997), 95.

76 Meriwether, *Proudly We Can Be,* 233.

77 "They'll Try Again: Nationalists Break Up NAACP's Harlem Rally," *Amsterdam News,* May 27, 1961, 13.

78 Meriwether, *Proudly We Can Be,* 209.

79 Harry G. Lefever, *Undaunted by the Fight: Spelman College and the Civil Rights Movement, 1957–1967* (Macon, GA: Mercer University Press, 2005).

80 Alistair Horne, *A Savage War of Peace: Algeria, 1954–1962* (New York: New York Review of Books Classics, 2011), loc. 2944 of 15340, Kindle.

81 Charles P. Howard, "Free Algeria at Crossroads; Faces French Legacy of Woes," *Baltimore Afro-American,* December 21, 1962, 20.

82 Robert H. Jackson and Carl G. Rosberg, "Why Africa's Weak States Persist: The Empirical and the Juridical in Statehood," *World Politics* 35, no. 1 (October 1982): 1–24.

83 Max Weber, *The Theory of Social and Economic Organization,* ed. Talcott Parsons (New York: Free Press, 1964), 155–56.

CHAPTER 5: "OUR PROBLEM IS YOUR PROBLEM"

1   Richard Heffner, "*Open Mind* with Richard Heffner, 1963," YouTube, accessed March 10, 2017, www.youtube.com/watch?v=QHPxQsjAp-k.

2   William Edward Burghardt Du Bois, *The Souls of Black Folk: Essays and Sketches* (Chicago: A. C. McClurg, 1903). See also Darlene Clark Hine, "Rape and the Inner Lives of Black Women in the Middle West," *Signs: Journal of Women in Culture and Society* 14, no. 4 (1989): 912–20, for the impact of a similar phenomenon: "dissemblance" on African American women.

3   Manning Marable, *Malcolm X: A Life of Reinvention* (New York: Penguin, 2011), 189–90.

4   The complete life story of Malcolm X is famously and vividly detailed in Malcolm X and Alex Haley, *The Autobiography of Malcolm X* (New York: Ballantine Books, 2015); Spike Lee, *Malcolm X*, narrative film (Warner Home Video, 1992); Orlando Bagwell and Judy Richardson, "Malcolm X: Make It Plain," documentary film (Blackstone, 1994).

5   The description of this meeting between Maya Angelou and Malcolm X is indebted to Marable, *Malcolm X*, 189–90.

6   Civil Rights Act of 1964, Pub. L. No. 88–352, 78 Stat. 241 (July 2, 1964).

7   Clayborne Carson, *In Struggle: SNCC and the Black Awakening of the 1960s* (Cambridge: Harvard University Press, 1995), 89.

8   John Lewis, "Original Draft of John Lewis' Speech [at March on Washington]," Moyers, July 24, 2013, http://billmoyers.com/content/two-versions-of-john-lewis -speech.

9   Carson, *In Struggle*, 94.

10   Lewis, "Original Draft."

11   Howard Zinn, *SNCC: The New Abolitionists* (Boston: Beacon, 1964), 208.

12   Zinn, *New Abolitionists*, 243.

13   John Lewis and Michael D'Orso, *Walking with the Wind: A Memoir of the Movement* (New York: Simon and Schuster, 1998), 244.

14   Lewis and D'Orso, *Walking with the Wind*, 101.

15   A. Peter Bailey, interview by Robin J. Hayes, Silver Spring, MD, 2005.

16   Sylvester Leaks, interview by Robin J. Hayes, Brooklyn, NY, 2005.

17   Marable, *Malcolm X*, 190.

18   Robert Franklin Williams, *Negroes with Guns* (Detroit: Wayne State University Press, 1962).

19   Marable, *Malcolm X*, 272.

20   Marable, *Malcolm X*, 273.

21   Marable, *Malcolm X*, 289–92.

22   Marable, *Malcolm X*, 294.

23   Malcolm X, letter to James Booker, April 25, 1964.

24   William Sales, *From Civil Rights to Black Liberation: Malcolm X and the Organization of Afro-American Unity* (Boston: South End, 1994), 72.

25 Robin J. Hayes, *Black and Cuba*, documentary film (Progressive Pupil, 2014).

26 Vicki Garvin, "Rough Copy of Address to Komozi Woodard's Class," in *The Black Power Movement* (Bethesda, MD: University Publications of America, n.d.), 26; Sales, *Civil Rights to Black Liberation*.

27 Ronald W. Walters, *Pan Africanism in the African Diaspora: An Analysis of Modern Afrocentric Political Movements* (Detroit: Wayne State University Press, 1997), 101.

28 Walters, *Pan Africanism*, 114.

29 Garvin, "Rough Copy."

30 Garvin, "Rough Copy."

31 Kevin K. Gaines, *American Africans in Ghana: Black Expatriates in the Civil Rights Era* (Chapel Hill: University of North Carolina Press, 2006).

32 Garvin, "Rough Copy."

33 Sales, *Civil Rights to Black Liberation*; Malcolm, *Autobiography*.

34 Malcolm, *Autobiography*, 411; "The Trip," In FBI File on Malcolm X.

35 James Booker, "Is Mecca Trip Changing Malcolm?" *Amsterdam News*, May 23, 1964, 3.

36 Malcolm, *Autobiography*, 410.

37 Marable, *Malcolm X*, 290.

38 Booker, "Mecca Trip Changing Malcolm?"

39 Alistair Horne, *A Savage War of Peace: Algeria, 1954–1962* (New York: New York Review of Books Classics, 2011), locs. 11882–930 of 15340, Kindle.

40 Malcolm, *Autobiography*.

41 Horne, *Savage War of Peace*.

42 Malcolm, *Autobiography*.

43 Malcolm, *Autobiography*.

44 Malcolm X, "Statement Announcing Formation of OAAU," In FBI File on the Organization of Afro-American Unity.

45 John Henrik Clarke's foundational works include *Marcus Garvey and the Vision of Africa* (New York: Vintage, 1974) and *Black Titan: WEB Du Bois* (Boston: Beacon Press, 1970). Gloria Richardson was most well-known for her involvement in SNCC's campaign to integrate facilities in Cambridge, Maryland. Sharon Harley, "'Chronicle of a Death Foretold': Gloria Richardson, the Cambridge Movement, and the Radical Black Activist Tradition," *Sisters in the Struggle: African American Women in the Civil Rights–Black Power Movement* (New York: NYU Press, 2001), 174–96.

46 Federal Bureau of Investigation (FBI), "A Statement of Basic Objectives of the Organization of Afro-American Unity," In FBI File on the Organization of Afro-American Unity.

47 FBI, "Internal Security—Miscellaneous Racial Matter," In FBI File on the Organization of Afro-American Unity.

48 Seth M. Markle, "Brother Malcolm, Comrade Babu: Black Internationalism and the Politics of Friendship," *Biography* 36, no. 3 (Summer 2013): 549.

49 Milton Henry, "Interview with Malcolm X," in *Malcolm X Speaks: Selected Speeches and Statements*, ed. George Breitman (New York: Grove, 1965), 81, 82–83.

50 Markle, "Brother Malcolm," 546, 550.

51 Markle, "Brother Malcolm," 550–51.

52 Henry, "Interview with Malcolm X," 82.

53 Federal Bureau of Investigation, Special Agent in Charge, New York, City Field Office. "Teletype to the Directory, FBI: Organization of Afro-American Unity," in FBI File on the Organization of Afro-American Unity.

54 Malcolm X, "Last Answers and Interviews," in *Malcolm X Speaks: Selected Speeches and Statements*, ed. George Breitman (New York: Grove, 1965), 202.

55 Malcolm X, "At the Audubon," in *Malcolm X Speaks: Selected Speeches and Statements*, ed. George Breitman (New York: Grove, 1965), 101.

56 FBI, "Teletype," FBI File on the Organization of Afro-American Unity.

57 Markle, "Brother Malcolm," 552.

58 Markle, "Brother Malcolm," 550.

59 Markle, "Brother Malcolm," 553.

60 Markle, "Brother Malcolm," 554.

61 Malcolm, "At the Audubon," 101.

62 Malcolm, "At the Audubon," 102.

63 Markle, "Brother Malcolm," 557.

64 Bailey, interview by Hayes.

65 Malcolm, "Confrontation with an Expert," in *Malcolm X Speaks: Selected Speeches and Statements*, ed. George Breitman (New York: Grove, 1965), 182.

66 Marable, *Malcolm X*, 180.

67 Malcolm, "Last Answers and Interviews."

68 Marable, *Malcolm X*, 403.

CHAPTER 6: "MISSISSIPPI EYES"

1 James Forman, *The Making of Black Revolutionaries: A Personal Account* (New York: Macmillan, 1972), 105.

2 Charles M. Payne, *I've Got the Light of Freedom: The Organizing Tradition and the Mississippi Freedom Struggle* (Berkeley: University of California Press, 1995), 101.

3 Howard Zinn, *SNCC: The New Abolitionists* (Boston: Beacon, 1964), 64.

4 Zinn, *New Abolitionists*, 64.

5 Zinn, *New Abolitionists*, 88.

6 Zinn, *New Abolitionists*, 88.

7 Doug McAdam, *Freedom Summer* (New York: Oxford University Press, 1988); Payne, *Light of Freedom*, 100.

8 Payne, *Light of Freedom*, 100.

9 Payne, *Light of Freedom*, 165–66.

10 Payne, *Light of Freedom*, 163.

11 Cleveland Sellers, *The River of No Return: The Autobiography of a Black Militant and the Life and Death of SNCC* (New York: William Morrow, 1973), 54.

12 John Lewis and Michael D'Orso, *Walking with the Wind: A Memoir of the Movement* (New York: Simon and Schuster, 1998), 260–61.

13 Sellers, *River of No Return*, 83.

14 Zinn, *New Abolitionists*, 95.

15 Zinn, *New Abolitionists*, 86–88.

16 "Fact Sheet on Greenwood," *Amsterdam News*, April 11, 1964, 26.

17 Barbara Ransby, *Ella Baker and the Black Freedom Movement: A Radical Democratic Vision* (Chapel Hill: University of North Carolina Press, 2003).

18 Carol Mueller, "Ella Baker and the Origins of 'Participatory Democracy,'" in *The Black Studies Reader*, ed. Jacqueline Bobo, Cynthia Hudley, and Claudine Michel (London: Psychology Press, 2004), 84.

19 Mueller, "Ella Baker," 85–87.

20 Stokely Carmichael and Michael Ekwueme Thelwell, *Ready for Revolution: The Life and Struggles of Stokely Carmichael (Kwame Ture)* (New York: Scribner, 2003), 319.

21 Payne, *Light of Freedom*, 154.

22 Payne, *Light of Freedom*, 154–55.

23 Sellers, *River of No Return*, 56.

24 Payne, *Light of Freedom*, 300.

25 Zinn, *New Abolitionists*, 15.

26 Payne, *Light of Freedom*, 332–33.

27 Iris Marion Young, *Justice and the Politics of Difference* (Princeton, NJ: Princeton University Press, 2011).

28 Sellers, *River of No Return*, 83.

29 Charles Cobb, "Some Notes on Education," n.d., Civil Rights Movement Veterans Archive, www.crmvet.org/info/cobb_education.pdf.

30 Student Nonviolent Coordinating Committee, "SNCC Position Paper: Women in the Movement," in *Let Nobody Turn Us Around: Voices of Resistance, Reform and Renewal*, ed. Manning Marable and Leith Mullings (Lanham, MD: Rowman & Littlefield, 2000), 422–25; Lewis and D'Orso, *Walking with the Wind*, 260.

31 Paulo Freire, *Pedagogy of the Oppressed* (London: Bloomsbury, 2000).

32 Payne, *Light of Freedom*, 303.

33 Payne, *Light of Freedom*, 202.

34 Payne, *Light of Freedom*, 303.

35 William Edward Burghardt Du Bois, *Black Reconstruction in America: Toward a History of the Part Which Black Folk Played in the Attempt to Reconstruct Democracy in America, 1860–1880* (New Brunswick, NJ: Transaction, 2013).

36 Isabel Wilkerson, *The Warmth of Other Suns: The Epic Story of America's Great Migration* (New York: Vintage, 2011).

37 The following description of counterinsurgent violence during Freedom Summer is indebted to Doug McAdam, *Freedom Summer* (Oxford: Oxford University Press, 1990).

38 Lewis and D'Orso, *Walking with the Wind*, 268.

39 Lewis and D'Orso, *Walking with the Wind*, 273.

40 Stokely Carmichael, *Stokely Speaks: Black Power Back to Pan-Africanism* (New York: Random House, 1971), 71.

41 Susan Ferriss and Ricardo Sandoval, *The Fight in the Fields: César Chávez and the Farmworkers Movement*, documentary film (Paradigm Productions, 1997).

42 Fannie Lou Hamer, "It's in Your Hands," History Is a Weapon, 1971, www.history isaweapon.com/defcon1/yourhandshamer.html.

43 "Aaron Henry," SNCC Digital Gateway, SNCC Legacy Project and Duke University, https://snccdigital.org/people/aaron-henry.

44 John Howard, *Men Like That: A Southern Queer History* (Chicago: University of Chicago Press, 1999).

45 Clayborne Carson, *In Struggle: SNCC and the Black Awakening of the 1960s* (Cambridge, MA: Harvard University Press, 1995), 108.

46 Carson, *In Struggle*, 108.

47 Carson, *In Struggle*, 278–79.

48 Carson, *In Struggle*, 278–79.

49 Carson *In Struggle*, 126.

50 Eric R. Burner, *"And Gently He Shall Lead Them": Robert Parris Moses and Civil Rights in Mississippi* (New York: NYU Press, 1994), 189.

51 Fannie Lou Hamer, "Speech to the Credentials Committee of the Democratic National Convention," 1964, www.americanrhetoric.com/speeches/fannielou hamercredentialscommittee.htm.

52 Hamer, "Speech to the Credentials Committee."

53 Robert (Bob) Moses, interview by Robin J. Hayes, Jackson, Mississippi, 2005.

54 Moses, interview by Hayes.

55 Lewis and D'Orso, *Walking with the Wind*, 282.

56 Moses, interview by Hayes.

57 Lewis and D'Orso, *Walking with the Wind*, 284.

58 Blackside, Inc., "Interview with Harry Belafonte," May 15, 1989, for *Eyes on the Prize II*, Washington University Libraries, Film and Media Archive, Henry Hampton Collection, http://digital.wustl.edu/e/eii/eiiweb/bel5427.0417.013harrybelafonte.html.

59 Lewis and D'Orso, *Walking with the Wind*, 284.

60 Blackside, "Interview with Harry Belafonte."

61 Fannie Lou Hamer, "I'm Sick and Tired of Being Sick and Tired," speech delivered with Malcolm X at the Williams Institutional CME Church, Harlem, NY, December 20, 1964, Civil Rights Movement Archive, Civil Rights Movement Veterans, www.crmvet.org/docs/flh64.htm.

62 Lewis and D'Orso, *Walking with the Wind*, 284.

63 Forman, *Making of Black Revolutionaries*, 409.

64 Harry G. Lefever, *Undaunted by the Fight: Spelman College and the Civil Rights Movement, 1957–1967* (Macon, GA: Mercer University Press, 2005), 206.

65 Forman, *Making of Black Revolutionaries*, 408.

66 Forman, *Making of Black Revolutionaries*, 410.

67 Lewis and D'Orso, *Walking with the Wind*, 286.

68 Carson, *In Struggle*, 134.

69 Carmichael and Thelwell, *Ready for Revolution*, 613.

70 For more on cultural retention, see Robert Farris Thompson, *Flash of the Spirit: African & Afro-American Art and Philosophy* (New York: Vintage, 2010).

71 Lefever, *Undaunted by the Fight*, 206.

72 Lefever, *Undaunted by the Fight*, 207.

73 Dona Richards, "Memo re: a SNCC African Project" (c. 1961–1967), in *Student Nonviolent Coordinating Committee Papers, 1959–1972* (Sanford, NC: Microfilming Corporation of America, [1982]).

74 Carson, *In Struggle*, 135.

75 Carson, *In Struggle*, 137.

76 Forman, *Making of Black Revolutionaries*, 409.

77 Richards, "SNCC African Project."

78 Forman, *Making of Black Revolutionaries*, 410.

79 Forman, *Making of Black Revolutionaries*, 207.

80 Ms. Richards later changed her name to Marimba Ani and became an anthropologist and African studies scholar.

81 Richards, "SNCC African Project."

CHAPTER 7: "LOVE OUR COMMUNITY"

1 Michael Dawson, *Behind the Mule: Race and Class in African-American Politics* (Princeton: Princeton University Press, 1997), 227–29.

2 George Breitman, *The Last Year of Malcolm X: The Evolution of a Revolutionary* (New York: Merit, 1967), 35.

3 Breitman, *Last Year of Malcolm X*, 35–36.

4 Breitman, *Last Year of Malcolm X*, 71.

5 Breitman, *Last Year of Malcolm X*, 79.

6 Manning Marable, *Malcolm X: A Life of Reinvention* (New York: Penguin, 2011), 401–2.

7 Marable, *Malcolm X*, 409.

8 Marable, *Malcolm X*, 410.

9 Marable, *Malcolm X*, 410.

10 Marable, *Malcolm X*, 416.

11 Marable, *Malcolm X*, 417.

12 Marable, *Malcolm X*, 419.

13 Marable, *Malcolm X*, 420.

14 Marable, *Malcolm X*, 428.

15 Marable, *Malcolm X*, 428.

16 Marable, *Malcolm X*, 430.

17 The description of this day's events in the Audubon Ballroom is indebted to Marable, *Malcolm X*, 434–37.

18 James Booker, "30,000 Mourn Malcolm X," *Amsterdam News*, March 6, 1965, 33.

19 Marable, *Malcolm X*, 458.

20 Marable, *Malcolm X*, 459.

21 "Malcolm X's Sister Takes Over," *Amsterdam News*, March 20, 1965, 8.

22 Robert (Bob) Moses, interview by Robin J. Hayes, Jackson, Mississippi, 2005.

23 Roy Reed, "'Bloody Sunday' Was Year Ago; Now Selma Negroes Are Hopeful," *New York Times*, March 6, 1966, 76.

24 "SNCC Workers Move to 9 Ala. Counties," *Amsterdam News*, May 8, 1965, 3.

25 Hasan Kwame Jeffries, *Bloody Lowndes: Civil Rights and Black Power in Alabama's Black Belt* (New York: NYU Press, 2010).

26 "SNCC Workers Move."

27 Stokely Carmichael, "Black Power Address at Berkeley," *American Rhetoric: Top 100 Speeches*, 1966, www.americanrhetoric.com/speeches/stokelycarmichaelblack power.html.

28 "An International Consciousness, Part 1," SNCC Digital Gateway, SNCC Legacy Project and Duke University, https://snccdigital.org/our-voices/internationalism /part-1.

29 Cleveland Sellers, *The River of No Return: The Autobiography of a Black Militant and the Life and Death of SNCC* (New York: William Morrow, 1973).

30 Gillo Pontecorvo, *The Battle of Algiers*, narrative film (Criterion Collection, 2004).

31 "International Consciousness, Part 1."

32 Jeffries, *Bloody Lowndes*.

33 Student Nonviolent Coordinating Committee, "Position Paper on Black Power," in *Modern Black Nationalism: From Marcus Garvey to Louis Farrakhan*, ed. William L. Van Deburg (New York: New York University Press, 1966), 119–26.

34 Clayborne Carson, *In Struggle: SNCC and the Black Awakening of the 1960s* (Cambridge: Harvard University Press, 1995), 151.

35 Carson, *In Struggle*, 151.

36 Carson, *In Struggle*, 308.

37 Blackside, Inc., "Interview with Harry Belafonte," May 15, 1989, for *Eyes on the Prize II*. Washington University Libraries, Film and Media Archive, Henry Hampton Collection, http://digital.wustl.edu/e/eii/eiiweb/bel5427.0417.013 harrybelafonte.html.

38 Student Nonviolent Coordinating Committee, "SNCC Position Paper: Women in the Movement," in *Let Nobody Turn Us Around: Voices of Resistance, Reform and Renewal*, ed. Manning Marable and Leith Mullings (Lanham: Rowman & Littlefield, 2000), 422–25.

39 Student Nonviolent Coordinating Committee, "SNCC Position Paper."

40 "Guevara, in Algeria, Sees Ben Bella for a Half Hour," *New York Times*, December 20, 1964.

41 Adam Bernstein, "Ahmed Ben Bella, Militant Leader in Algeria's Struggle for Independence, Dies at 96," *Washington Post*, April 11, 2012.

42 Alistair. Horne, *A Savage War of Peace: Algeria 1954–1962* (New York: New York Review of Books Classics, 2011), locs. 11882–11930 of 15340, Kindle.

43 Charles P. Howard, "Ghana Plot Was Engineered from Outside," *Africa and the World* 2, no. 20 (May 1966): 16.

44 Simon Anekwe, "Tells Why Ghana Ousted Nkrumah," *Amsterdam News*, October 15, 1966, 1.

45 Howard, "Ghana Plot Was Engineered," 20.

46 Anekwe, "Ghana Ousted Nkrumah," 31.

47 Howard, "Ghana Plot Was Engineered," 16.

48 Kwame Nkrumah, "My Dear Brother and President: Thank You Letter to Toure After Coup," 1966, containers 154–9, p. 4, Kwame Nkrumah Papers, Manuscript Division, Moorland-Spingarn Research Center, Howard University, Washington, DC.

49 Christopher Andrew and Vasili Mitrohkin, *The World Was Going Our Way: The KGB and the Battle for the Third World* (New York: Basic Books, 2006); John Stockwell, *In Search of Enemies: A CIA Story* (New York: W. W. Norton, 1978), 201n; Seymour Hersh, "CIA Said to Have Aided Plotters Who Overthrew Nkrumah in Ghana," *New York Times*, repr. in *Dirty Work 2: The CIA in Africa*, ed. Ellen Ray, William Schaap, Karl Van Meter, and Louis Wolf (Secaucus, NJ: Lyle Stuart, 1979), 159–62; John Prados, *Safe for Democracy: The Secret Wars of the CIA* (Chicago: Ivan R. Dee, 2006).

50 Nkrumah, "My Dear Brother."

51 Doug McAdam, "The Framing Function of Movement Tactics: Strategic Dramaturgy in the American Civil Rights Movement," in *Comparative Perspectives on Social Movements: Political Opportunities, Mobilizing Structures, and Cultural Framings*, ed. Doug McAdam, John D. McCarthy, and Mayer N. Zald (Cambridge: Cambridge University Press, 1996), 338–55; Mayer N. Zald, "Culture, Ideology and Strategic Framing," in McAdam, McCarthy, and Zald, *Comparative Perspectives on Social Movements*, 261–74.

52 Carson, *In Struggle*, 105.

53 Charles J. Stewart, "The Evolution of a Revolution: Stokely Carmichael and the Rhetoric of Black Power," *Quarterly Journal of Speech* 83, no. 4 (1997): 429–46.

54 Stewart, "Evolution of a Revolution," 433.

55 The following description of this event is indebted to Stewart, "Evolution of a Revolution," 433–34.

56 Stewart, "Evolution of a Revolution," 433–34.

57 Carson, *In Struggle*, 276–77.

58 "Interview with Stokely Carmichael" (1967), *El Djeich: Magazine of the People's National Army of Algeria*, in *Student Nonviolent Coordinating Committee Papers, 1959–1972* (Sanford, NC: [1982]).

59 James Booker, "Black Power Goes Political: Pouncing Panther Portrays Power," *Amsterdam News*, September 10, 1966, 1, 2.

60 "The Position of SNCC on Its Black Power Philosophy Has Shaken the U.S.," *Amsterdam News*, September 10, 1966, 31.

61 Kwame Ture and Charles V. Hamilton, *Black Power: The Politics of Liberation in America* (New York: Vintage, 1992).

62 "Position of SNCC," 31.

63 Stokely Carmichael, *My Dear President Nkrumah: Carmichael Writing from Cairo*, containers 154-3, p. 2, 1967, Kwame Nkrumah Papers, Manuscript Division, Moorland-Spingarn Research Center, Howard University, Washington, DC.

64 Carson, *In Struggle*, 201.

65 Carson, *In Struggle*, 255.

CHAPTER 8: "WE HAVE COME BACK"

1 Peniel E. Joseph, "Dashikis and Democracy: Black Studies, Student Activism, and the Black Power Movement," *Journal of African American History* 88, no. 2 (2003): 187.

2 Joseph, "Dashikis and Democracy," 187.

3 Donna Jean Murch, *Living for the City: Migration, Education, and the Rise of the Black Panther Party in Oakland, California* (Chapel Hill: University of North Carolina Press, 2010).

4 Huey P. Newton, *Revolutionary Suicide* (New York: Penguin, 2009), 2.

5 Bobby Seale, "Bobby Seale Speech at Free Huey Rally, February 1968," Pacifica Radio/UC Berkeley Social Activism Sound Recording Project, https://guides.lib .berkeley.edu/c.php?g=819842&p=5923284.

6 *Black Panther*, documentary film (California Newsreel, 1968).

7 James Forman, *The Making of Black Revolutionaries: A Personal Account* (New York: Macmillan, 1972), 531–32.

8 James Forman, "For Immediate Release: Statement from SNCC Delegation at the United Nations Conference on Racism, Colonialism and Apartheid" (August 28, 1967), in *Student Nonviolent Coordinating Committee Papers, 1959–1972* (Sanford, NC: Microfilming Corporation of America, [1982]).

9 Stanley Nelson, *The Black Panthers: Vanguard of the Revolution*, documentary film (PBS Independent Lens and Firelight Films, 2016).

10 Peniel E. Joseph, *Waiting 'Til the Midnight Hour: A Narrative History of Black Power in America* (New York: Holt Paperbacks, 2007).

11 Seale, "Speech at Free Huey Rally."

12 Carole Lyles, "Joan Gets Out," *Amsterdam News*, July 11, 1970, 1, 37.

13 Catherine Breslin, "One Year Later: The Radicalization of the Panther 13 Jury," *New York Magazine*, May 29, 1972, 3.

14 Alondra Nelson, *Body and Soul: The Black Panther Party and the Fight Against Medical Discrimination* (Minneapolis: University of Minnesota Press, 2011).

15 "Panthers Feed Kids," *Amsterdam News*, May 31, 1969, 1; "Panthers to Clothe the Poor," *Amsterdam News*, August 23, 1969, 2.

16 William L. Van Deburg, *New Day in Babylon: The Black Power Movement and American Culture, 1965–1975* (Chicago: University of Chicago Press, 1992).

17 Van Deburg, *New Day in Babylon*.

18 "Ten Point Program and Platform of the Black Student Unions," in *The Black Panthers Speak*, ed. Phillip S. Foner (New York: DeCapo, 2002), 1–6.

19 John H. Bunzel, "Black Studies at San Francisco State," in *The African American Studies Reader*, ed. Nathaniel Norment Jr. (Durham, NC: Carolina Academic Press, 2001), 202.

20 Van Deburg, *New Day in Babylon*, 67.

21 Van Deburg, *New Day in Babylon*, 71.

22 Van Deburg, *New Day in Babylon*, 65–66.

23 Robert L. Harris, "The Intellectual and Institutional Development in Africana Studies," in *The Black Studies Reader*, ed. Jacqueline Bobo, Cynthia Hudley and Claudine Michel (New York: Routledge, 2004), 15–20; Delores P. Aldridge and Carlene Young, *Out of the Revolution: The Development of Africana Studies* (Lanham: Lexington Books, 2000).

24 Barbara Easley-Cox, interview by Robin J. Hayes, Philadelphia, July 22, 2005.

25 Easley-Cox, interview by Hayes.

26 Melvin Dickson, interview by Robin J. Hayes, Berkeley, November 22, 2007.

27 David Hilliard and Lewis Cole, *This Side of Glory: The Autobiography of David Hilliard and the Story of the Black Panther Party* (Boston: Little, Brown, 1993).

28 "An International Consciousness, Part 2," SNCC Digital Gateway, SNCC Legacy Project and Duke University, 2017, https://snccdigital.org/our-voices/inter nationalism/part-2.

29 "International Consciousness, Part 2."

30 "International Consciousness, Part 2."

31 "International Consciousness, Part 2."

32 "International Consciousness, Part 2."

33 *CBS News with Walter Cronkite*, breaking news announcement (Columbia Broadcasting System, April 4, 1968).

34 Stokely Carmichael, "Press Conference," digitized newsreel footage (Huntley Film Archives, April 5, 1968), YouTube, accessed October 21, 2019, www.youtube.com /watch?v=dwYYvOjsxjE.

35 Robert Eratz, "Hoover Note Revealed Fear of Carmichael as 'Black Messiah,'" *Chicago Tribune*, February 10, 1976, 3.

36 Ward Churchill, "'To Disrupt, Discredit, and Destroy': The FBI's Secret War against the Black Panther Party," in *Liberation, Imagination and the Black Panther Party*, ed. Kathleen Cleaver and George Katsiaficas (New York: Routledge, 2014), 89–92; Joshua Bloom and Waldo E. Martin, *Black against Empire: The History and Politics of the Black Panther Party* (Berkeley: University of California Press, 2013), 122–23.

37 Karen Grigsby Bates, "Bobby Hutton: The Killing That Catapulted the Black Panthers to Fame," NPR, April 6, 2018, www.npr.org/2018/04/06/600055767/bobby -hutton-the-killing-that-catapulted-the-black-panthers-to-fame.

38 Eldridge Cleaver, "Affidavit #2: Shootout in Oakland," in *Post-Prison Writings and Speeches*, ed. Eldridge Cleaver and Robert Scheer (New York: Random House, 1969), 80–94.

39 Dickson, interview by Hayes.

40 "This Day in History—April 6, 1968: Bobby Hutton Killed by Oakland Police," Zinn Education Project, www.zinnedproject.org/news/tdih/murder-of-bobby-hutton.

41 Kathleen Cleaver and Julia Wright Hervé, "Interviews Kathleen Cleaver," *Black Scholar* 3, no. 4 (1971): 56.

42 Robyn C. Spencer, *The Revolution Has Come: Black Power, Gender, and the Black Panther Party in Oakland* (Durham, NC: Duke University Press, 2016).

43 Elaine Brown, *A Taste of Power: A Black Woman's Story* (New York: Anchor, 2015).

44 Josh Meyer, "Ex-Fugitive Agrees to 12 Years in 1969 Hijacking," *Los Angeles Times*, May 17, 2001.

45 Kathleen Neal Cleaver, interview by Robin J. Hayes, New Haven, CT, May 16, 2006.

46 Robin J. Hayes, *Black and Cuba*, documentary film (Progressive Pupil, 2015).

47 Henry Louis Gates and Eldridge Cleaver, "Cuban Experience: Eldridge Cleaver on Ice," *Transition* no. 49 (1975): 33.

48 Kathleen Neal Cleaver, "Back to Africa: The Evolution of the International Section of the Black Panther Party (1969–1972)," in *The Black Panther Party (Reconsidered)*, ed. Charles E. Jones (Baltimore, MD: Black Classic, 1998), 217.

49 Nathan Hare, "A Report on the Pan-African Cultural Festival," *Black Scholar* 1, no. 1 (November 1969): 2–10.

50 Hare, "Pan-African Cultural Festival," 3.

51 Hare, "Pan-African Cultural Festival," 3.

52 Elaine Mokhtefi, *Algiers, Third World Capital: Black Panthers, Freedom Fighters, Revolutionaries* (New York: Verso Books, 2018).

53 "First Pan-African Festival Opens in Algiers," digitized newsreel footage (AP Archive, July 22, 1969), YouTube, accessed January 25, 2019, www.youtube.com/watch?v=to_FiiDceZc.

54 Hare, "Pan-African Cultural Festival," 8.

55 Other musicians in the performance included Clifford Thornton, Grachan Moncur III, Dave Burrell, Alan Silva, and Sunny Murray. Archie Shepp, *Live at the Pan-African Festival*, BYG Records, 1971.

56 Michael L. Clemons and Charles E. Jones, "Global Solidarity: The Black Panther Party in the International Arena," in *Liberation, Imagination and the Black Panther Party: A New Look at the Panthers and Their Legacy*, ed. Kathleen Cleaver and George Katsiaficas (New York: Routledge, 2001), 29.

57 Cleaver, "Back to Africa," 227.

58 Cleaver, "Back to Africa," 229.

59 Cleaver, "Back to Africa," 220.

60 Cleaver, "Back to Africa," 229.

61 Bruce Weber, "D. L. Cox, a Leader of Radicals during 1960s, Dies at 74," *New York Times*, March 13, 2011.

62 David Rosenzweig, "Ex-Panther Says He Saw Cleaver Kill a Man," *Los Angeles Times*, February 24, 2001, http://articles.latimes.com/2001/feb/24/local/me-29765.

63 Mokhtefi, *Algiers, Third World Capital*.

64 Rosenzweig, "Ex-Panther Says."

65 Mokhtefi, *Algiers, Third World Capital*, 102.

66 Mokhtefi, *Algiers, Third World Capital*, 195.

67 Cleaver, "Back to Africa," 230; Clemons and Jones, "Global Solidarity," 29.

68 Cleaver, "Back to Africa," 235.

69 Sanche de Gramont, "Our Other Man in Algiers," *New York Times Magazine*, November 1, 1970, 228.

70 Eldridge Cleaver and Lee Lockwood, *Conversation with Eldridge Cleaver: Algiers* (New York: Dell, 1970).

71 Easley-Cox, interview by Hayes.

72 Nacio Jan Brown, photograph of Huey Newton upon his release from prison, May 29, 1970.

73 Huey P. Newton, "The Women's Liberation and Gay Liberation Movements: August 5, 1970," in *To Die for the People: The Writings of Huey P. Newton* (New York: Random House, 1972), 152–53.

74 George Todd, "Panthers Bitter over Police Attacks: Reprisals May Result," *Amsterdam News*, September 14, 1968, 23.

75 Les Matthews, "Panther Backers Get Set," *Amsterdam News*, April 26, 1969, 26.

76 Huey P. Newton and Bobby Seale, "Petition to the United Nations," in *The Black Panthers Speak*, ed. Philip S. Foner (New York: DeCapo, 1995 [1970]), 254–55.

77 Ward Churchill and Jim Vander Wall, *The COINTELPRO Papers: Documents from the FBI's Secret Wars against Dissent* (Boston: South End, 2002); Nelson, *Vanguard of the Revolution*.

78 Cleaver and Wright Hervé, "Interviews Kathleen Cleaver," 59.

79 "The Black Panthers Warring," *Amsterdam News*, April 24, 1971, 3.

80 Cleaver, "Back to Africa," 249.

81 Cleaver, "Back to Africa," 229.

82 Gramont, "Our Other Man in Algiers."

83 Hilliard and Cole, *This Side of Glory*, 267.

CHAPTER 9: "READY FOR THE REVOLUTION"

1 Fannie Lou Hamer, "The Special Plight and the Role of Black Women," in *Let Nobody Turn Us Around: Voices of Resistance, Reform and Renewal*, ed. Manning Marable and Leith Mullings (Lanham, MD: Rowman & Littlefield, 2000 [1971]), 420.

2 Stokely Carmichael, "Stokely Carmichael Speaks at Howard Part II" (1972) Dr. Huey P. Newton Foundation, Inc., Collection, Department of Special Collections, Stanford University Libraries, Stanford, CA.

3 Michael L. Clemons and Charles E. Jones, "Global Solidarity: The Black Panther Party in the International Arena," in *Liberation, Imagination and the Black Panther Party: A New Look at the Panthers and Their Legacy*, ed. Kathleen Cleaver and George Katsiaficas (New York: Routledge, 2001), 37–38.

4 Aaron Matthews, *A Panther in Africa*, documentary film, POV (PBS, 2004).

5   Matthews, *Panther in Africa.*

6   Clemons and Jones, "Global Solidarity," 37–38; Matthews, *Panther in Africa.*

7   "An International Consciousness, Part 3," SNCC Digital Gateway, SNCC Legacy Project and Duke University, 2017, https://snccdigital.org/our-voices/interna tionalism/part-3.

8   "International Consciousness, Part 3."

9   "International Consciousness, Part 3."

10 Unlike, for example, the African National Congress, which was recognized as the true people's government in exile.

11 "International Consciousness, Part 3."

12 La TaSha Levy, "Remembering Sixth-PAC: Interviews with Sylvia Hill and Judy Claude, Organizers of the Sixth Pan-African Congress," *Black Scholar* 37, no. 4 (2008): 39–47.

13 Julius K. Nyerere, "President Nyerere's Speech to the Pan-African Congress" (1974), Courtland Cox Papers, David M. Rubenstein Rare Book and Manuscript Library, Duke University, Durham, NC.

14 Courtland Cox, "Sixth Pan African Congress," *Black Scholar* 5, no. 7 (April 1974): 32–34.

15 Cox, "Sixth Pan African Congress," 33.

16 "An International Consciousness, Part 4," SNCC Digital Gateway, SNCC Legacy Project and Duke University, 2017, https://snccdigital.org/our-voices/inter nationalism/part-4.

17 Levy, "Remembering Sixth-PAC," 41.

18 Walter Rodney, "Pan-Africanism: Struggle against Neo-colonialism and Imperialism—Documents of the Sixth Pan-African Congress," in *Aspects of the International Class Struggle in Africa, the Caribbean and America. Proceedings of the Sixth Pan African Congress, Tanzania, Dar es Salaam* (Toronto: Afro-Carib Publications, 1975), 18–41.

19 Michael Dawson, *Behind the Mule: Race and Class in African American Politics* (Prince-ton: Princeton University Press, 1994), 64–68.

20 Rodney, "Pan-Africanism."

21 Frantz Fanon, *The Wretched of the Earth* (New York: Grove, 1963 [1961]); Cathy Cohen, "Punks, Bulldaggers, and Welfare Queens," *Gay Lesbian Quarterly* 3 (1997): 437–65.

22 Ashley Farmer, "Black Women Organize for the Future of Pan-Africanism: The Sixth Pan-African Congress," *Black Perspectives*, July 3, 2016, www.aaihs.org/black -women-organize-for-the-future-of-pan-africanism-the-sixth-pan-african-congress.

23 Levy, "Remembering Sixth-PAC," 44.

24 Cleveland Sellers, *The River of No Return: The Autobiography of a Black Militant and the Life and Death of SNCC* (New York: William Morrow, 1973).

25 United African Community Alliance Website, accessed August 12, 2020, www .uaacc.net.

26 Matthews, *Panther in Africa.*

27 Cynthia Young, *Soul Power: Culture, Radicalism, and the Making of a US Third World Left* (Durham, NC: Duke University Press, 2006).

EPILOGUE

1 For a more comprehensive survey of developments since independence, see Paul Nugent, *Africa since Independence* (London: Macmillan International Higher Education, 2012).

2 Achille Mbembe, *On the Postcolony* (Berkeley: University of California Press, 2001).

3 Jeffrey S. Ahlman, *Living with Nkrumahism: Nation, State, and Pan-Africanism in Ghana* (Columbus: Ohio University Press, 2017).

4 Minkah Makalani, "Black Lives Matter and the Limits of Formal Black Politics," *South Atlantic Quarterly* 116, no. 3 (2017): 529–52.

5 Eduardo Bonilla-Silva, *Racism without Racists: Color-Blind Racism and the Persistence of Racial Inequality in the United States* (Lanham, MD: Rowman and Littlefield, 2006).

6 "Demands," Ferguson Action, http://uucsj.org/wp-content/uploads/2016/05/Ferguson-Action-Demands.pdf.

7 Opal Tometi, "High-Level Thematic Debate on UN@70," paper presented at the Human Rights at the Centre of the Global Agenda—General Assembly, New York, July 12, 2016.

8 Sewell Chang, "Black Lives Matter Activists Stage Protest across Britain," *New York Times*, August 5, 2016; Glen Ford, "'Black Lives Matter' Resonates in Johannesburg," *Black Agenda Report*, March 31, 2015, www.blackagendareport.com/category/africa/south-africa; Susie Armitage, "2016 Was the Year that Black Lives Matter Went Global?" *BuzzFeed*, December 8, 2016, www.buzzfeednews.com/article/susiearmitage/2016-was-the-year-black-lives-matter-went-global.

9 Zane Schwartz, "How a Black Lives Matter Toronto Co-founder Sees Canada," *Macleans*, July 8, 2016.

10 Jordan T. Camp and Christina Heatherton, eds., *Policing the Planet: Why the Policing Crisis Led to Black Lives Matter* (New York: Verso Books, 2016); Alicia Garza, "A Herstory of the #BlackLivesMatter Movement," in *Are All the Women Still White?: Rethinking Race, Expanding Feminisms*, ed. Janell Hobson (Albany: State University of New York Press, 2016), 23–28.

11 Some widely used resources in these discussions include Patrisse Khan-Cullors, *When They Call You a Terrorist: A Black Lives Matter Memoir* (New York: St. Martin's Press, 2018); Robin DiAngelo, *White Fragility: Why It's So Hard for White People to Talk about Racism* (Boston: Beacon, 2018); "Undoing Racism Community Organizing Workshop," People's Institute for Survival and Beyond, accessed August 11, 2020, www.pisab.org/programs.

INTERVIEWS, ARCHIVAL MATERIALS, AND PERIODICALS

INTERVIEWS

A. Peter Bailey
George Barner
James Booker
Richard Brown
Clayborne Carson
Kathleen Neal Cleaver
Melvin Dickson
Barbara Easley-Cox
Hardy Frye
Arthur Gathings
Maria Gitin Torres
Benjamin Graham
Darlene Gramigna
Matt Herron
George Houser
George Koch
Sylvester Leaks
Reginald Lyles
Theodore Merriwether
Robert (Bob) Moses
Prexy Nesbitt
Edward Peeks
Michael Cetewayo Tabor
Richard Tolliver

ARCHIVAL MATERIALS

BOOKS ON MICROFILM

The Black Power Movement, Parts 1–4. Bethesda, MD: University Publications of America, 2000–2004.

FBI File on Malcolm X. Wilmington, DE: Scholarly Resources, 1995.

FBI File on the Organization of Afro-American Unity (OAAU). Wilmington, DE: Scholarly Resources, 1995.

Student Nonviolent Coordinating Committee Papers, 1959–1972. Sanford, NC: Microfilming Corporation of America, [1982].

Universal Negro Improvement Association, Central Division, New York. Records, 1918–59. Schomburg Center for Research in Black Culture, New York Public Library, New York.

COLLECTIONS

African National Congress Archives. University of Fort Hare, Alice, South Africa.

Convention People's Party Papers. Public Records and Archives Administration Department of Ghana, Accra.

Courtland Cox Papers. David M. Rubinstein Rare Book and Manuscript Library, Duke University, Durham, North Carolina.

Martin Luther King, Jr. Papers Project. Martin Luther King, Jr. Research and Education Institute, Stanford University. https://kinginstitute.stanford.edu/king -papers.

The Malcolm X Collection: Papers. Manuscripts Archives and Rare Books Division, Schomburg Center for Research in Black Culture, New York Public Library, New York.

Dr. Huey P. Newton Foundation, Inc., Collection. Department of Special Collections, Stanford University Libraries, Stanford, California.

The Papers of Kwame Nkrumah, 1957. Manuscript Division, Moorland-Spingarn Research Center, Howard University, Washington, DC.

George Padmore Papers. George Padmore Research Library of African Affairs, Accra, Ghana.

PERIODICALS

Amsterdam News, 1959–72
Baltimore Afro-American, 1959–72
Black Panther, 1967–70
Chicago Defender, 1959–72
Student Voice, 1960–65
Voice of Africa, 1961–74

INDEX

A

Abyssinian Baptist Church, 37

advanced marginalization, 28, 175

African diaspora, 3, 4, 15, 18, 22, 42, 75, 80, 133, 180, 188, 189

African independence, 9, 15, 16–17, 20, 23, 24, 26, 34, 55, 57, 60, 67, 85, 88–89, 101, 135, 148, 175, 179; continuing struggles, 182–85; definition of, 6–7; influence on Black Lives Matter, 185–88; remaining non-self governing territories, 182. *See also* Algeria; Democratic Republic of Congo; Ghana; Guinea; Tanzania

African Liberation Support Committee (ALSC), 15, 176–77, 178

African Student Association of US and Canada, 40

Afro-American. See Black press

Afro-American Association (Bay Area), 143, 148

Alabama, 38, 57, 64, 105, 106, 109, 130, 131, 145; Birmingham, 64, 101, 135, 186, 188; Dexter Avenue Baptist Church, 38; Lowndes County, 126–27; Montgomery Bus Boycott, 37–38; Selma, Alabama, 123, 126, 130, 135–36, 153. *See also* Freedom Rides; King, Martin Luther Jr.; Lewis, John; Student Nonviolent Coordinating Committee (SNCC)

Algeria, 10, 14, 23, 44–47, 51, 52, 67, 69, 72, 74, 76, 87–88, 98, 128–29, 132–33, 139, 148, 156, 157–59, 161, 162, 164, 167, 180, 183, 184; Algiers, 9, 14, 32, 48–50, 52, 96, 98, 122, 131, 133, 135, 150, 156, 157, 158, 159, 160*fig*, 161–63, 165, 166–68, 173, 181; Casbah, 48, 49, 50, 158, 168; *les indigènes*, 45; *les pieds-noirs*, 45, 47, 48–49; Revolutionary Council 167. *See also* Algerian Revolution; Frantz Fanon; *Front de Libération Nationale* (National Liberation Front, FLN)

Algerian Revolution (War for Independence), 10, 47, 52, 74, 76, 98, 129, 132, 148, 167; Battle of Algiers, 10, 44, 47–51, 52, 158; Evian Peace Agreement 87. *See also* Frantz Fanon; *Front de Libération Nationale* (National Liberation Front, FLN)

All-African People's Conference (AAPC), 11, 22, 74–76, 96, 117, 128, 146, 157, 173

All-African People's Revolutionary Party (AAPRP), 14, 176, 177

Alliance des Bakongo (ABAKO), 73

allyship (against anti-Black racism), 12, 109–10, 112–13, 121, 127, 130–31, 140–41, 156, 169, 187

American Indian Movement (AIM), 154

Amsterdam News. See Black press

Angelou, Maya, 11; in Cultural Association of Women of African Heritage

transnational advocacy networks (TANs, concept by Margaret Keck and Kathryn Sikkink), 25
Tristan da Cunha, 182
Tshibanda, Raymond 184
Tshombe, Moïse, 73, 81, 84, 91
Tunisia, 51, 52, 87, 129
Ture, Kwame. See Carmichael, Stokely
tutoyer, 45 *See also* France: colonization of territories in Africa, Asia, and the Americas
Twi, 23

U

United Farm Workers Union, 106, 113
United Gold Coast Convention (UGCC), 40–41
United Nations (UN), 12, 15–16, 83, 86, 100, 145–46, 164–65, 182, 186; Declaration of Human Rights, 37, 78; Geneva Conventions, 10, 49; intervention in Congo 81–82, 85–86; Year of Africa, 69–85
Universal Negro Improvement Association (UNIA), 39
University of Mississippi, 136
U Street Corridor (Washington, DC), 151

V

Vietnam War, 47, 51, 170
Voting Rights Act (1964), 24, 90, 136

W

wade-ins, 58, 116
Walker, Alice, 61–62
Watson Commission, 41
WBAI-FM, 122

Wesley, Cynthia. *See* Four Little Girls
Western Sahara, 182
White Fragility (theory by Robin DiAngelo), 187
White privilege, 93, 140, 187
Williams, Robert F. 55, 86, 136, 144
Wretched of the Earth (Fanon), 128–29, 130, 150, 153, 175, 183
Wright, Richard 53, 158

X

X, Malcolm (also Malcolm Little), 11, 13, 83, 86–87, 90–91, 94–96, 99–100, 103–04, 121–24, 133, 141, 143, 144, 145, 146, 149, 153, 154, 157; 163, 164, 171–72; assassination of, 13, 124–25, 188; *Autobiography of Malcolm X* (film by Spike Lee), 96; in Algeria, 98; in Cairo 12, 100–101; in Ghana, 11–12, 96–98, 133; in Tanzania, 102–03, 151, 172. *See also* Organization of Afro-American Unity

Y

Yacef, Saadi 48–51, 87
Yaya, Muhammad 159
Yazid, Muhammad 162
Young Lords Party, 148, 154
Yoruba, 23, 28

Z

Zambia, 8, 146, 167, 188
Zanzibar, 100
Zedong, Mao, 144
Zimbabwe, 157, 177
Zinn, Howard 57, 61, 106, 110
Zinn, Roslyn, 61–62

CPSIA information can be obtained
at www.ICGtesting.com
Printed in the USA
BVHW032226110721
611540BV00001B/3